OPERATION CLEEVES

For my boys, you know who you are.
Pugnare et vincere in mari.

OPERATION CLEEVES

SOE's

FORGOTTEN WARTIME TRAGEDY IN THAILAND

KATHLEEN REID-SMITH

Pen & Sword
MILITARY
AN IMPRINT OF PEN & SWORD BOOKS LTD.
YORKSHIRE – PHILADELPHIA

First published in Great Britain in 2024 by
PEN AND SWORD MILITARY
An imprint of
Pen & Sword Books Limited
Yorkshire – Philadelphia

ISBN 978 1 03610 979 0

A CIP catalogue record for this book is available from the British Library.

Typeset in Times New Roman 11/14 by
SJmagic DESIGN SERVICES, India.
Printed and bound in the UK by CPI Group (UK) Ltd.

Pen & Sword Books Limited incorporates the imprints of Atlas, Archaeology, Aviation, Discovery, Family History, Fiction, History, Maritime, Military, Military Classics, Politics, Select, Transport, True Crime, Air World, Frontline Publishing, Leo Cooper, Remember When, Seaforth Publishing, The Praetorian Press, Wharncliffe Local History, Wharncliffe Transport, Wharncliffe True Crime and White Owl.

For a complete list of Pen & Sword titles please contact
PEN & SWORD BOOKS LIMITED
George House, Units 12 & 13, Beevor Street, Off Pontefract Road,
Barnsley, South Yorkshire, S71 1HN, England
E-mail: enquiries@pen-and-sword.co.uk
Website: www.pen-and-sword.co.uk

or
PEN AND SWORD BOOKS
1950 Lawrence Rd, Havertown, PA 19083, USA
E-mail: uspen-and-sword@casematepublishers.com
Website: www.penandswordbooks.com

FSC
www.fsc.org
MIX
Paper | Supporting responsible forestry
FSC® C013604

Contents

Preface

This is the story about a Second World War covert operation you have never heard of; a long-forgotten battlefront you did not know existed; and the whispering of unheard voices in unmarked graves still resting somewhere deep in the jungles of Southern Thailand.

Thailand remains one of the least-known covert battlegrounds of the Second World War. For some European civilians living and working across the Southern Provinces in December 1941, it would be the adventure of their lives, and for others the end of theirs. Under the auspices of Operation Matador, which was Britain's plan to defend Malaya, many were recruited by the Special Operations Executive in the Far East to undertake a series of complementary, small-scale tin mine denial sabotage operations known collectively as Operation Cleeves. Cleeves' activities were to be undertaken either side of the Singora Line, a British military delineation further dividing Southern Thailand into north and south areas of operation. All became moot points on 8 December 1941, when Japan simultaneously invaded Malaya and Thailand, and it was Southern Thailand's tin mining communities that bore the brunt of Japan's first waves of violent assault.

While the little-known Battle of The Ledge may seem of relative unimportance to Second World War history, the degree of importance to British Malaya's first battlefront increases when other unknown truths come to light. For example, more is known about how bad the monsoonal weather was when Japan invaded, than is known about how by Christmas 1941 most of Southern Thailand's remaining European population had been dead for weeks. Christmas Day came and went as worried friends and families continued waiting with bated breath, and in vain hope that they might get some news, any news, about what had happened to their loved ones. It took the fall of Singapore in February 1942 for the Allies to understand the gravity of the situation. It took three more months for the forgotten SOE Operation Cleeves and its operatives to literally be written out of history.

Five years of research across five countries has gone into this book, and it took this long because much of the original documentation that should have been available in archives, war museums and libraries, is either missing or buried deep within what can only be described as camouflaged filing. One of the major problems in tracking many SOE operations related to the Far East in general, but Operation Cleeves and South Thailand in particular, is that most paper trails were destroyed by the British themselves during the chaotic retreat from Japan's blitzkrieg advance. To overcome these limitations a synthesised analysis of original research, combined with recently discovered archival and other primary sources including never-before-seen photographic evidence, provides the historical canvas upon which the tragedy of SOE's first sanctioned operation in Southern Thailand is slowly coming into view. This work is an attempt to start addressing these and other substantial gaps in the historical literature, and in its own small way, try to provide some closure for some of the families of those victims who never came home.

Kate Reid-Smith
Kew Gardens, 2023

Chapter 1

Paradise Asleep

War is Coming

In mid-1940, not long after Adolf Hitler had announced his intention of invading Britain under his ambitious Operation Sea Lion, and while regular Allied forces were being decisively routed from Europe, Britain's military chiefs began looking at alternative war-fighting strategies. While regular warfare still dominated military planning, it was the successful exploitation of irregular warfare in Poland, Greece and elsewhere that had caught the attention of Britain's Joint Chiefs of Staff. Not only because partisan-style actions were seemingly effective in altering Axis military planning, but also in the way small-scale sabotage operations were both cost effective and highly disruptive to enemy positioning across occupied territories. On realising the potential value to Allied defensive and offensive operations, the War Cabinet endorsed the Joint Chiefs of Staff's recommendations that a special organisation, accompanied by an equally special planning and training wing, was needed as a complementary war-fighting strategy. British Prime Minister Sir Winston Churchill agreed, quickly sanctioning the establishment of the Special Operations Executive (SOE).[1]

Set up under the control of Hugh Dalton's Ministry of Economic Warfare (MEW) and with a mandate of setting Europe ablaze, it was to be both a special and clandestine organisation, and focused exclusively on mounting covert operations within enemy territories.[2] Dubbed the 'Ministry of Ungentlemanly Warfare', SOE focused on two forms of behind-enemy-lines resistance.[3] The first was organising covert armies for longer-term guerrilla warfare operations including subversion. The second was in recruiting clandestine groups for smaller-scale, industrial sabotage attacks. Once Churchill began realising how valuable SOE operations might become to Britain's war-fighting efforts, he too supported the additional requirement of a larger and separate SOE training section. By the end of 1940 that came to fruition, when Brigadier Colin Gubbins assumed the newly-established position of head of SOE training. His focus was on co-ordinating subversion and sabotage actions against the enemy outside of the British Isles, and the timing could not have been better.[4]

As areas of SOE operations expanded as the war progressed, so too did the requirement for Special Training Schools (STS) to meet operational demands. Of particular focus was small-scale industrial sabotage, targeting actions that were proving their worth in providing advantageous nuisance value. The aim was to increasingly hamper specific enemy abilities to conduct war, mainly by disrupting access to vital war-fighting resources. That meant rather than haphazardly destroying certain types of machinery, a more tailored tampering approach focusing on disabling essential component parts might be preferred. It would be especially effective if it could force the enemy to waste precious time in repairing or replacing necessary parts. As some actions in France were already showing, blowing up bits of railway track, and denying Axis powers ready access to replacement parts, sometimes offered the Allied forces much-needed tactical and operational breathing space for other concurrent operations. This was especially so when planning future offensives, some of which often required something other than what conventional warfare could provide. It was a delaying tactic that if co-located or co-implemented inside alternative enemy-influenced areas, such as within neutral nations, might aid in the disruption of vital enemy supply lines and in providing the Allies with certain battlefield advantages.[5] Fortuitously for Gubbins, substantial work had already been done on mounting these types of operations, and it was STS 17 at Brickendonbury Manor in Hertfordshire that was leading the way.[6]

When Gubbins took over SOE's training mandate, STS 17 was already honing a specialised six-step approach to smaller-scale operations. Churchill was keen to expand those efforts where necessary into other potentially emerging conflict zones.[7] There had already been some lessons learned in Europe, especially how mounting a sequence of small-scale sabotage operations could help initiate debilitating flow-on effects across wide-ranging enemy capabilities. Put bluntly, the more annoying those efforts could be towards disrupting the enemy's support or back lines, the more time the Allies could use in exploiting and attacking the enemy's front lines. That also suggested that if SOE could find and recruit operatives with at least some working knowledge of the technologies in question, it might prove cost and time beneficial to field operations.

Having some familiarity with how to disrupt both was preferable, but at the very least training operatives in some type of generic demolitions work was often a reliable last resort. In this way, combined acts of passive or active sabotage might prove more useful and beneficial to future Allied strategising, especially if used in ways that stopped short of any offensive-style operations. That could include active sabotage activities, such as deliberately losing essential machinery component parts, or acts of passive sabotage, which might be something as simple as just not pushing the 'on' button on time. The idea being that targeted machinery sabotage in enemy-occupied, or at least soon-to-be enemy-occupied areas, might take on a defensive measure with an end goal of preceding any larger-scale advancing operations. If used in this way, smaller-scale sabotage operations might then be used in paving the way for a larger pre-emptive offensive military strike. The real question by the end of 1940 was whether or not it might work in other potential battlefields, particularly those in defence of external British colonial territories, including in the Far East.

As Britain's Second World War battlefields were expanding into diverse soldiering terrains ranging from sea to desert, to mountainous snow and ice, STS 17's industrial sabotage training was already taking those environmental differences into account, and Gubbins too was paying attention. Firstly and foremostly that included establishing different types of training measures, with particular attention being paid to where potential small-scale sabotage operations might be implemented. That meant the STS location was important, because it had to be somewhere where the arrival of bombs, bullets and body bags would not raise too much public attention. The venue itself need to be larger in size than the average house, and preferably situated in open country, which is why in most cases a sprawling landed estate with its own large grounds was generally best suited. That way on-site provision of self-contained practical capabilities suitable for training, accommodation, staff offices, classrooms, recreation areas, and other 'hands-on' educational facilities and so on, might not raise too much outside suspicion as to the types of training that were actually going on inside.

While SOE training for the war progressed, one essential emerging key was in expanding successful field-operator training, part of which included keeping limited demolitions and denial actions as simple, and as user-friendly, as possible. But as with all things during wartime, recruitment for industrial sabotage operations relied heavily on personnel and resource availability. While military personnel provided most of the STS training, it was often civilians who made up the bulk of SOE operatives, and they were usually given at least nominal equivalent British Army ranks. Sometimes a group of individuals selected for one particular operation were awarded these through block waiver, meaning the local military command authority in a particular area had discretionary powers to do so. In wartime Malaya for example, that responsibility fell to the General Officer Commanding (GOC), but that did not necessarily mean the requisite paperwork often made it back to the Ministry of Defence, let alone the War Office. The other major problem was actually being able to find individuals with wider specialty experiences, within a specifically targeted industry, and who might be available to be released for SOE work.

If anybody with years of practical experience with any particular machinery could be found, and if they could be spared from military service, SOE recruiters often found themselves in close competition with the War Office or other security organisations over human resources. But if certain professionals could be spared among those who were producing vitally important war resources, including tin for example, then perhaps SOE just might be lucky enough to find a potential ready-made, small-scale sabotage team lying in wait. In Britain's Far East, many professionals associated with the mining industry such as engineers, metallurgists, chemists, surveyors, and even specialised mining accountants and so on were exempt from military service whether they liked it or not. While the war continued ravaging Europe in 1941 many of these people were still living and working in Malaya and Southern Thailand; the former being Britain's rubber 'cash-cow' and the latter being the same in tin.[8] By keeping the training as repetitive and almost rote learning, in theory at least less time might be needed in training potential operatives for certain small-scale industrial sabotage activities.

That 'big picture' approach was important to evaluate as well as calculate what types of smaller-scale sabotage might be more useful to Britain's overall war effort. For instance, small-scale disabling or disrupting of machinery, particularly if made in relation to raw tin resource production, might prove more useful in Britain's envisaged post-war future than complete destruction of entire mine sites in the long run. In this way denial operations focusing on constant irritation and annoyances to the enemy, especially in terms of costly repair and replacement of necessary component parts, could become more advantageous in terms of nuisance value by morphing into tactical worth. Both of these could also influence future British military, economic and political planning outcomes as the war progressed. None of that was new in terms of Imperial Empire building in any post-war relationship-building era, because Britain had been successfully exploiting all three for centuries.[9]

By this reasoning, it might be more prudent if specialised component parts essential to vital resource production, such as mining dredge equipment in tin ore production for example, might be given a higher priority in terms of post-war rebuilding. If those promises could be made, especially to the private companies that owned and ran whatever particular resource industry, then it would take less time to get Britain's 'cash-cow' operations back up and running again in minimum time. Noting that Britain relied heavily on its far-flung colonies for supplying all of its vital war resources including tin, rubber and anything else that helped support the war effort, it made sense that SOE and STS operations should also be concomitantly expanding to protect British raw resources wherever they might be located. By early 1941, and with a new threat looming on the horizon to British interests in the Far East, that argument would soon be put to the test in defending British Malaya's backyard.

Chapter 2

Paradise Awake

Old Neighbours, New Foes, Indifferent Friends

For Britain's colonies in the Far East, the expansion of the European theatre of war from mid-1940 onwards had unforeseen consequences. When Nazi-occupied Paris ushered in Nazi-friendly Vichy France, the flow-on effects of that situation also began impacting French colonies around the world, and French Indochina was no exception. After France had little choice but to sign an armistice with Nazi Germany in June, and the French parliament had voted full powers to Marshal Philippe Pétain, that effectively meant the Third Republic was dead.[1] That also meant that while most of metropolitan France was under German occupation, France's far-flung colonies remained under Pétain's Vichy government control. The added corollary being that the now Axis-friendly Vichy French Indochina, and the new Vichy-aligned Hanoi capital, was just the start of Britain's Far Eastern defence woes neighbouring the Malay Peninsula.

Once the Tripartite Pact between Germany, Italy and Japan forming a new Axis-aligned bloc was signed in September 1940, more influences of Europe's war were creeping further into the region, and it was tied up with Malaya's closest next-door neighbour, Thailand. Just prior to the fall of France, Paris and Bangkok had been in tense negotiations for months over three north-western boundary regions. They had historically been vassal states of Thailand, but a few decades earlier were ceded to France during the reign of King Chulalongkorn (1868–1910).[2] After France's capitulation to Hitler, Thailand had reasoned that Germany's military occupation of metropolitan France had possibly rendered any hold on its French colonial possessions at best tenuous. The now isolated French colonial administration in Hanoi was essentially cut off from outside French colonial help. With this in mind, Thailand had mounted a short border war against what was now Vichy French Indochina, seeking to reclaim territorial possessions. The short-lived Franco-Thai War (October 1940–January 1941) achieved just that, but it was not the traditional regional arbiters of Western diplomacy that ended the conflict, but rather Japanese mediation. The post-war outcome resulted in the return of the western provinces to Thailand, but also Thailand's concessionary loss of other areas to Vichy French Indochina along what is today the contemporary Thai–Laos border.[3] By early 1941, Tokyo's diplomatic success between the two helped in gaining a stronger foothold across the region, including wielding increasing influence on Hanoi's political, diplomatic, military and economic fronts, and it was Vichy Hanoi's nearest neighbour, Bangkok, that was paying closest attention.

In 1932 a political coup had stripped the Thai monarchy of absolute power. After much internal turmoil and infighting, fascist-leaning Colonel Plaek Phibunsongkhram, more popularly known as 'Phibun', and his supporters had emerged victorious.[4] It was a forcible change of government that immediately changed the direction of Thailand's governance. As the military-dominated leadership gained momentum in the years that followed, ultra-nationalist Phibun now reigned virtually supreme in a quasi-dictatorship. Holding the major portfolios of foreign affairs, defence, and the interior, he exploited all three, not only in his dealings with Britain's long-standing representative in Bangkok, Sir Josiah Crosby, but also with his counterparts in Tokyo, Vichy Hanoi, and even in Berlin. Phibun had taken note of Hitler's hegemonic thirst for power ravaging Europe from 1938 onwards, and now as Thailand's self-styled leader, he too was consolidating his own grip on power. That was helped in part when the Second World War broke out in 1939, and when a year later Thailand subsequently declared its own version of neutrality.

Copying Hitler's playbook, Phibun continued advocating that Thailand's economy had to become more insular, self-reliant, and self-sufficient to protect its national sovereignty.[5] To achieve that it had to first rid itself of comparable problems similar to that of Nazi Germany, including the ousting of liberal rivals seen as being 'too weak' to help govern Thailand.[6] This was only achievable if the nation rid itself of Thailand's two major afflictions. The first was eradicating the undermining influences of minorities, which in Thailand's case were the Chinese. The second was putting a stop to other nations' exploitative monopolies of Thai resources, and that centred around British domination over Thai tin.[7] Both of these in Phibun's and his ultra-nationalist supporters' eyes were continuing problems undermining the longevity of Thailand's independence.

Against the background of the still-raging Sino-Japanese War, it seemed as if Japan was seeking as many avenues as possible to isolate China. Taking advantage of the defeat of France and its forced armistice with Germany, and Tokyo's forced mediation over the border confrontation, Japan was already giving Vichy Hanoi ultimatums. That included demanding the closure of all supply routes through Vichy French Indochinese territories into China. Such actions were also accompanied by the arrival of large numbers of Japanese civilian and military advisors. The biggest red flag was that Japan was also demanding free and unfettered access across Indochina.[8]

Within three months Japan had secured basing rights for their Navy, Army and Air Force assets across the country, and secured permission to station troops at forward staging posts in Indochina. Tokyo had secured Vichy Hanoi's reluctant permission to use all of Indochina's sovereign territory as a transit corridor for the war's duration. By late 1940, thousands of Japanese troops were swarming into the country, including amphibious infantry units, accompanied by hundreds of commercial transport convoys, warships, aircraft carrier fleets and so on. Japanese land-based aircraft too were arriving in droves, and being housed in a wide variety of what were formerly French Air Force aerodromes. In quick succession Japan now controlled Indochina's geostrategically important Haiphong port, and the vitally significant Kunming–Haiphong railway, which effectively closed off most of China's supply route access to arms, fuel and other resources from Malaya and Thailand, and vice versa.[9] That practically severed the Chinese government's last secure overland link to the outside world, which also meant the only effective supply route still left to the Chinese was through Burma. But that was not all Japan wanted from Vichy Indochina, as the ensuing months would show.

At the same time as Japan was busily assembling its massive troop build-up within French Indochina's borders, it seemed Washington, London, British Malaya and even Berlin were watching with apparent indifference and from afar. Bangkok, on the other hand, was not. Phibun's government in Bangkok was paying closer attention, especially when Japan was now actively promoting its Greater East Asia Co-Prosperity Sphere.[10] The proposed objectives were aimed at ensuring economic self-sufficiency and co-operation among member states, along with resisting Western interference. The premise being that if all Asian countries worked together, then they could support one another in expelling Western imperialists, and capitalists, from their lands. After that each would share in the mutually exclusive trade, resources and commodities between themselves. All of which was literally music to the ears of fascist-leaning Phibun. In what was becoming a burgeoning geopolitical vacuum in Southeast Asia, Tokyo was already warmly embracing its new-found role as regional mediator, while Western influences were doing the opposite. Indifferent Washington was still self-absorbed with its own isolationist self-protection, while London and Paris were distracted with their own respective national survival. For British Malaya on the other hand, it was business as usual.

By early 1941, it seemed that Thailand was moving further away from its relationship with Britain, and leaning closer into its new-found best friend in Japan. That had been helped along in part by Britain's ongoing refusals to Thailand's repeated requests for military aid. Japan, on the other hand, had no such qualms. With the Japanese having already consolidated their military advisors and large-scale occupation of Vichy Indochina, it was also beginning to do the same in Thailand but in different, flattering ways.[11] In Bangkok, for example, assorted Japanese military attachés were being invited in, and arriving in droves with their credentials. Japanese-supplied armoured vehicles, tanks, army trucks, weapons and ammunition were increasingly being used for newly established Thai–Japanese military training purposes.

Elsewhere across Thailand, and just as Germany had done in previous years, it was now Japanese industrial specialists, engineers and other technological advisers building up Thailand's roads, railways, ports, harbours and bridges. Accompanying that expansion was a concomitant rise in the Japanese civilian population, many of whom had been relocating in large numbers from Malaya at least since mid-1941. Japanese cafes, barbers, bicycle shops, travel hotels and tourist entrepreneurs were popping up everywhere, and in some of the more remote places including the southernmost railway towns of Haad Yai and Yala, Japanese chemists, doctors, businessmen and shop owners were also setting up shop. Even disused tin mines and redundant rubber plantations were being snapped up by Japanese investments. These were activities that were raising some concerns among locals, including long-time Yala resident Dr Sam Thomas.[12]

For months Thomas had been trying to raise his concerns with British authorities about what was going on, especially how there had been a sudden influx of a large number of Japanese relocating from Malaya into Southern Thailand, but he had continually been rebuffed by both Crosby in

Bangkok, and the British authorities down in Singapore.[13] He had continued trying to raise the alarm, especially about a Dr Seto, who although a long-standing Singora resident, seemed to be paying too close attention to where the European tin mines and rubber plantations were located in Southern Thailand. It was only after he had taken his concerns over the border to one British Immigration Officer, a Captain Cauvin based in Padang Besar, and another British Deputy Immigration Officer in Kedah named JD Borrity, that he found any interest from anyone within official British circles.[14] It probably helped that Captain Louis Patrick Trevelyan Cauvin also just happened to be a member of Britain's Inter Services Liaison Department (ISLD), and was actually in Malaya as part of Britain's Secret Intelligence Service (SIS).

The other conundrum was that although the Sino-Japanese War from 1937 onwards had warranted some of London's and by default Malaya and Singapore's attention, the widely held belief of any nefarious Japanese intentions towards the Malay Peninsula remained vague. It seemed the main view out of the colonial Far East was that any latent Japanese aggression was probably going to remain restricted to areas far removed from British Hong Kong, Burma or Malaya. Aside from China, Japan may have been too preoccupied with its other ongoing skirmishes with Russia to the far north to be even bothered worrying about anything south. It was almost a similar attitude spilling over into the Malay Peninsula, when it seemed even less attention was being paid to what had been happening in British Malaya's immediate backyard, not the least of which included Tokyo's new up close and increasingly cosy relationship with Bangkok.

Arguably that may have been largely due to Britain's interwar years, when in the disastrous economic aftermath of the First World War, the far-flung Empire had fallen into three distinct areas of importance. Firstly and foremostly was defence of the British Isles; secondly was securing British interests in the Middle East and North Africa; and lastly, and lowest down the geostrategic pecking order, were Britain's colonies in the Far East. At the lower end of that rung was the Malay Peninsula, which aside from Singapore was considered as being somewhat of a colonial backwater. Singapore was the jewel in the Southeast Asian tiara, and Singapore's island defence centred around the maritime Fortress Singapore analogy. The Malay Peninsula's defence, on the other hand, hardly rated a mention. By the time anybody in London was paying attention to what those implications might mean for the Far East and the Pacific it was already too late. Bangkok, along with Vichy-Hanoi, was firmly in the clutches of Tokyo.

Chapter 3

Paradise Alert

Thailand Tin and Japanese Chagrin

Although the Sino-Japanese War had warranted some of London's attention, the general belief seemed to be that Japanese aggression was still considered remote from Britain's Far Eastern colonies. There was also the same presumption for British Malaya's immediate defence that the more things changed, the more any British dominant status quo would remain the same. What London and Singapore had either abrogated, ignored, or were just incapable of envisaging, was that pre-war British international relationships in this part of the world were changing, and they were changing fast, and there was nothing the Government let alone the Foreign or Colonial Office could do about it. Neither, it seemed, could Crosby, as long-time leader of Britain's Legation in Bangkok, quite come to grips with the changing situation. Thailand's recent history was proving that point. While Phibun was busily dismantling Western-influenced constitutional methods of democracy, bureaucracy and meritocracy, and replacing them with Japanese-style militant nationalism, Crosby was equally adamant that the Anglo-Thai relationship remained strong. It was the latter that almost begrudgingly came under more intense scrutiny in London in early 1941, especially when by now the ways and means of protecting British access to Thailand's dominant raw resource of tin, and British ownership of Thailand-based tin mines, were being challenged by forces outside of London's control.

Within months, and despite the much-vaunted Atlantic Charter being signed by Washington and London aimed at curbing Japan's increasing influence in the region through economic sanctions, it neither pressured Japan into abandoning its war in China, nor deterred Japan from any further expansionism. What it did do, however, was provide Japan with further incentive to overcome the freezing of its financial assets, and find other ways of accessing vitally important oil, tin and rubber supplies. Japan merely expanded its search for alternative markets, and Thailand's neutrality guaranteed its own right to trade in its own resources, including tin, with whomsoever it pleased. Although tin was vital to Britain's war effort, large amounts of Thailand's tin supplies were now being redirected away from deliveries in Liverpool, to alternative destinations in Hamburg, and in some instances via Hamburg to Yokohama.

Not only that, the Japanese Government was already making direct contact with various tin mining company interests in Thailand, and trying to open up their own markets. The Yuasa Trading Company, for example, had contacted Nawng Pet Tin's Nakorn Si Thammarat office in Thailand, stating that Japan was keenly interested in the importation of their tin and tungsten.[1] They qualified that statement by asking if Nawng Pet Tin could not help them, could they please recommend other tin mining companies who would. Nawng Pet Tin's immediate reply thanked the Japanese Government for its interest, but then immediately qualified that statement with a polite 'no thank you'. Their tin mining company was under strict contractual obligations that they were to keep selling their tin ore commodities to the Straits Trading Company, and that they would not and could not 'dream of disposing of it to anyone else …'.[2] By now it was becoming increasingly clearer, at least to the War Office, that Japanese political, economic, and more worryingly military influences were making steady advances into the Malay Peninsula region, and it had the domestic infrastructure to back it up.

In less than a decade, Japan had reversed its predominance of light industry in favour of heavy industry. Its stranglehold military grip on North China and Manchuria continued, providing Japan's military industry with much-needed coal and bauxite resources, and increasingly, varieties of non-ferrous metals and ferro-alloys were likewise being supplied from occupied Manchuria and Korea.[3] Even Japan's production of organic high explosives was such that it had outstripped that of both America and Britain. Now that Japan's production focus had shifted to wartime materials including in the motor vehicle industry, land weapons, tanks, armoured fighting vehicles (AFVs), aircraft, ammunitions, merchant ship expansion, naval ship building and so on, Japan had also been busily stockpiling those essential raw materials to which it did not have primary access, and most scarce of all was tin. Although Japan's regional imperative in relation to accessing raw resources seemed to be changing, Britain's contemporary focus remained the same.

British and some Australian tin mining interests dominated Southern Thailand's lucrative and highly profitable tin trade, yet it seemed little effort had been expended on securing and protecting those resources vital to Britain's war effort. With many in both Britain and Australia still considering Singapore, Penang, Hong Kong and Shanghai as far safer places to be than London or Sydney, it provided firm reassurances to British Malaya's politicians, policy makers and practitioners alike that there was probably nowhere safer to be in the Empire than in any of the Far Eastern colonies.[4] Besides, Japan's military capabilities were nothing more than outdated technologies, supported by antiquated hardware and untrained personnel, and even the military bible *Jane's* 1940 edition supported that argument. Combined with the fact that the nearest potential Japanese air threat was more than 2,700km (1,700miles) away in Japan, if the Allies were adhering to the conventional war-fighting theory that capability plus intent always equals threat, then Japan was of no threat to Malaya whatsoever.

After the Japanese attempts to access Thailand's tin were continually rebuffed by private tin mining company's trade refusals, there were other movements beginning in Tokyo. With the ever-tightening grip being enforced by ongoing Western sanctions on raw resources, Tokyo was starting to make similar bully-boy pressures on Bangkok as it had on Vichy Hanoi. Put bluntly, Japan wanted Thai tin, but unlike the Vichy Hanoi–Tokyo relationship it did not have any bargaining chips to exploit, other than filling even more geopolitical voids that were appearing, and many of them had been caused by Britain in the first place. These were points of contention Crosby in Bangkok was making the most of, as he continued openly disparaging the War Office for not taking a harder stance with Thailand's government. His view was that Britain should tell Phibun that if Japan attacked Thailand, then Britain would promise his Government that they would help them to resist, but if Japan was to begin threatening Thailand's territorial sovereignty then Britain should also inform Phibun that they might occupy Thai territory if necessary.[5] Why Crosby maintained this argument remains questionable, mainly because London was continually advising Crosby that both were impossible due to the ever-expanding areas of operation in Europe, the Middle East and North Africa. If there were not enough troops or resources to go around for their home defences, let alone Malaya's defence, then there were even fewer available to help in defending a neutral neighbouring country.

Things were no different on the diplomatic front either, and again largely centred around the Bangkok-centric Crosby's advice. His view was that due to the longevity of Britain's diplomatic relationship with Thailand, and Thailand having already self-proclaimed its neutrality, he deemed it highly unlikely that Thailand would not remain firm friends with Britain. In his reporting back to London, Crosby was emphasising that the Anglo-Thai relationship was solid, and Japan was not having as much influence as London was presuming. He qualified this opinion by reasoning that he had already managed to allay Phibun's fears about Britain's newest air base, recently built in Kota Bharu, as being too close to Thailand's southernmost borders. Despite Crosby's advice, it was the latter that came under more intense scrutiny in London by early 1941, when ongoing plans for the defence of Malaya changed tack, and as a new more all-encompassing Malay Peninsula defence strategy began taking shape.

Chapter 4

Operations Sandwich, Etonian and Matador

Meet the Malayan Maginot Line

In direct contrast to Crosby, Britain's Ambassador to Japan, Sir R Craigie, had been warning London for months that Britain should start preparing to cope with an ever-expanding Japanese footprint in the region. Not only in Vichy French Indochina, but also into Thailand.[1] He politely disagreed with Crosby's confirmed opinion that Thailand would remain pro-British and honour any potential non-aggression pact. Craigie made the point that if Japan exerted undue pressure on Bangkok as they had in Hanoi, then there was every chance Japan could have military access on both east and west coasts of the Kra Isthmus in the very near future.[2] If that happened, it would allow Japan to bypass Singapore altogether, and perhaps prey on British shipping in the Indian Ocean, and that would ultimately render Fortress Singapore, and also by default Fortress Penang, impotent. More importantly, if Japan gained control of Thailand, it could afford Japanese forces a most favourable location to attack Singapore or Burma, and perhaps even cut off Malayan access to essential food supplies, including Thai rice.[3] Essentially, Craigie was arguing that Malaya's most significant weakness was its outer defences, and he was worried that British Malaya was falling into some sort of contemporary Maginot Line psychology.[4]

Craigie was not the only diplomat sounding the alarm in early 1941. Bernard Kuskie had joined Australia's Department of External Affairs earlier in the year, and had found himself sent to Japan as part of the establishment team of Australia's Legation to Japan. Kuskie, among others, had been reporting not only on the military build-up in Japan, but also how rapidly changing the general Japanese populace's attitude was towards Japan's southern military expansion.[5] The Australians too had been noticing there had been a significant shift in Japan's interest in Southeast Asia, specifically towards the resource-rich Netherlands East Indies and Southern Thailand, more so than in coveting European colonies of French Indochina or British Malaya.[6]

It was also becoming obvious to both British and Australian representatives in Tokyo, that the newly elected Japanese government was more than well aware of how substantial shortages were afflicting not only the domestic population, but also hampering Japan's military advancements. The basic argument ran that there was something going on between Japan and the rest of the region and it appeared directly related to both. Against these reasonings, and as a more holistic approach to Empire was being taken by Britain at least, the War Office was soon realising that a more comprehensive approach to Britain's colonial military assets scattered around the world needed to be taken. After taking Craigie's observations on Japan's activities in the Far East on board, in British Malaya the newly arrived Commander-in-Chief Far East (CICFE), Air Chief Marshal Sir Henry Brooke-Popham, was tasked with reporting on his proposed disposition of Malayan and other forces at hand. Aside from specific requests as to what was locally available in terms of military assets, and what might be some of their logistical limitations, the War Office also wanted to know if there might be some scope to exploit the use of resistance or subversive movements, should Malayan defences need them.[7]

Brooke-Popham's reply focused primarily on protecting British military assets in those Malay states bordering Southern Thailand. From his perspective, the south-east coast of Kelantan was only important to protect British use of the Kota Bharu aerodrome; similarly it was only those south-westernmost frontier states of Perlis and Kedah that lay closest to the RAF bases at Alor Setar and beyond in Penang that mattered.[8] At least Brooke-Popham, as an Air Force man, was realising the drastic need for Malaya's air defences to be taken up a level. He also added that, unlike coastal Kelantan however, Perlis and Kedah's bordering regions were criss-crossed by dense belts of jungle, a topography that suggested it was useless for rear positioning of any infantry or tanks and so on, and hence probably lent itself to some natural defence. He also pointed out that if there was any enemy pre-positioning along any of the Thai–Malay border regions up north, then it would place Malaya at an immediate disadvantage.

His logic was sound, mainly because where British Army, Air Force and other Allied military assets were already positioned on the peninsula, meant a combination of the tyranny of time and distance restricted them from mobilising to any part of Malaya's northernmost frontiers without having at least two to three days' notice to deploy. He agreed with the War Office's suggestion of using smaller operational units in frontier areas, arguing that the only way to combat a nightmare scenario of enemy forces making their way across the border in haste, was to deploy small-scale sabotage units in and around the Thai–Malay border.[9]

With these recommendations in hand, the feasibility of occupying the southernmost part of the Kra Isthmus in defence of Malaya was gaining traction. The War Office was especially worried that if Japan was granted a similar military footprint in Thailand as they now had in Vichy French Indochina, then Japan would be able to amass land and air troops at will, wherever and for whatever purposes they wanted. The sobering reality was that if that did eventuate, then it might be necessary for British forces to make preliminary moves into Southern Thailand before any potential Japanese invasion. Such pre-emptive actions might at the very least limit any Japanese invasionary force capabilities, by denying them access through Thailand with intentions of using Malaya to invade Burma, Singapore, or ultimately India.[10]

Any developments around various scenarios of British forces advancing into Southern Thailand needed by necessity to take several diplomatic nuances into account. Any British actions further north towards the cosmopolitan city and seat of government in Bangkok, for example, might prove too contentious, and could equally be interpreted as a deliberate offensive act against the nation's capital. In the remote and heavily jungled rural south, on the other hand, Phibun's government might just be that little bit more amenable to any smaller localised British military presence. That might be negotiable if it was nothing more than a token force presence, and exclusively focused on defending the Malay side of the Thai–Malay border. It was a new defence posturing for British Malaya, in light of what was seemingly an ever expanding Japanese footprint over the region. A new kind of viable forward Malayan defence strategising had to be found, and that also meant a new appraisal of Malaya's viable war-fighting capabilities had to be reached. Given the paucity of military personnel and hardware available, that meant it would be impossible to offer any offensive options in the mix, but Malaya's defence just might get away with plenty of defensive ones.[11]

In British Malaya, Brooke-Popham and the General Officer Commanding (GOC) Malaya, Lieutenant-General Arthur E. Percival, were leading the Malayan side of the initial planning. They remained fully confident some of their local British forces could hold some front-line positions, but only if and when their requested troop and hardware reinforcements arrived. Their combined assumptions remained that London would find additional reinforcements from somewhere, if and when they were needed. Despite the ongoing to-ing and fro-ing between them requesting reinforcements from London, and the War Office continually telling them there were none coming, it seemed to indicate that Malaya's military planning lacked initiative in thinking outside of the conventional war-fighting box. It was almost as though they both hoped their combined and individual continued requests for reinforcements would ultimately wear the War Office down, and London would be obliged to honour its commitments to colonial Malaya's defence if Japan attacked.[12]

Operation Sandwich

Despite this, and amid the perpetual lack of human, hardware and other military resources being the proverbial elephant in the room, Percival and Brooke-Popham, and often in consultation with Crosby up in Bangkok, continued on with their version of Thai–Malayan border defence planning. Their main focus remained in securing British Malaya's northernmost border, which skirted all of Thailand's southernmost provinces. The westernmost Thai–Malay border was close to the already existing military bases of Fortress Penang, Alor Setar and so on, and was in close proximity to British military forces. It was not the same on the easternmost frontier, on the other hand, where aside from the almost completed and skeleton-staffed air base at Kota Bharu, there were no other reliable adequate British or Allied military assets to speak of. The obvious influence that might have, at least in terms of forward defence planning, was that some type of expanded British military footprint would need to made somewhere in southernmost Thailand.

There was only one area that could be of any real use to British forces under those circumstances, and that was Thailand's southernmost east coast harbour town of Singora. It had a sheltered harbour for all-weather maritime access, and was linked directly by train with the town of Haad Yai, which was the main railway nexus running north from Bangkok and south to Singapore. Alongside the railway ran one of only two passable roads linking Southern Thailand with Malaya. As the closest major town to British Malaya's easternmost northern border, it could become a forward staging post for British forces if Phibun agreed to Malaya's terms. Despite nobody having as yet broached the subject with the Thai Government, Brooke-Popham's proposal back to the War Office visualised Singora as becoming the hub from which British forces could mount a defensive barrier against any Japanese Army transit. He proposed a forward Malayan defence plan named Operation Sandwich. The War Office agreed in principle, but after more discussions thought Operation Sandwich should be subsumed within a newer proposed operation, and one that had a more in depth approach to Malaya's defence. That new plan was Operation Etonian.[13]

Operation Etonian

Now Malaya's defence planners needed to workshop complementary operations designed not only to defeat an enemy attack, but to gain valuable time and breathing space, while at the same time economising the use and deployment of a paucity of military forces. Malaya's air and ground forces, paltry as they were, needed to be working together cohesively and concisely in mounting defensive operations. It was the only way Malaya might develop conditions on the ground, and eventually aid British forces' transition to envisaged operations targeting halting any Japanese advance. But Malaya's military strength was still hampered by insufficient aircraft, aircrews and trained pilots, and the entire RAF air fleet was made up of poorly maintained and ageing aircraft types. The various hodge podge of Allied armies recently cobbled together did not fare much better, with troops from Australia, New Zealand and British India, while sharing defence responsibilities with their British Army cohorts, mostly operating under their separate commands. In many cases, most of the newly arrived Commonwealth soldiers were literally raw recruits, had never seen action nor been in armed combat, and had at best the most basic of recruit school training. The only available reinforcement solution that was subsequently offered by the War Office was the offer of extra units from the 11th Division India Infantry, to which both Percival and Brooke-Popham readily agreed.

The reality of Operation Etonian's planning, however, even with the arrival of different elements of the 11th Indian Division, was that Malaya's standing fighting force was still only roughly twenty or so battalions, which was in no way, shape or form capable of mounting any offensive operations. On sheer numbers alone, it also meant Etonian planning needed to remain purely defensive in intent, and both Brooke-Popham and Percival seemed to be missing that point. Underlying the latter, the Foreign Office was also continually reminding the increasingly belligerent Crosby that Britain's policy was to avoid war at all costs with Japan, and not to alienate Britain's only neighbouring friend on the peninsula in Thailand. It would also be good if he would stop continually bringing up the British military aid question.[14] Within months, Etonian's replacement was an even more encompassing Malayan defence plan known as Operation Matador.[15] Although focused exclusively on defensive operations, it also now contained twin components of protecting British access to essential Thai raw resources, and denying Japanese access to the same. London's focus seemed to be shifting more away from any potential armed conflict with Japan to a sequence of limited denial activities.

Operation Matador

It was against this background that British military and security intelligence circles both in London and in Malaya, began workshopping different types of border infiltration plans under Operation Matador for Thailand. From the outset, the War Office was realising that the hardest part was going to be in selling a proposed operation of defending Malaya by incursion into Thailand by British forces, and how to at least get that idea off the ground without creating too many internal fissures in either country. As it was, colonial Malaya was already a highly competitive decision-making ivory tower arrangement, with each area, whether military, security or civil services, competing for London's attentions and vying for the Foreign Office's affections. The last thing war-ravaged Britain wanted was a worsening, far-away, internal colonial squabble on their hands. But, as with most regional sensitivities over local chains of command, it was deemed best by persons unknown in the upper echelons of the War and Foreign Office, if the request for certain clandestine operations in defence of Malaya might come from the man at the top himself, the CICFE Brooke-Popham.[16]

In early 1941, that seed was planted by persons unknown in Singapore, and soon after Brooke-Popham obliged London with a strategic overview of what he deemed was an 'infiltration' plan for Operation Matador that might serve the War Office's purposes. Although lacking definition let alone any timeline as to the how, when, where or what type of goals were to be achieved, at least now there was a formal paper trail from his office to the War Office. When London advised that his proposed 'infiltration' plan was now on the table in his military area of responsibility of the Far East, they also advised that they needed his version to be substantially honed down. The suggestion was that the plan needed to be more directly focused on militarily combatting potential enemy invasion, rather than in mounting precursory covert 'infiltration' operations *per se*, the latter of which would require further investigation and input from other interrelated organisations including SOE.[17] Although the War Office had agreed in principle that part of Operation Matador's planning should include select small-scale industrial sabotage operations in Malaya, they needed the CICFE to forward an outline plan of the type of operation being proposed, where and when he envisaged it might work, and how it might complement any pre-existing SOE planning.[18] Brooke-Popham's official CICFE reply a few days later addressed none of their questions.

His answer was merely another expanded version of what he perceived were covert operations in general, but little else. That approach may have helped influence Churchill to personally back the establishment of a new SOE offshoot in the Far East sooner rather than later. Although it was a latent responsive action to circumstances by Churchill towards a rapidly changing region, at least some attention was being given to Japan's ever expanding and large-scale military footprint getting closer to Malaya's jungled hinterland. Part of Churchill and the War Office's reasoning was more not if, but when, some type of special warfare in Malaya might be needed. That came to fruition just after New Year's Day in early 1941, when various Malayan military and civilian authorities were informed that SOE activities in the Far East had been authorised, an organisation was going to be set up in Singapore to co-ordinate operations, and a specialised training centre would be accompanying it.[19] To this end Operation Puma would be the code name for setting up the Special Operations Executive (Far East) (SOE (FE)) known as the Oriental Mission, and Operation Scapula would be the establishment of the accompanying STS101 training establishment.

Chapter 5

Operation Puma (Oriental Mission)

Lions and Tigers and Bears and Flies

The Oriental Mission's official cover was to be as an Economic Mission responsible to the Ministry of Economic Warfare, with an ostensible mandate of collecting economic and industrial trends throughout the region.[1] The immediate operational focus was to stretch from Thailand's Kra Isthmus to the southern tip of the Malay Peninsula, with other areas of interest including Burma and Hong Kong to eventually follow. Heading up the organisation was Valentine St John Killery, a First World War veteran now a civilian and a former manager of Imperial Chemical Industries (ICI) China.[2] He was going out to Singapore as the chief representative of SOE in the Far East. Contingency planning for the Oriental Mission was that Killery and his staff would all remain headquartered in Singapore for the war's duration, but from the outset the prospects of being able to achieve anything in Malaya were discouraging.

When London had first advised the Governor of the Straits Settlements, Sir Shenton Thomas, that plans for undertaking covert actions in the Far East were well under way, he along with GOC Malaya Percival, and CICFE Brooke-Popham, were not pleased.[3] Thomas refused the concept outright, arguing that it might have drastic consequences for the Colonial status quo, especially if some of those being trained were Communist sympathisers. Besides, any hint of possible Japanese invasion might also lead to the unthinkable, such as the unheard nonsense of British vulnerability. The Straits Settlements' government thought it was a waste of time and money, but the government of the Federated Malay States (FMS) seemed to have welcomed the news. The Treasury countered that argument by reinforcing the fact that the Oriental Mission would fall outside of both Army and Colonial Government expenditures, reassurances that meant any expenditures would not pose a threat to colonial Malayan purse strings.

When Thomas was also advised that Killery and his team would be arriving sometime in March 1941, he was tasked with finding and providing some sort of office space and equipment set-up for them prior to their arrival. The Governor's headquarters seemingly initiated a go-slow campaign and ultimately failed to provide either.[4]

Thomas's other arguments against SOE operations were also tied up with what he saw as his main focus, and that was preservation and protection of British trade and commerce in the region. Because both were dominated by Malayan rubber and Thailand tin, and each was of vital importance to Britain's war effort, he argued that if SOE was planning to recruit British planters and tin miners they would not be spared. They would by necessity be required to stay at work and provide much-needed war support resources, rather than playing silly little war games in the jungle.[5] His other bone of contention was that if STS101 was planning on training non-Europeans, that could severely damage the existing colonial status quo.[6] Thomas was further advised that Killery and his mission would co-operate with his office on general political or economic matters, but anything outside of that including special field missions, or anything else military or defence related, would be discussed and fall under full control of the CICFE Brooke-Popham.[7]

That was somewhat problematic, because neither GOC Malaya nor Brooke-Popham wanted Killery or his Oriental Mission there in the first place.[8] Both men were less than happy when notice was received that a large cache of weapons, ammunition, explosives and other battlefield supplies was being sent out to Malaya, but only exclusively for Oriental Mission use, before Killery or any of his staff had even arrived.[9] Percival was even less impressed when he was told that he had to find certain stores that London could not provide for them, including detonator parts.[10] Brooke-Popham took it a step further, still arguing that it was regular troops and conventional war-fighting methods that would ultimately be at the forefront of Malaya's defence in the longer run, not select and special, small-scale sabotage, denial operations, whatever they were.[11]

Crosby too was unhappy because he felt that both the War Office and SOE London had overstepped their mark, especially if this new Oriental Mission was going to have anything to do with Thailand. For almost a decade he had been the official Foreign Office 'go-to' guru on all things Thai, and if anybody should have been consulted on this decision, he considered it should have been him. He cited his position as head of the British Legation in Bangkok, and Britain's lead Ministerial representative in the region, as both cases in point. Crosby was making it well known back in London that, in his considered opinion, any and all Thai-related components of Operation Matador, and more particularly anything whatsoever Killery and the Oriental Mission had to do with Thailand in general, should be his responsibility.

On top of these complaints, there was also competition arising between all three over the Oriental Mission's chain of command, and that was even before Killery had left London. Shenton Thomas, as Governor of the Straits Settlements, presumed he would have command of Killery and any of his missions, so too did Crosby in his Ministerial position in Bangkok. Having been given ultimate decision-making authority as to when to commence any actions under Operation Matador's mandate, Brooke-Popham thought he had absolute authority over everyone and everything, including unilateral authority to initiate and deploy whatever operations, including covert operations, he deemed fit. Percival chose to stay out of this affray, but did ultimately defer to Brooke-Popham's command version, at least when relevant to Operation Matador. Things came to a head when it was made known to all and sundry that Killery would not be drawing from any local military, security or Colonial Office talent to form the Oriental Mission. Helping him along at various times to set up the 'certain economic mission' both from London and in Singapore would be his own hand-picked crew.[12]

That included the British diplomat, commercial councillor and historian of pre-modern Japan, Sir George Bailey Sansom. Sansom was particularly well known for his concise historical surveys and comprehensive understanding of Japanese society and culture. Next was SC Miskin, a career civil servant with links to SIS and SOE, and one-time employee of the Asia Petroleum Company in China. He was followed by the world-renowned botanist, explorer, plant collector, author and covert specialist for the British India Office, Frank Kingdon-Ward. Kingdon-Ward had only recently returned from a scientific botanical trip along the Thai–Burma border, and had brought back with him some interesting reporting on Japanese activities there. Lastly were Messrs AB Butler and PC Wren, two civil servants with substantial combined embassy and Foreign Office experience, and both of whom were OTC Graduates. In order to offer some protection if hostilities against Japan broke out, Killery was given a field commission of a British Army Lieutenant Colonel.

Enroute to Singapore, Killery had stopped off in Karachi to meet up with British Indian Army Intelligence, as well as also catching up with Burma's Deputy Director of Defence Bureau along the way.[13] Both areas had been working on building their own respective covert intelligence operations, and as Killery was the new kid on the SOE covert block in the region, it was imperative that all three started working together to be on the same page should any Japanese threat eventuate. This was especially because the Oriental Mission's timeline in Singapore was expected to take up to at least three months to get the headquarters established, and a little bit longer to get the accompanying training school up and running.[14] Because there was a general feeling that Killery would have a full twelve months to establish a consolidated and cohesive Singapore-based SOE network, there was not an immediate sense of urgency in getting missions up and running as soon as possible. That timing had been predicated on what was known about the region's seasonal weather patterns. September to March was the traditional, disruptive and most atrocious monsoonal season in both Malaya and Southern Thailand, and nobody was envisaging Japan, or any other enemy for that matter, would be interested in undertaking any operations over those bad monsoonal months. Yet most notably, and even before leaving London, Killery was already advising MEW to open up negotiations with Thai tin mining companies.[15] That suggested seasonal planning for any potential industrial tin mining sabotage in Thailand was probably already well under way by MEW and SOE before the War Office even knew about it.

This may have been part of the reasoning as to why Killery had been hopeful that prior to his arrival he might have been able to enlist the aid of other potential SOE recruits across the region. Just before leaving London he had sent letters to the Borneo Company, asking whether or not certain of their staff members in Singapore and Bangkok as well as in Kuching in Sarawak, might possibly be released for future Oriental Mission operations.[16] That SOE hunt for regional expertise fell short, although future discussions between himself and other local Borneo Company representatives was not completely dismissed out of hand. Unfortunately for Killery, the company's present circumstances were inextricably tied up with supporting Britain's war effort in vital resources such as timber, and nobody could be spared. Nonetheless, he had better luck in Hong Kong, where an old acquaintance from his time in China suggested a few associates that might help in finding contacts in Vichy Indochina.[17] All of these were promising leads in setting up the wider SOE Far Eastern extension through the Singapore-based Oriental Mission, but none of them were helpful in setting up contacts in Southern Thailand.

As the command kerfuffle had shown, Killery was probably also a bit worried about how much the Oriental Mission differed from the SOE in

London. Unlike their operations, which were almost exclusively initiated, planned and executed solely by SOE personnel, in British Malaya Killery would have to run the gamut of competing ivory towers, and navigate inflated egos, whilst all the time attempting to maintain operational security in covert operations.[18] The other problem Killery had to contend with was that the Oriental Mission's close-held operational security might be ruffling many competing powerbase feathers in Malaya. Killery's arrival was so contentious that the War and Foreign Offices had to eventually advise Governor Thomas, Percival's Malaya Command and Brooke-Popham's General Headquarters, that Killery's Mission was only there to complement Malaya's Defence, and not compound it.[19] On this at least, it seemed Brooke-Popham and Percival agreed, but the sticking point remained that there was an urgent need to establish a good working relationship between Special Operations and standard military practices, the emphasis being that neither could, nor should, operate in isolation of the other. To bridge the gap, Royal Marine Lieutenant Colonel Alan F Warren was appointed Liaison Officer between General Headquarters and the Oriental Mission.[20] He had already been in Singapore for nearly a year on an SOE scoping mission anyway, and was well versed in the nuances of local power politicking.[21] Warren was not going in blind in placating competing sensitivities when it came to setting up SOE or STS facilities. He had his own STS experiences to draw upon, but there had already been lessons learned through the recent groundwork of the Mawhood Mission in Australia.

Colonel JC Mawhood's No. 104 Mission to Australia and New Zealand's primary purpose included establishing both a Special Intelligence (SI) wing and STS area on Wilsons Promontory in Victoria, Australia.[22] It also included the training of Australian Independent Companies, meaning military units specialising in specific in-country, behind-enemy-lines types of activities. Their envisaged role was to initiate defensive action against enemy paramilitary forces, as well as offensive actions in territories that might possibly be occupied by hostile enemy forces.[23] Training elements were provided by demolitions expert Captain 'Mad' Mike Calvert; fieldcraft was by noted adventurer and mountaineer Captain Freddie Spencer Chapman; Staff Sergeant Stafford was the weapons specialist; and Staff Sergeant Frank Misselbrook provided wireless expertise.[24] Now their jobs in Australia were done, some of Mawhood's Mission members, namely Chapman and Misselbrook, were being redeployed under the auspices of Operation Scapula, to help set up STS101 in Singapore.

Chapter 6

Operation Scapula (STS101)

Bombs, Bullets and Body Bags

Under the auspices of Operation Scapula, demolitions expert and Freddie Spencer Chapman's fellow mountaineer and pioneer in guerrilla warfare, Lieutenant Colonel JML (Jim) Gavin of the Royal Engineers, was given command of the new SOE (FE) training facility and with a broader training mandate.[1] Chapman was to become his second in command. STS101 objectives were to recruit and train personnel, European and Asian, civilian and military, in basic guerrilla warfare tactics, intelligence gathering, sabotage, as well as any other such activities as required. While those in the know referred to STS101 as the Oriental Mission's training school, to nearly everyone else it was referred to by its cover as the Royal Engineers' School for Demolitions.[2]

Located at Tanjung Balai on the east coast about sixteen kilometres (roughly ten miles) west of Singapore town, SOE's latest training venture was housed in a very large art deco mansion, only recently requisitioned from an Armenian businessman.[3] The sprawling estate was fit for purpose with its own small jetty, a workable boat ramp and convenient access to the sea for maritime operational training. It had good road connections linking directly into Singapore's heavily jungled interior, as well as running along the sandy shore-lined coast and beaches straddling either side. The house itself and various outbuildings and storage sheds were surrounded by a combination of densely covered mountain jungle, flat fields, and everything in between. It provided not only a good all-terrain training facility, but a very private one as well. Logistically, not only did it have ample storage space for an assortment of vehicles, motor bikes, boats, stores, mess halls, galleys, armouries, accommodation, and recreational facilities, best of all it was far from any potential prying eyes.

To all outward appearances the uniformed staff suggested to the casual onlooker that it was indeed a British military training facility, mainly because all of the training staff wore varying types of British military uniforms. Aside from the routine cloak and dagger introduction to operational security, training courses centred around weapons handling, demolitions, and general courses on enemy delaying or denying tactics including small-scale industrial sabotage. At the core lay using standard made-up explosive charges, how they should be initiated, connected to other incendiary devices, and what they would or could not do against different materials used in the construction of particular types of machinery.[4] More importantly, training would include how manipulating the charge, leads and initiators would not need to be undertaken by scientists, sappers or other specialists, but could be done by a wider range of field operatives. To this end, the perception management of STS101 being a purely military organisation was well maintained, especially when recruiting and training over the next few months started including more civilians, including tin miners and rubber planters.

Part of the way STS101 and the Oriental Mission held cover was how some operatives were being recruited. One of the few British Army areas Killery was not having trouble with was Lieutenant General Sir Lewis 'Piggy' Heath. He had arrived in Singapore in April 1941 to take command of III India Corps.[5] While he often clashed with Percival, he had a different relationship with Killery, and he seems to have supported what it was the Oriental Mission was trying to achieve. That was a problem because Malaya was a War Office responsibility, and not a British Indian Army one, and despite not having a dedicated intelligence section *per se*, Heath still found ways to enhance Killery's work and protect both his and the Oriental Mission's legend.[6] For example, it was often his troops who talent-scouted potential Oriental Mission recruits from among the civilian community, and it was nearly always his uniformed personnel, probably from III Corps Kuala Lumpur headquarters, who were involved in any liaison leading to recruitment. Even administratively, that was usually supported by all form filling being of the notorious British Army kind. These were just some of the reasons as to why most civilian personnel eventually recruited for Oriental Mission work firmly believed that they were working for the British Army, and not some nefarious covert intelligence organisation. That many were given 'secret' Army Officer and Non-Commission Officer (NCO) field commissions only helped reinforce the perception.

The reality was that although the Oriental Mission was receiving considerable pushback from Crosby and others, and there was substantial animosity between Crosby and Killery, it was the opposite with Heath and his III Indian Corps.[7] From Killery's arrival onwards, they had been instrumental in helping set up the organisation and he had been working closely with their headquarters for months.[8] In some cases it had been members of Heath's staff who had particularly helped in addressing many local concerns over the Oriental Mission, some even using personal relationships with many of the upper echelons in the community, not only in allaying doubts about Killery or the MEW's validity, but also the importance of what it was they were trying to achieve.[9] At least with Heath and his III Corps support, Killery was finally getting operational planning back on track, or so he thought until the month after Heath arrived, when Brooke-Popham decided to take Oriental Mission covert operations into his own hands.

Chapter 7

Playing Hide and Seek

Brooke-Popham's 'Infiltration' Mission

Synthesising internal and external information into workable intelligence was the type of knowledge all military planning relied heavily upon. Not only in determining any offensive or defensive actions that might be needed to achieve a particular battlefield goal, but also as to what type of responsive enemy actions might be expected. In the Far East in general, and the Kra Isthmus and Malay Peninsula in particular, British intelligence was practically deaf, dumb and blind. The Secret Intelligence Service (SIS) cuts throughout the 1930s onwards had not helped, which meant most foreign intelligence London was working with was either outdated or just plain wrong.[1] Sometimes the only intelligence of any note even the SIS could muster was negligible, and usually from secondary Netherlands East Indies sources, selective titbits passed on from the Americans, or French Indochinese information sources, the latter of which were now firmly compromised. If Britain could call on a cache of highly trained infiltration operatives positioned close to Thailand, with extensive local in-country experience and knowledge, then any current information directly relevant to the Thai–Malay border might also contribute to the type of defensive posture that could be implemented.

But for now, any small-scale sabotage planning and training in relation to Operation Matador remained fairly vague and overly simplistic. The military premise remained the same, an overwhelming confidence that British regular troops could hold out for at least six months against any Japanese invasion in Malaya's north, especially if Britain's forward staging platform was in Singora.[2] That looked good on paper, or over chatter at the Long Bar in Raffles, but it did not help that there were still ongoing arguments as to what type of Oriental Mission operations might be involved. From Malaya's military side, that not only involved trying to hone down what areas might become liable to be overrun by enemy forces, but from

Killery's covert side, that was also in determining which places might best benefit from embedded small-scale industrial sabotage cells.[3] Despite ongoing discussions still ensuing between the Oriental Mission, STS101 and everybody else, at least London had seen a clear path forward, and by now had given Killery the green light to start preparing tin mine denial plans for Southern Thailand. He was also officially tasked with starting up liaison with local tin mining companies, and for the first time was given discretionary powers in dealing directly with Crosby in Bangkok.[4]

The trouble was that even before any talent spotting for operatives could begin, let alone any recruiting or eventual training could take place, there needed to be current, concise and cohesive information about the status quo of the Southern Thailand tin mining industry itself. Nobody in Britain's military or any of the other security services on the Malay Peninsula had any of that intelligence on hand. This was not being helped by the fact that as a self-declared neutral country, Thailand was now facing two self-made dilemmas over any actions it might take in terms of resources. If Bangkok bowed to Western pressure, then Japan might consider its access to much-needed high-value raw resources such as tin could potentially lie in the hands of a new Thai enemy. On the other hand, if Bangkok bowed to Japanese pressure, then the problem was alleviated at least for Tokyo, but that also might mean Thailand would no longer be a friend of the British Empire. Even worse, it would no longer be Malaya's buffer zone. With the pre-war colonial status quo already coming into serious question, and an almost complete lack of up-to-date intelligence on what was actually going on in the region, British wartime military and intelligence planners were starting to highlight in depth just how bad Malaya's defence weaknesses appeared to be. To address this, and a series of other information shortfalls relevant to the Thai–Malay border quandary, Brooke-Popham drafted a proposal of what he considered might be an adequate fact-finding mission to the War Office.

His scheme centred around not sending civilian Oriental Mission operatives into Southern Thailand, but British military ones.[5] He also followed that up with the timing caveat that such actions would only occur twenty-four hours in advance of any potential Japanese incursion. Under his proposal, military personnel were to wear civilian clothing and, posing as tourists, make their way over the border from Malaya into Thailand, and on return report their observations directly to his headquarters in Singapore. After that had been achieved, his operatives' secondary theoretical focus would then be in helping secure Thailand's southernmost ports and aerodromes. But again, Brooke-Popham offered nothing on the tactical nor operational front as to how they were going to achieve these lofty goals, and he had advised London of the same. In no uncertain terms, he stated that he had no plan, no detailed methods of penetration, and no idea as to how individual cover was going to be arranged. In his view that was not his job in his senior Command position, but rather it remained the onerous burden of SOE London or someone else to sort out; and besides, he could not foresee any problems co-ordinating 'his' 'infiltration' operations within 'theirs'.[6] He immediately followed that statement up with the news that after consulting with Percival, Crosby in Bangkok, and the British Consul in Burma, he had already started practice run 'infiltration' operations into Thailand.

Without consulting the War Office, the SIS, the Foreign or Colonial Office or SOE in London, let alone Killery, in May 1941 Brooke-Popham had taken a unilateral decision and deployed roughly twenty or so of Percival's British military personnel into Southern Thailand. Dressed and acting as tourists in accordance with his directions, the troops were to take short return trips over the three main southern Thai–Malay land border crossing areas. They were to begin their travels on the Malayan side, with some leaving from Kroh and crossing the border into Betong, then on to Yala and Pattani; another group left from Padang Besar and crossed the border near Sadao and then on to Haad Yai and eventually Singora; while another group travelled from Kota Bharu up to Pattani and then on to Singora and beyond. It remains unknown what their taskings were, but it seemed the general orders given were to take notes and observe anything and everything they saw, heard and experienced, and then report that information back to CICFE's headquarters.

Whether they travelled together, alone or in smaller parties is not known, but it seems all travelled either by road or rail and none of them travelled by sea. Whatever 'findings' were reported back also remains open to debate, other than the most relevant observation was that they had apparently met several Japanese 'tourists', doing exactly the same type of information-gathering exercises as they were doing along the way. In what little of note was reported back, there seemed to be a plethora of Japanese-speaking 'tourist' guides and all seemingly working within exclusive Japanese 'tourist' accommodation, and only using any number of 'tourist'-friendly Japanese-run taxis, cafes and restaurants. For reasons unknown, Malaya's northernmost states of Perak and Kedah, bordering Southern Thailand, had also become part of the latest trend in what might only be described as 1940-style off the beaten track tourism.[7]

As Dr Sam Thomas and others had already been noting, the large numbers of Japanese tourists flooding into rural and remote backwaters across Southern Thailand was astounding. Especially when it seemed the monsoonal time of the year, at least since 1940, was quite popular. What, if anything was being done with any of the information, let alone any analysis or dissemination of what was being reported outside of cloistered British Malayan defence and government circles, can only be surmised.

At the same time Brooke-Popham had deployed his 'infiltration' into Southern Thailand, he had also refused twin offers from the Foreign and Colonial Office for additional civilian staff, and that was also causing problems. London had high hopes that creating the position of CICFE might expand the two new areas of engagement London wanted brought online. One was to widen regional political contacts outside of the Bangkok-centric Crosby, and the other was to start identifying any areas within which Japan might begin challenging British commercial and trade domination.[8] They had presented Brooke-Popham with the additional specialised staff for these two specific reasons. The Foreign Office had offered to provide him with a dedicated Thailand economic advisor, and the Colonial Office with a Political Officer specialising in Thailand's international politics. When Brooke-Popham immediately turned both of them down, he did so citing his own decision-making reasons to London.[9] His first refusal was based on the fact that as he was in regularly close contact with Killery, and part of MEW's responsibility included establishing a Far East-wide economic information collection agency, his headquarters did not need any additional staff on that front. On the second issue of an additional Thai political specialist, Brooke-Popham advised he already had a very good close working relationship with Crosby in Bangkok, which made any such offer redundant. According to his reasoning, if Japan did invade, all of the various consular and diplomatic officials from Bangkok and elsewhere in Thailand would gather in Singapore anyway. In his eyes that meant he would have the best economic and political advisories 'you could hope to obtain…' in this part of the world.[10]

His having been given overall command and authority over Operation Matador might go some way to explaining as to why Brooke-Popham had only advised London of his 'infiltration' operation weeks after the fact. It might also be why he did not feel the need to concur with Killery, or why he thought he could turn down additional staff in defiance of London. Now that London had been informed about these unsanctioned 'infiltration' exploits, and his refutation of their proposals, in a polite but tersely worded reply the War Office requested Brooke-Popham 'please explain' on all three fronts.[11]

Chapter 8

Never Complain, But Always Explain

From the outset, the War Office, SOE London and a plethora of other departments were not happy that Brooke-Popham had not only undertaken his 'infiltration' mission, but that he had done so only after consulting with, and taking advice from Crosby in Bangkok, Percival, and, on the further periphery, another civil servant in the form of the British Consul in Burma.[1] All sorts of clarification was being sought on just what Brooke-Popham actually meant about having sent his own 'infiltration' team into Thailand, and everybody wanted to know the intricate details. Special Operations added their take, arguing that professional infiltration operations were usually a slow process, often taking weeks if not months as a minimum to not only get War Office or SOE approval, and valuable lead-in time was of vital importance to organise, recruit, train, equip and then put into place operatives where and when required. The Foreign and Colonial Office joined in the admonishment chorus by pointing out that their offer of additional staff was less about Brooke-Popham's personal viewpoint, or what he deemed as being inimical to his headquarters' requirements, and more about what London urgently needed. That included gathering some measure of vitally important economic, social, cultural and political current intelligence about Thailand in general, but more so Southern Thailand in particular.

On the diplomatic front, many were worried that Brooke-Popham's knee-jerk actions might be misconstrued not only by Thailand, but also by Japan. If so, it could create a major incident of any sort; implications that would only serve Phibun's Thai ultra-nationalistic political interests, and Japan's 'Asia for Asians' geopolitical mantra, both of which were rapidly gaining traction amongst pro-independence movements in both Malaya and Thailand. The other disquiet was that Brooke-Popham's actions had potentially opened up major problems for Britain and across multiple fronts. Aside from any flow-on military or other security sensibilities possibly opening up in this part of the world, Brooke-Popham's unilateral actions might have instigated the very antithesis against British Malaya's Operation Matador defence. Opening up another unwanted battlefront on the other side of the world was not something Britain needed right now.

But as it was, Brooke-Popham's unsanctioned 'infiltration' operation had been over and done with for weeks, and there was nothing London could do about it now, other than contingency planning for the inevitable diplomatic fallout from Bangkok. In this at least, there had been nothing but silence from Phibun's government, and neither had there yet been any noticeable commentary from Japan over the events as they were unfolding. The former, perhaps, was the Thai Government's way of avoiding any embarrassment of being relegated to mere observer status in their own sovereign territorial backyard. The latter probably was Japan's own way of not drawing unnecessary attention to its own similar activities across the same region. Nonetheless, something had to be done to try and prevent this happening again, and the best way forward on offer by the War Office and Chiefs of Staff was to immediately clarify the chain of command in the Oriental Mission's covert operations.

That started with a polite educational campaign via highly classified cypher communications to Brooke-Popham of the intricacies surrounding intelligence work. Using layman's terms, Special Operations highlighted some of the subtle and not so subtle differences between differing types of non-conventional operations, especially those relative to complementing conventional warfare. He was given examples of how any military personnel being caught in civilian clothing behind enemy lines could lead to allegations of espionage, and possibly their execution, and that the Judge Advocate General (JAG) was probably not happy about any of the potential legalities that might fall out of his 'infiltration' operation. None of this was something Britain's covert war-fighting world welcomed. The other significant downside was that there may have been a chance that civilians who were neither military nor covert operatives, and who were already living and working in Southern Thailand, might be misidentified by potentially hostile forces as being enemy combatants. That premise was one of the most problematic, especially if Britain had gone to war with either Japan or Thailand while the British military teams were still in-country.

The Foreign and Colonial Offices, on the other hand, were adopting a more conciliatory tone. Both were focusing on the potential political semantics and diplomatic sensitivities of it all. Citing recent Thai legislative changes to the protection of British nationals in Thailand, both were advising how these might directly impact on how British populations might be viewed in the region in the near future. A significant case in point was that the earlier protections made under the 1906 Anglo-Thai Treaty, especially those affording preferential judicial and other treatments for British populations, had actually been rescinded by the Thai Government in 1940.[2] Although it was not stated outright, the other implication was that Crosby of all people, on that point at least, should have known better.

All of these potential scenarios were the dangerous types of actions that if left unattended, might contribute to fracturing what was becoming an increasingly volatile Anglo-Thai diplomatic relationship. In his eventual reticent reply, Brooke-Popham conceded that point at least, but then went on to gloss over the deficiencies and obvious potential threats his 'infiltration' plan may have instigated. Rather than addressing those issues, he then suggested that perhaps it was best if those types of 'infiltration' jobs he was envisaging might be left to some of the newly established military Independent Companies everyone was hearing so much about. He even put forward the suggestion that perhaps those undertaking specialist training at STS establishments elsewhere, including those recently set up by the Mawhood Mission in Australia, could be made responsible for his type of 'infiltration' missions into Southern Thailand.

It was sound reasoning from a military perspective, because these highly trained, specialised, and well-disciplined operatives from all ranks had already carried out similar reconnaissance and reconnoitre duties under hazardous circumstances in the Middle East, North Africa and elsewhere. If need be, these troops could fight their way out of a firefight as a cohesive force and if they had to, do everything and anything needed to survive behind enemy lines while also helping in facilitating pathways for military troop advance. But again, London reminded Brooke-Popham that the manpower shortages in defending the British Isles were already so vast that nobody could be spared, let alone any troops for covert or any other operations including those under Operation Matador. Brooke-Popham countered that argument by again arguing the case that if he was to be successful in mounting Malaya's defence he would need military reinforcements to do so.

The War Office stood firm and their advice remained the same. They would try to help where they could at least in terms of military resources associated with defending Malaya, but also made the point that no matter how many times he asked, there were not enough resources to go around. Brooke-Popham's frustration at London's latest rejection to all of his suggestions and requests for reinforcements came to the fore in his next less than gracious reply back to London. He again reaffirmed that it was not his responsibility as Commander-In-Chief of the Far East to delve into the finite details of any covert planning minutiae, that was their job.[3] As the to-ing and fro-ing between London and Brooke-Popham continued, it was left to Wing Commander Sir Frank Nelson of the War Office to put the problem into perspective. London was realising that intelligence operations in general, and covert infiltration operations in particular, lay 'outside the scope of existing divisions of staff…' in Malaya.[4]

Chapter 9

Operation Matador and the Singora Line

After the infiltration debacle had settled, and Crosby had been more or less put in his place regarding covert operations relevant to Malaya and Thailand, and as more consultations, negotiations and heated discussions ensued, by June 1941 Operation Matador's proposed scope of operations was starting to take shape. The core focus remained centred around harrying enemy forces wherever possible, but Thailand's sprawling geography, coupled with Malaya's paucity of military defence forces, suggested a more delineated geostrategic approach was going to be needed. Given that operations around the capital Bangkok's immediate area had already been dismissed, and central Thailand was too far from Malaya's northernmost frontier to quickly mount any British occupying force, it was decided mounting actions in Southern Thailand would have to remain the main focus. Not only did it straddle all of Malaya's northernmost frontier regions, it also housed the majority of Thailand's tin mines, and more importantly, it was an area that was completely undefended.

Southern Thailand was bounded by the four British Malaya states of Perlis, Kedah, Kelantan and Terengganu. Two branches of Thailand's south railway connected up with Malaya's railways in Malaya's northern frontier stations of Padang Besar and Sungai Golok. Only two main roads crossed the frontier; the first was at Sadao that ran directly to Singora, and the second ran from Betong to Kroh and was the gateway to Penang and beyond. There were numerous footpaths and bike paths crossing the frontier in all four adjoining states, including through rubber plantations straddling both.

In April 1941, the European population across Southern Thailand was estimated to be comprised of forty-five British and Australians, as opposed to almost double that number of Japanese.[1] The majority of the former were tin miners, the latter were overrepresented in infrastructure projects, including construction or improvement of certain roads including the Pattani to Betong highway. Despite several Japanese businesses like the fifteen-man Japanese Mitsubishi Company owned Kopkeb tin, or other Ban Nassan and Kohsabar tin mines failing badly, all still retained maximum staff, and they were all Japanese.[2] In fact, it had been the Ishihara Mining Company that had supplied useful information not only on Malaya's geography, but on other areas as well including the impact of weather on potential coastal disembarkation sites, to Japan's pre-invasion planners.[3]

The area of British operations being planned, essentially, encompassed all of Thailand's southernmost and narrowest section of the Kra Isthmus. It began roughly around Chumphon's 11° degree north line, and ended just south of Pattani's 6° degree line. In between lay a plethora of British and Australian-owned tin mining investments. Whether Brooke-Popham used the British Army's Military Geography (MI2) most recent geographic report of Southern Thailand below the eleventh parallel is unknown, but it seemed his proposed Operation Matador operating areas followed similar delineations. Line A stretched from Singora to Pattani and westward to Haad Yai, encompassing the entire Yala District as well as the two border towns of Sadao and Betong on the southernmost Thai–Malay frontier. Line B lay just north of Bandon, while Line C stretched across the Kra Isthmus through Chumphon. After several discussions between London, the Oriental Mission, GOC Malaya and CICFE, Lines B and C were determined to be too distant in terms of Britain's ability to move forces into those areas in time. Line A, on the other hand, fulfilled operational, tactical and strategic requirements.

Now identified as the Singora Line, it was further divided into two main areas of operations. The first stretched northwards from the main coastal harbour and trade port of Singora to Ronpibon and Phuket, encompassing the major railway nexus of Haad Yai, the Thai border town of Sadao, and the border crossing that led on to Padang Besar on the Malay side. The second ran south of Singora, encompassing the smaller east coast market harbour town of Pattani, running through the smaller railway town of Yala and frontier town of Betong, and then over the border on to Malay's border town of Kroh. The entire area was a rich tin and rubber resource landscape.

At the Singora Line's northernmost reaches (Singora Line North), lay Ronpibon, Phuket and other tin mining sites. Further south and closer to the western border region of Haad Yai and Sadao lay smaller mines, including the Takuapa Tin Mine's Ban Pru dredge. In and around Singora itself lay a handful of mining concessions including the Teh Seh and Bandinlan tin mines. South of Singora (Singora Line South) near Pattani were others. Just south of Yala lay the most advanced state-of-the-art, lode tin mining concession in Southern Thailand in the Pinyok Tin Mine.[4] Down the road sat the Ayer Weng tin ore survey site, and further south-west nearer to Betong and the border, lay the Kampong Toh Tin Mine.

Lying between all of these tin mines was dense jungle interspersed with vast tracts of rubber plantations. Either side of Pattani, Singora, Betong and Sadao, Japanese investors had bought up hundreds of acres of rubber plantations.[5] Accompanying the mass purchases had been the concomitant setting up of three Japanese rubber buying agencies with exclusive interest in Southern Thailand. In 1941, some of the largest major rubber plantations flanking either side of the Thai–Malay border, and stretching from Sadao in Thailand to Padang Besar in Malaya, and likewise from Betong and over the border to Kroh, were owned by the Japanese. The only other vast rubber plantation nearby was the British-owned Yala Rubber Estate, lying alongside the Kedah border.

The Yala District was the halfway point that lay between Pattani and Betong, and it was home to some of the highest limestone mountains in Thailand. Nearby was the highest point of the Sankalakhiri Mountain Range, stretching all the way across from central Thailand into northernmost Malaya. Roughly forty-one kilometres (twenty-five or so miles) south of Yala township, a new surveyed and graded terrace had been cut into the western bank of the Pattani River. A shelf had been successfully cut into the hillside, and a new road was now running along the top of a sixty-one metre (200 feet) drop into the river below. Nestled just behind it, and on the other side of the same mountain chain area, was the Pinyok Tin Mine. The Ledge was the highest roadway portion of the 122 kilometres (seventy-six mile) long Yala to Betong highway, and it was not a drive for the faint-hearted. On reaching its crest, however, it offered maximum range in both line of sight, and a good high-angled trajectory position over both northern and southern approaches. The route running further south and into Betong was a tortuous, winding road, full of repeated sharp turns and 'S' bends.

Singora was considered as the only port of consequence in Southern Thailand, and as such would undoubtedly be any invading force's main landing point. From there, the presumption was that Japan would then push on to the east–west railway hub of Haad Yai, and that might be the best place to confront Japan's forces before they reached the border.[6] In strategic terms it made sense, because it was one of the shortest distances in Thailand that crossed from the east to the west coast, and the closest place to cross into Northern Malaya. Not only that, as the main railway nexus for both north–south and east–west trains, Haad Yai would be an obvious target in terms of establishing control for faster troop transport and other resource movements. The other major point of importance was that this particular Thailand to Malaya train line shared a single-line metre gauge, that in peacetime had a daily capacity of at least nine trains running each way.[7]

Alongside the track also ran the better of the two southern roads linking Southern Thailand with Northern Malaya. Although it was narrower in parts to the one further south running from Yala to Betong, it was straighter, and had less of the jungle twists and turns. It was also well maintained, fully metalled, and ran almost parallel to the railway. All of which suggested that if there was going to be any place that was an imperative to seize, hold and control, it was Singora. That would be the centrepiece to the British Army securing a Line of Control (LOC) north of Kedah and Perlis, and cutting off a potential Japanese advance westward into Northern Malaya.[8] That is, of course, if the Japanese Army was planning on moving down the Kra Isthmus from Bangkok, and not across it. Pattani, for the most part, was not considered a viable landing option. Nonetheless, at least now that an area of operations had officially been decided in military geography terms, Killery's next step could turn to the operational planning of small-scale, tin mine denial sabotage actions. In Southern Thailand that would be known collectively as Operation Cleeves.

Chapter 10

Operation Cleeves

Herding (Tin Mining) Cats

Operation Cleeves' primary goals had not changed since the original ideas about small-scale tin mine denial operations had been talked about earlier on in the year.[1] Under the auspices of Operation Etonian, the threefold SOE approach had already been identified, and it was only later when it was replaced by Operation Matador that some Oriental Mission approaches changed. While Operation Cleeves' Southern Thailand-focused imperative still centred around tin mine denial operations, it had now expanded to include those same teams finding other ways of helping any British Army advance into Thai territory. The caveat remained the same however, insomuch as that both should only happen in response to any potential Japanese invasion.[2] Of these newly designated Operation Cleeves objectives, however, top-level planning both in London and Singapore had agreed that in the event of a Japanese invasion into Southern Thailand, it was to be tin mine denial operations that were to take precedence and to be put into effect immediately should Japan invade.

Aside from these actions, there was now some scope around whether additional responsibilities could be included, such as engaging teams in a series of targeted and pre-positioned delaying tactics. That might involve disrupting communications and transportation, with an end goal of maximising as much disruption to Japanese intentions as possible. The only areas that were off limits for Operation Cleeves operatives were strict instructions to neither contaminate nor destroy water supplies or foodstuffs. They would be needed by the advancing British Army along the way. The idea was that Operation Cleeves' field agents might be able to set up roadblocks, cut telephone lines, blow up bridges and so on, but also have enough time to disable as many tin mines as possible, as well as making sure the mining machinery was not completely destroyed. Their final tasking if and where possible was in assisting and evacuating Europeans out of Thailand if necessary.

Now that the Singora Line had been delineated as Operation Matador's area of operations, it made the Oriental Mission's specific tin mine denial targeting under Operation Cleeves that much easier. This was helped in part now that overall delegation for enacting Operation Matador remained the sole responsibility of Brooke-Popham, while military operations would remain under Percival as GOC Malaya's command. Significantly, potential covert, sabotage and denial missions also fell under Brooke-Popham's command, but to achieve that he would need to rely heavily on input from Killery and his Oriental Mission's area of expertise in these small-scale industrial sabotage operations.

One of the earliest hurdles Killery had to get over was that unlike regular military operations that relied on basic soldiering assumptions including command and control, it soon became apparent that corralling a myriad of civilian tin mining companies into some sort of covert unit was more like herding cats than mustering troops. Once this was realised back in London, it was only then that Killery was given freer rein to get Operation Cleeves up and running, and he was soon advising them with the good news that it was finally progressing and would be under way shortly.[3] But first there was the question of garnering the support of tin mining companies, and Killery could not progress in any recruiting, training or organising objectives for Southern Thailand tin mine denial planning until he had at least tacit agreement from the companies themselves.

It was around this time that Killery opted to send Kingdon-Ward out on a scoping mission into Southern Thailand. Hopes were high that because of his previous travels into other frontier regions, this foray would not raise suspicions among local Thai authorities or potentially Japanese observers. His presence on either side of the Thai–Malay border in the towns of Kroh in Malaya and Betong in Thailand, for example, or his forays up into and around The Ledge, might just be considered another scientific jungle expedition if they were lucky. The trouble was, however, that Killery had despatched Kingdon-Ward not long after Brooke-Popham's 'infiltration' fiasco, and needless to say that particular large-scale influx of fit, agile British military personnel in civilian dress, crossing the border at the three main overland border regions in Southern Thailand and preferring to drive rather than sail up the coastline or take the train, was more than a bit peculiar. These may have been among some of the reasons as to why Kingdon-Ward was repeatedly held up at the border, often facing a barrage of questions as to what he was doing there. When he was finally allowed into Southern Thailand, things did not go to plan, as the local authorities were viewing him with suspicion. He cut the trip short and returned to Singapore, which was not the type of news Killery wanted.

After this event, Killery's contingency planning was now looking into more unorthodox recruiting approaches. He knew the majority of the thirty or so working tin mines in and around the Singora Line were dominated by British and Australian tin mining investments. That implied that if any denial operations were going to get off the ground in the first place, then securing their parent company co-operation and support was vital to any operational success. Not only that, if Operation Cleeves was to have any chance at all over such a scattered jungle area of operations then the recruiting alternatives were obvious. Working on the timescale principle alone meant he would need to be able to utilise a majority civilian participation among those living and working on the tin mines; that was, of course, if he could get local tin industry support. But that was not going to be as straightforward as Killery had been envisaging, especially when in 1941 in British Malaya and Southern Thailand armed conflict had not yet been felt in this part of the world. Aside from what was happening in French Indochina further north, and the friendly but rapidly de-escalating diplomacy in Thailand, war had not been declared against Japan and, as far as anybody knew, neither were they at war with Thailand.

To this end, Killery had realised early on that getting the tin industry support he badly needed was not going to be easy, mainly because supporting the war effort was still a highly lucrative, profitable, and not to mention safe trading platform for tin mining stakeholders in the Far East. But he had a few things up his sleeve, and that included his own substantial company expertise as a former chief executive officer in the corporate world. He would use that particular skillset to bridge the civilian with the military in the current wartime world, especially as he knew that without any of the tin mining industry's corporate support any tin mine denial operations of any kind would be over before they had even started. Noting that tin mining was one of many professions where some workers had been given exemptions from military service, especially because they were considered essential services critical to Britain's war effort, Southern Thailand's European tin mining communities were no exception. For Killery, that meant he might be able to recruit operatives from among a bevy of professionals already within the tin mining industry, and at least give Operation Cleeves a fighting chance in what was already a precarious human resource situation.

From the outset the Oriental Mission's planning hinged on two essential achievements. The first was garnering majority civilian support and participation, not only from all aspects of the Thailand tin mining industry, but between the twin locations of both the Kra Isthmus and within the Malaya Peninsula. That was because while the actual tin mining itself was physically being undertaken in Southern Thailand, the headquartered company control of tin mines was based in Malaya. The second was in gathering as much top-down mining industry support as he could muster, and that was where the relationship with Crosby started to deteriorate quickly. Since arriving, Killery had routinely been reporting his progress back to London as negotiations progressed, and there had been an additional suggestion that perhaps MEW contact Crosby direct and inform him that any and all tin mining industry liaison relevant to Thailand was going to be undertaken by the Oriental Mission.[4] The relationship with Killery soured even further when Crosby was also informed that Killery might be given discretionary power to inform him, as head of the British Legation in Bangkok, when all the agreements had been completed. With that arrangement in place, Killery next turned to finding and appointing staff from within the tin mining management community for the next two crucial stages. Phase one included identifying specific tin mines and their locations for denial operations, and phase two was identifying, selecting and recruiting tin mining staff as operatives. To Killery's credit, he was already addressing several of these factors by exploiting what was the most common denominator to all tin mining stakeholders in Southern Thailand, and that was tin smelting.

Chapter 11

Oriental Mission (Penang Headquarters)

It was one thing to mine the tin and get it out of the ground, but it was another thing entirely to transform the raw resource into a manageable export commodity. All tin produced in Southern Thailand was sent to the two main smelting works on the peninsula. One was the Eastern Smelting Company (ESOY) located in Penang, and the other The Straits Trading Company (STC) with smelters both in Penang and Singapore. STC's Singapore's smelter in particular had earned a reputation for producing high-grade tin that was shipped and sold on the world's market in the usual form of ingots. Internationally recognised as the purest-quality tin in the world, production was so lucrative that both smelting companies were purchasing ore in ever-increasing quantities from Thailand, and attracting additional investment from around the world. By successfully gaining the co-operation of these two main smelting operators, Killery would already be laying the groundwork for encouraging participation from within the wider tin mining community. First to come on board was Franklin Donovan Bisseker, head of the Eastern Smelting Company (ESOY) based in Penang.

Bisseker had only been in Malaya for a few years. Fluent in both Chinese and Malay, he had spent the previous twenty years or so in China working with the British American Tobacco Company based in Shanghai.[1] On arrival in Malaya in the late 1930s, he had soon established a good working relationship with the then GOC Malaya, Major General William Dobbie, and both men were concerned at the paltry situation of Malaya's defences. Dobbie was continually raising his alarms on the military side, while Bisseker did the same regarding the civil defence side on the other.[2] Now a few years later, there was a new reality that both might become a future defence reality, especially if Southern Thailand was to become Japan's stepping stone into Malaya.

After Dobbie's forced retirement and despatch back to Britain in 1940, it was Bisseker who was left to take up the mantle, albeit it from a civilian perspective. That same year, when he found himself elected as the Penang commercial community's representative on the Straits Settlements Legislative Council, he had continued questioning Malaya's appalling lack of local civil defences. Without Dobbie's backing, however, he soon found himself as the proverbial lone voice in the wilderness, and an ongoing thorn in the side of Malayan defence planners. By publicly criticising both their attitudes towards Malaya's lack of civil defence, and Malaya's general unsatisfactory preparations for war, Bisseker was not winning any local military or political friends. So when Killery approached him with a proposal to actively participate in some sort of defence arrangements, particularly those involving civilian defence components, Bisseker jumped at the chance. He was one of the first in the local community to not only support Killery and Operation Cleeves, but also to allow the Oriental Mission to use some of his company resources.

That was why it was at Bisseker's ESOY Penang smelting works located at 73 Dato Kramat Road on Penang Island that the Oriental Mission found its Penang home.[3] Bisseker even provided Killery's staff with offices in the company's headquarters at nearby Birch House, which became the Advanced Operational Headquarters for Oriental Mission business and administration in northern Malaya.[4] The smelting works, too, would eventually offer some limited STS101 consolidation training and the location was ideal because the factory lay set back from the main road, in the middle of what was then a deep valley, surrounded by a variety of low-ceilinged houses all crammed together. Aside from the main roadway out front, the only other main form of transport was a small, nondescript freight railway line linking the factory with Weld Quay and Penang Harbour.[5] Using the Birch House office location made sense in terms of conducting Oriental Mission business this close to the Thai–Malay border, because Penang was geographically closer to and had quicker access to Southern Thailand than Singapore. Not long after gaining Bisseker's support, STC headed up by Sir John Bagnall was also persuaded to support the scheme.[6]

Getting these two men on side from the outset was a shrewd move by Killery. Not only because he now had the backing of the two major operators monopolising the smelting of all tin resources, but also because both men had substantial sideways influence over the two largest tin mining investors in Southern Thailand – one being the British-owned and operated Thailand Tin Mines, and the other the Australian-owned and operated Anglo-Oriental Tin Mining Company. Moving forward and in consultation with Bisseker and Bagnall, Killery then put forward a contact plan as to how each man might help in getting Operation Cleeves under way, mainly because there was still the need to gain at least in principle support from both companies. Of the two, it was the British-owned Thailand Tin Syndicate that immediately offered support, while the Australian-owned Anglo-Oriental Tin Mining Company hesitated.

In a confidential meeting co-hosted by Bisseker and Killery's representative, Kingdon-Ward, held in Birch House in late August 1941, fraught discussions began in earnest to address some of the stumbling blocks being raised.[7] That included understanding just what it was Killery was asking them to do, not the least of which was what type of potential participation was being requested of the mines themselves. Other important details were also being worked out, including what did small-scale sabotage mean, what was the difference between destruction and disruption, and what did all of this portend for the future preservation of the tin mines and their on-site machinery. Some of the other underlying sticking points were what immediate influences Operation Cleeves preparations might have on daily tin mine production and outputs, what were the safety plans being put in place for tin mining community operatives, and how did these outcomes expect to support Britain's longer-term war effort? Generally speaking, companies were considering their own risk assessments should they participate in any tin denial operations, and the last thing they wanted to do was put the lives of their employees and investments any more at risk than they had to.[8]

In addressing some of these very real issues Bisseker had assured the mine managers attending the meeting, that the Oriental Mission had negotiated a definitive agreement that a Royal Navy ship would be despatched to the west coast to evacuate Singora Line North European populations, including operatives, when and if required. Those located around Singora Line South with easy access to road and rail systems would in all probability be able to merely drive out, or catch a train, once the job was done. Other affirmations were made that there would be no cost to post-war rebuilding of any of the tin mines being denied, because the British government would provide higher prioritisation in the supply of essential component parts after the war.[9] Kingdon-Ward gave further assurances that in those circumstances once the war was over, whatever parts would be needed could be ordered directly with the Oriental Mission. Written lists for parts were to be placed in an envelope and specially marked 'M.100', and after being endorsed by FJ Steggall of ESOY in Penang, they would then be sent on to the Oriental Mission headquarters in Singapore.[10] There was no need to mention the arrangement to MEW London, or to involve others including the Ministry of Supply over the arrangement, because everything would be handled locally and in-house.[11]

Further to these ongoing discussions were what other impacts Operation Cleeves requirements might have on maintaining ongoing vital tin outputs for the war effort, especially as there were real problems with ongoing tin mine professional labour force shortages in the region. Writing home to his wife Iris in November 1941, the Pinyok Tin Mine Superintendent, Harding Thomas, had opined that not only was he doing his own job, but he was also doing the job of three others as well. With this additional human resource problem looming, it seemed garnering tin mining community support might be harder than realised, but that too was helped by Bisseker. Earlier in the year, Governor Thomas had appointed him responsible for sorting out that Malaya-wide problem. A responsibility that suggested Bisseker could tailor the impact of training requirements for Operation Cleeves, while still maintaining the favourable daily running of the tin mines themselves. Noting that most tin mining professionals were considered as essential services personnel, and thereby critical to Britain's war effort in maintaining vitally important tin mining production, Bisseker knew at least in this way he could probably fix both problems in one go.

Some employees already had official exemptions from military service whether they liked it or not, and many were not happy with that situation. Killery surmised that on that point alone many like himself might then be keen to jump at the chance and do 'their bit' in support of the war, and not just the war effort. That helped in narrowing down the recruitment stakes, as well as cutting down some of the envisaged training times that might be needed at STS101. Any workplace absences could be manageable with the right approach, especially in mitigating any potential Oriental Mission demands, along with alleviating any possible interferences with the very tin production the Empire demanded. These were the very same arguments some of the upper echelons including Governor Thomas, Crosby and others had been harping on about since the Oriental Mission had been officially sanctioned.

The other main argument was inextricably linked with the individual mine technologies themselves. Some of Southern Thailand's tin mines had the latest and most expensive state-of-the-art hydraulic dredge machineries in the world. Any wanton destruction would not be welcomed by the companies, and neither would unfair competitive disadvantage be endorsed. Even with Bisseker and Bagnall's help, Killery was still facing tin mining executives seeking assurances, and reassurances, that the mines and dredges would not be destroyed, but merely disabled. This lay at the core of all of Operation Cleeves' small-scale sabotage denial operations anyway. That seemed to remain a main sticking point for the Australian-owned Anglo-Oriental, as arguments dragged on surrounding if their machinery was incapacitated by removing essential operating parts, what type of compensatory or other claims could they expect from the British Government, and in the aftermath of the potential fulcrum of war, and so on. While Anglo-Oriental had qualms about supporting Operation Cleeves, Thailand Tin was the opposite, and they were fully supportive of what Killery and the Oriental Mission were trying to put in place from the outset.

Because the majority of those who might potentially become involved with Operation Cleeves were already living and working across Southern Thailand, and would by necessity still be needed in maintaining their particular company's tin mine daily workings, a full-time organiser and common point of contact would need to be found. Killery delegated another Oriental Mission operative, WD Reeve, to help sort that out.[12] Although Reeve had extensive experience in the Far East, he was more experienced with Burma than Thailand, so Bisseker successfully enlisted the aid of Thomas R Weir, the Eastern Director of Thailand Tin, to help Reeve out.

Weir's appointment, like Besseker's, would prove to be the more beneficial in terms of garnering the tin mining community's engagement. Unlike Anglo-Oriental's Kuala Lumpur-based representative Adolphe Alois Henggeler, for instance, Weir actually had more autonomy than others when it came to committing Thailand Tin Mine resources to Operation Cleeves. Thailand Tin's London head office had already given him authority to utilise company personnel, and commit company resources, as he saw fit in accordance with any potential Japanese invasion.[13] That included any liaison he deemed necessary with the Oriental Mission or anyone else for that matter. The other responsibility given to Weir was that he also had full company authority to follow the CICFE's directions if and when required under Operation Cleeves, and in support of Operation Matador. On top of that, he also had additional company authority that should alternate circumstances demand something else be put in place, whatever that may be, he could act unilaterally over his company's tin mines in Southern Thailand.

Meanwhile, Reeve began his tasking by undertaking a few scoping missions and visiting a handful of Southern Thailand's tin mines over the next few weeks. He was checking in with mining staff and looking at some of the exigencies of their respective locations, and local Thai officials were noticing this latest, new face travelling between the various tin mine communities in this part of the world, even though he was not a tin miner. When Reeve returned to the Oriental Mission by late September, he brought with him some conflicting news. On his travels into some tin mining communities, including those owned by Anglo-Oriental, it did not seem to be the coalface that was the problem. It was becoming clearer that there were other fissures emerging, and they were mostly upper management and locally based. There seemed to be an information chasm between Anglo-Oriental's chairman, Swiss national Henggeler in Kuala Lumpur for example, and his head offices back in Australia. The information Australia was receiving was that Britain was requesting the large-scale complete destruction of their Southern Thailand tin mines, and that request was being made prior to any declaration of war being made against Japan, Thailand or anybody else. That explained why the Australians had then taken their concerns to the Australian Federal Government, and made formal protests to the British High Commissioner in Canberra. Once the War Office weighed into the argument and Operation Cleeves' aims were formally outlined, the Australians finally agreed to help support the denial operations.

With that matter settled, Weir's follow-up visits into Southern Thailand's tin mining communities did not raise the same level of suspicion as Kingdon-Ward or Reeve had done. In contrast to others venturing into the area of late, his sojourns were not out of the ordinary, and any of his travelling to and from all of Southern Thailand's tin mines anywhere on the Kra Isthmus or Malay Peninsula was neither suspicious nor out of place at any time of the year. That was because Weir was a well-known employee of Thailand Tin and routinely visited the mining company interests at Huey Moot, Takuapa and in Renong and elsewhere. He was also a familiar tin mining identity throughout the region, and any of his involvement in visiting various tin mines including those of his competitors would provide Killery with much-needed valuable insight. Weir could look into what types of tin mine denial or other small-scale sabotage operations might be undertaken, and into which mines could or would potentially be able to complete other taskings. Only a month after bringing him on board, the Oriental Mission was already reaping the benefits of Weir's local and professional tin mining knowledge, because it was also not out of the ordinary for him to routinely travel up to Bangkok and visit with Crosby on a regular basis. In mid-1941, Crosby's increasing animosity to Killery and the Oriental Mission was getting out of hand, and it was Weir who went up to Bangkok to meet with him and attempt to smooth the stormy waters.[14]

It was good news for Killery when Weir returned from his lengthy visit. Not only had he managed to talk Crosby around and into some sort of tacit agreement over the Operation Cleeves component, he had also convinced him of how it was an important and essential support component of

Operation Matador. He managed this by explaining to the British Legation head how his own company, Thailand Tin, was making necessary planning steps in immobilising its tin mines in Southern Thailand, and that contrary to what Anglo-Oriental was promulgating, nobody was being asked to destroy them. In doing so, Weir had given Crosby a better understanding of what was actually going to be needed, and that had included the security of tin mine property, dredge machinery and most importantly of all, the protection and safety of mine personnel.[15]

Weir had also managed to achieve what Killery and others could not, and that was getting Crosby to realise that the Oriental Mission was not trying to step on his Bangkok-centric toes. Rather, they were trying to improve Britain's bad intelligence deficit on Thailand, and find ways to prevent any Japanese commercial monopolies emerging in direct competition to Britain's pre-existing ones. He cited the importance of the tin mining industry in Southern Thailand to Britain and to the war effort as just one of them. Weir also made the point surrounding the tyranny of distance that afflicted the locations of the tin mines themselves. On this point at least Crosby acceded to Weir's suggestion, that for obvious reasons of timeliness and location, evacuation would need to be controlled from his office in Penang, and not from Singapore or Bangkok. His other advice to Crosby was that ancillary arrangements for the protection of non-European mine staff had also been put in place, including provisions made for those workers who might choose to stay behind and safeguard company property. Others who would not be involved in the scheme would be released immediately before any operations began.

The other information Weir sent to his London offices was that although he acknowledged Crosby's view that some of Thailand's authorities feared the Japanese, and that while Crosby himself maintained the assumption that there was a strong desire among the Thais to maintain strict neutrality, Weir himself was not convinced. After his last trip to Bangkok, he was not too sure that Phibun's government wanted to remain as good a friend to Britain as Crosby was depicting. It was one of the reasons why he next advised his head office in London that, should the time come, he and several other of their Thailand Tin employees, each with substantial local knowledge and regional expertise, would be offering their services to local British authorities if an actual crisis emerged. It was part of the reasoning as to why some Thailand Tin Syndicate employees including himself were among some of the first to volunteer for Oriental Mission recruiting, and why others would shortly be undertaking STS101 training in support of Operation Cleeves.

Chapter 12

Radio Hits of 1941

Signal Tunes and Missing Files

Now that the 'who' and the 'where' had been sorted out, the last piece of the mission puzzle was the 'when'. How Operation Cleeves was to disseminate CICFE's orders to commence operations was a bit of a problem in Southern Thailand, given that the Thai authorities had of late started cracking down on anybody with shortwave radio sets. The easiest and probably most time-effective method was to exploit that which was already in place, the radio. English language radio programmes were broadcast daily from either Radio Delhi or the Malay Broadcasting Commission (MBC) down in Singapore. At the August meeting, an agreed system of announcement signal tunes and messaging had been worked out to be played over MBC airwaves. The two signal tunes decided upon and chosen by the tin mining communities themselves, were 'Abide with Me' and 'Keep the Home Fires Burning'.[1] If and when the time came that Brooke-Popham as CICFE gave the command to commence operations, they were to be broadcast without hesitation from the MBC station down in Singapore.

The first tune of 'Abide with Me', was to be a planned broadcast indicating a timing of between seven to ten days prior to any probable expected invasion date. That was going to be the signal alerting Operation Cleeves parties to get ready, begin their pre-preparations and planning sequences to commence operations, and then standby for the second signal tune. The second tune of 'Keep the Home Fires Burning' was supposed to be given within twenty-four hours of what was considered zero hour. Zero hour was military speak for being the probable time an invasion might actually start. That would be the signal tune for operatives to literally start commencing their denial and disruption operations in their respective areas.

On top of these two signal tunes, there was a third additional communication order to be broadcast for certain team leaders. Sometime after 'Abide with Me' had been played, and sometime either before or after 'Keep the Home Fires Burning' was heard, an emergency news story would be released about an unnamed junior Army officer in Singapore.[2] It would report how the said junior officer had been foolhardy and careless, and had through incompetence and a lack of security lost some very important files from Malaya Command. He had left them on the front seat of his unlocked car with the car windows down, and while he had left the vehicle to attend to some obscure personal business somewhere in the centre of Singapore town, they had gone missing. The newsreader would then painstakingly read out each of the missing files' numbers in the vain hope someone might find them and hand them in to the nearest Army headquarters.

In reality that final broadcast was to contain additional coded instructions for cell leaders. It was about the Oriental Mission communicating specific co-ordinates, orders and exact individual instructions as to what each Operation Cleeves party was to do, how it was to be done, and in what order each operative's area of responsibility should be implemented. Each participating tin mine denial party was to have a working list of possible objectives applicable to that particular mine, and within a dedicated area of relatively close proximity in which teams would be able to carry out operations in a timely manner. It would be a pre-planned and allocated numerical code that cell leaders would have to decipher themselves, and then translate those particular sequences of actions into specific operations. It was a way of communicating Operation Cleeves orders for targetted operational cells. The numbers would be giving exact individual instructions, as to what to do, when to do it, where to do it, and in what order each action should take place, in allocated operational areas of responsibility.

In those tin mining areas where there were not dedicated Operation Cleeves operatives, the songs carried equal warning arrangements, and they too had been made with individual mine managers of other tin mines participating in the scheme. Some of those supporting the scheme were not formally part of Operation Cleeves, or received any training or supplies from the Oriental Mission, but would on their own account deny their tin mines if they could. Depending on their locations, some of those further inland on hearing the first song were advised to evacuate immediately. Anyone not engaged with any of the tin mine sabotage operations, including others living in various European tin mining enclaves such as wives, were also to leave as soon as possible on hearing 'Abide With Me'. For others closer to the border, on hearing the second tune of 'Keep the Home Fires Burning' they were to do the same. Again, it was presumed by Operation Cleeves' planners that everyone else, because of their proximity to main transport routes, would have ample time to leave as soon as operations had been completed. With all the procedural applications now more or less in place, it was time for the Oriental Mission to start recruiting.

Chapter 13

Smuggling, Trafficking and Grassroots Planning

As the practicalities of successfully implementing Operation Cleeves were coming together, so too was the organisational grassroots stakeholder support expanding. The Oriental Mission was already realising that a co-ordinating point of grassroots contact was going to be a necessary part of the action, so Weir released one of his mine managers, Maurice C Kain, to take up that position on the civilian tin mining community liaison side.[1] While Weir took on the higher-level mine management co-ordinating role, Kain's responsibilities became more focused on the practical implementation details, which was why it was Kain's Birch House offices that became the main point of contact as the Oriental Mission's Penang liaison.

One of Kain's core responsibilities was in finding ways of incorporating various Operation Cleeves' requirements into routine tin mining activities. That might have included exploiting customary workplace behaviours, such as moving staff between tin mines, or rotating them into and out of districts on a regular basis. These were well-known and familiar practices, not only among the tin mining communities, but also among the wider European community in general. Over the past few years Weir and Kain had been involved with both, and now of late were doing more of the same. It was not unusual in some of the newer and more modern, state-of-the-art tin mining ventures in Southern Thailand, such as Pinyok Tin Mine for example, that there was a ramping up of rotational rosters as mining production increased. Over the past few months they had been doing just that, attracting a wider variety of European tin mining professionals from around the world, and sometimes interchanging them between the same parent company's different tin mining-related work sites. In Ayer Weng Tin Survey Fields, for example, not far down the road from the Pinyok Tin Mine, a newly developing tin mine survey operation was being undertaken by Australian mine surveyor

Thomas B Donnelly, who would probably often travel between his survey site, Pinyok and the other mines in the district in the routine undertakings of his position.

As most of the on-site tin mine placements were usually based on short-term contracts or 'on-loan' agreements between workforces, it often meant a high turnover of staff was also not out of the ordinary. Additionally, mine managers, accountants, supervisors and other employees were always to-ing and fro-ing between their respective tin mines and their various company head offices in Penang, Kuala Lumpur or Singapore. Travelling between local mining headquarters and different company tin mines was also a regular occurrence and not unusual, as much as it was quite routine that certain employees would be constantly touching base with local tin mining employment agencies. The main one in Southern Thailand was the General Mining and Agency Company (GMAC). Several of those employed on multi-interest mine sites including Kampong Toh Tin Mine, or further north in Ronpibon and Phuket tin mining areas for example, had only recently been placed in their positions by the mining workforce placement agency. Over the past few months there had been plenty of rotations and resignations, as the impact of war was increasingly taking its toll on the tin mining profession. That meant that given the ongoing labour shortages of tin mining personnel, it would be routine for any new tin mining professionals to turn up at any given time, or to transition between different mines on different dates. In fact, it would be deemed as odd if there was not an ongoing rotation amongst the tin mining sites on a regular basis, or ongoing new faces turning up among the various European tin mining enclaves. All of this would work in Killery's favour, when he soon began placing Operation Cleeves operatives into Southern Thailand's tin mines.

On top of that, most Southern Thailand tin mining travelling was often accompanied by ongoing supply runs, not only between the various tin mines themselves but also into and out of the local district and beyond. That included driving back and forth over the border into Malaya, towards the east coast harbour market towns of Pattani and Singora, west to the more cosmopolitan respites offered in Penang, or even further south to Kuala Lumpur. Driving trips or railway journeys that were not only consistent, but were as regular as clockwork. Constantly moving staff and supplies between mines to accommodate Operation Cleeves, and any other potential Oriental Mission requirements, could be done without arousing too much suspicion. On both of those counts Weir and the Thailand Tin Mines had already started leading the way, especially in exploiting well-worn jungle pathways for what were essentially covert weapons smuggling operations.

Using a combination of routine relocations of tin mining personnel and routine supply runs, Operation Cleeves' arms and materials had already started being smuggled over the Thai–Malay border into Southern Thailand. Not only along the two main roads, or the various criss-crossing backroads that linked various rubber estates, but moreso over unmapped dirt roads and roughly hewn jungle tracks. These were the same hidden pathways villagers on both sides of the border had been using literally for centuries. Numbered in their hundreds, they could be found at any given point along the entire Thai–Malay border. They were well known to many, and had long been used for all sorts of nefarious activities, including blackmarketeering among other things. Now they were a series of access routes that were working well and in Operation Cleeves' favour in several ways. For example, some of the more adventurous tin mine denial operatives, when returning from Oriental Mission Penang meetings, or later, their STS101 training in Penang or Singapore, often chose to travel along the offroad tracks in specially altered motor vehicles. Some of the mine cars had been refurbished with new undercarriage concealment storage areas, where all sorts of weapons were strapped underneath. Others had special store areas hidden in pockets such as in car seats, that held smaller items including detonators. In some instances, special explosives were packed with the usual stores on the back of trucks for routine supply deliveries to the mines.

Sometimes other mine vehicles such as open-backed lorries would take the main Kroh to Betong border road, then head for the ferry near Yala. From there they would cross the Pattani River and head for Pattani. Others would take the other route, travelling from Padang Besar and on to Sadao, passing through Haad Yai before eventually arriving in Singora. One key trick learned from the tin miners themselves, was that on trips involving transporting specific items such as ammunition, it was best if it was packed into large, filthy drums of dirty grease.[2] One of the reasons was that it was well-known in the always unlocked Betong border gate crossing area for example, that if members of the tin mining community were stopped by Thai border guards or the local police, which was hardly ever, most of the guards shared peculiar proclivities of not wanting to rummage around in dirty, greasy, old and well-weathered oil drums.[3] This was something that was working very well in the Oriental Mission's covert favour, especially when most of the time the European tin miners were already well-known to the guards, and would more often than not be routinely waved through after passing through customs and immigration and happily sent on their way.

Within months, the Thai–Malay border smuggling operations had been so successful that at least three Operation Cleeves weapons caches were already on site, and at their select locations a month or more before Japan invaded. Up north at Ronpibon and at the Ban Pru, Huey Moot and other tin mine offshoots, Operation Cleeves teams were already in possession of two rifle pistols, six revolvers, 400lb of high explosives, as well as other ancillary materials and devices. Across at Phuket they had their eight Tommy guns, twenty rifles, thirty-one revolvers and 250 grenades already securely stored. Alike Ronpibon they too were allocated 400lb of high explosives. Pinyok's weapons and explosives list, on the other hand, was different. They had four Tommy guns, twelve revolvers, twenty-four grenades, as well as an undisclosed number of demolition stores for all of their taskings in the Pinyok–Yala area, yet paradoxically they were not allocated a secret wireless telegraphy (W/T) set, nor a W/T specialised operator. Both of those had been reserved for the only two Operation Cleeves sites allocated W/T transmitting sets at Ronpibon and Phuket. Those two sites had been deemed of more importance, probably because they were further north and closer to Bangkok. The sets had been sent in the care of the only two known regular Army communications specialists detached to Operation Cleeves and working undercover. Sergeant ES Wright, who had previously been teaching communications down at STS101, was attached to Nawng Pet Tin Mine under cover as a tin miner; and Sergeant Frank Misselbrook, who too had been part of Mawhood's Australian mission and also on staff at STS101's communicator training, had been sent to Phuket to do the same. The next thing that had to be sorted out was operational taskings and responsibilities.

Chapter 14

Mining, Missions and Multi-tasking

In roughly only four months the Oriental Mission had managed to cobble together twenty-nine Operation Cleeves tin mine denial operatives, into eight operational cells relative to Southern Thailand's Singora Line.[1] In direct contrast, there had been little progress in northern and central Thailand, which Killery lay squarely on problems associated with Crosby. Crosby remained suspicious of anything to do with any SOE-like operations, and he was continually badgering the Foreign Secretary, who in turn was continually badgering SOE London, for definite assurances that no SOE-like operations or projects would be undertaken in Thailand. That is, not without first securing prior agreement of the local British Government representative, who was of course, Crosby himself.[2] SOE London had let Killery know that they had repeatedly given the Foreign Secretary that assurance, and nobody was sure why Crosby could not let the matter drop, unless he felt that anybody other than he who might be approaching the higher levels of Thailand's society or government, were somehow creating a diplomatic *faux pas*. Given Crosby's close personal friendships with many of Britain's upper echelons in Bangkok, Killery thought the lack of progress up north was probably a consequence of the Bangkok-centric Crosby's relationships, which may also have accounted for the good progress being made down south, because they were progressing independently of other areas in Thailand.[3]

Of the twenty-nine, twenty-three of them had been trained in demolition and in the use of small arms, grenades and so on, and of the remaining six, it was noted that at least half were First World War veterans. The largest cell consisting of twelve operatives was based out of Ronpibon, and included other operatives working further south at the Takapua Valley Tin Mine's Ban Pru dredging operations, the smaller mining location closer to Haad Yai. The Pinyok Tin Mine was next with six, Phuket Island with five, and

Huey Moot operations with four. Huey Yot, Renong, Bandinlan and Tah Seh each had one operative in place. In theory, all of Operation Cleeves' cells were to reach out and enlist the help of other Europeans residing in their respective neighbourhoods, as well as do the same with any and all types of local Thai officialdom in support of operations. That probably included helping out those mines without Operation Cleeves operatives, who were also committed to their own promised tin mine denial activities.

While the majority of Operation Cleeves personnel had been recruited from the tin mines themselves, including Pinyok Mine's Welsh Superintendent Harding Thomas or Ronpibon's point of contact WJ Parsons, eleven others had been recruited in Malaya by the Oriental Mission and subsequently placed into key tin mining installations. Aside from the two Army communication specialists placed further north, at the Pinyok Tin Mine for example, the Oriental Mission, through Kain and Weir, had secured the placement of English metallurgist Frank Butler-Jones as mining manager. They had done the same with the Danish-born Georg Laub, who had also recently arrived as the mine's chief chemist. Although the balance of tin mine denial cells was to be made up ostensibly of British miners also living and working at the same mine site, that invitation was also extended to other members in the Commonwealth Defence family, including Australians, New Zealanders and South Africans and others. In addition to the tin mine denial cells, there were other Oriental Mission operatives also placed into Southern Thailand and associated ostensibly with Operation Cleeves, but who in reality were undertaking other kinds of SOE work. Most of them were stationed alongside the Thai–Malaya border. One of them was New Zealander Horace Travis Cummins, who had only recently arrived to take up his cover position as the manager of the vast Yala Rubber Estate.

Three unidentified operatives had been especially trained in liaison duties for the Oriental Mission's offshoot in Penang. Two of them may have been in all probability Weir and Kain. An as yet unknown third was based in Kuala Lumpur, who may have been part of the III Division set up. Either way, the tasking of all three personnel was linked directly to their ability to travel into Southern Thailand at short notice and without raising too much attention. They were to be the essential points of contact between the tin mine denial cells, while also functioning as the Oriental Mission's advance headquarters including for recruiting, administration and so on. A further five unknown trained operatives including one W/T operator were held in reserve, but they were also to remain available for infiltration to any point within Southern Thailand at short notice.

Although the primary purpose of all cells remained the same, insomuch as the main focus was on tin mine denial, the feasibility of an expanding secondary focus was also being investigated among the larger Operation Cleeves cells. That consisted of ways in aiding the advance of British troops into Thailand if required, while at the same time delaying as much and for as long as possible any potential Japanese advance through Thailand into Malaya. Each cell's location held the key to their potential individual team responsibilities, which was also reflected in the types of weapons, ammunition and demolition supplies they received. Ronpibon's cell was to focus on derailing a train in the Ronpibon tunnel, along with washing out the railway embankment almost a kilometre to the north and destroying the railway bridge linking it similarly to the south. Elsewhere, the main Huey Moot–Tungsong section of the railway line was also to be cut. Those closest to Haad Yai such as at Ban Pru, aside from sabotaging their tin mining dredges were tasked with dislocating and disrupting all telephone and telegraph communications between there and Huey Moot, Tungsong, Kantang and Nakai, and all the way down to the Thai–Malay border. Their focus was in helping to facilitate British troops advancing from Padang Besar and Chunlun on the Malayan side, over the border into Sadao, Haad Yai and eventually Singora.

Phuket's responsibilities included enlisting the support of the Thai Governor, congregating the roughly one hundred or so Europeans from the district at the aerodrome, taking control of and holding that same aerodrome against potential Thai opposition, and then doing the same against potential Japanese plane or parachute landings. Their other main role was to assist in and provide general assistance to any Royal Air Force landings and so on. The trouble was that Phuket was practically the last of the cells to have been formed, and although it had only just received its weapons and other operational supplies in the week before Japan invaded, it was still more or less in an operational wilderness. Training had not been undertaken, dedicated operatives had not been selected, nor had specific sabotage targets been identified. That Phuket still did not have a standing tin mine denial cell in place was only compounding the problem, but at least they had highly experienced British Army Sergeant Misselbrook, who already had the W/T set unpacked and up and working. His communications base was located out of the Phuket Post Office, and it was only just before midnight on

Saturday, 6 December 1941 that he made his first successful transmission to Singapore.[4]

Pinyok's responsibilities, aside from tin mine denial sabotage, were also to take control of the single-car ferry crossing over the Pattani River near Yala, and prepare to blow up the bridge just north of the ferry linking it with the main Betong highway. They were also required to mount some sort of blackout information operations. Not only were they to disrupt and prevent any information getting out regarding British troop movements anywhere along the Betong to Yala highway, they were also to stop any news reaching the Tanicom Penal Settlement. Located further down the road and a few kilometres outside of Betong, it housed the only wireless transmitting station in the entire Yala District, and Pinyok was to make sure no information of any British advance could get out. Next door to it lay the Tanicom workers' village, some of whom were in the employ of the Kampong Toh Tin Mine down the road. On top of that, the Pinyok cell was to collect all available transport in the entire Yala District, and then start amassing any and all such vehicles near the ferry. Like their Ronpibon and Phuket cohorts, they too were supposed to obtain the co-operation of local authorities and other local European communities, when and wherever they could.

With these main mission taskings now in hand, it seemed Operation Cleeves, at least in theory, was almost at a state of readiness. That was until, in the early hours of Monday, 8 December 1941, Japan began its invasion into Thailand and Malaya, and Southernmost Thailand became Japan's first and bloodiest battlefield on the Malay Peninsula.

Chapter 15

Running from the Rising Sun

Offshore
East Coast
Southern Thailand
Monday
8 December 1941
0030

On late Sunday night, 7 December 1941, the 5th Division of the 25th Imperial Japanese Army under the strategic command of Lieutenant General Tomoyuki Yamashita were streaming towards Southern Thailand.[1] They had been deployed from Hainan Island four days earlier and were now joining the rest of Japan's invasionary forces that had been amassing at Phú Quốc Island for weeks.[2] This tiny, French Indochinese island lying roughly 430 kilometres (267 miles) north-east of British Malaya was a small, nondescript landmass located just off the west coast of what is today Vietnam. With the blessings of Vichy Hanoi, it was a strategic stepping stone, providing the quickest and most direct maritime route across the Gulf of Thailand. Now, it was Japan's major forward jumping off platform into British Malaya.

The main architect of the three-pronged invasion, Lieutenant Colonel Masanobu Tsuji, had chosen this part of east coast Southern Thailand for a number of reasons.[3] Not only would Japan prove that which Britain could not achieve by successfully disembarking troops during the worst monsoon season in years, it would also exploit Japan's textbook surprise attack to full tactical advantage. Tsuji knew there was no rush in undertaking the landings because unlike the deeper western coastal anchorages on the other side of the peninsula, this side of the east coast held shallower waters. In Pattani even smaller fishing junks had to routinely anchor a few kilometres off shore all year round, and Singora's sheltered harbour provided little room for battleships let alone submarines, to play hide and seek.[4] There would not be anywhere any large British fleet presence, let alone Allied warships, would have any chance of coalescing or using the approach as a holding ground against the Imperial Japanese Forces.

He was also confident in pre-war Japanese Intelligence reporting that both chosen beach landing sites were undefended, and there were no landward military threats to speak of because there were no fixed shore defences. Other than a couple of rundown wooden structures straddling the mouth of the Pattani River, the location around which the small town of Pattani had been built, there was nothing even resembling pillboxes or observation posts. Without any wire entanglements to speak of it should be easy going making it on to Pattani's coast line without any harassment. The other significant advantage was that on this side of the peninsula there were no military Direction Finding (DF) Stations, either above Singora, below Pattani, or anywhere in between.[5] That meant other than aerial reconnaissance, there was little chance of any early warning being raised as to the presence of Japan's convoy fleets. These were just some of the sound reasonings as to why Tsuji was fairly confident that his landing plan would work, because there was probably no immediate threat of British naval guns looming over the horizon.

The men wading ashore on this particularly wild, wet, and windy morning, were among some of the most highly experienced, veteran troops in Japan's arsenal. Most had only recently been redeployed from the Sino-Japanese theatre of war, and the more experienced of the 25th Division's reconnaissance units had already cut their battle teeth fighting in Nanjing and Manchuria. The majority of the first and front-line troops had recently completed advanced jungle warfare training on Hainan Island, followed closely by a period of intensive consolidation training in the jungles of Vichy Indochina. As a result, nearly all of them excelled in unarmed guerrilla-style combat. This little bit of saltwater discomfort meant nothing in the greater scheme of things, especially given the lucrative profits Japan stood to gain. It was not only the importance of the Greater East Asia Co-Prosperity Sphere helping fill Japan's dwindling economic pockets, it was also their contributions in supporting Japan standing proudly in its own hegemonic glory, including, if needed, honourable death in battle.[6]

The 5th Division's joint tasking after landing was to break through to the Thai–Malay frontier as fast as possible. That included crushing any potential enemy positions they might come across within Southern Thailand along the way. Troops would then coalesce at the Perak River, which was the planned central meeting point for Japan's main invasionary forces, after which all would make haste towards the main prize of Singapore.[7] The night was cloudy as the first Japanese convoy approached Southern Thailand's eastern coast, and shortly after midnight around fourteen ships under Imperial Japanese Navy escort dropped anchor just off Singora Beach. They were carrying the main Singora landing forces, including the Saeki Detachment. Lieutenant Colonel Shizuo Saeki was a former head of the Japanese Army's Cavalry School, and a highly experienced Cavalry and Reconnaissance Officer. His detachment had been tasked with protecting the troops' landings, and then later securing the Sadao border crossing.[8] The other three transports that had already diverged further south-east were also arriving off the Pattani coast, and they carried the feared Ando Detachment.[9] Led by their namesake, Regimental Commander Colonel Tadao Ando, they were known as Japan's 'Distinction Division' and were the equivalent of British irregular war-fighting experts, excelling at commando-style combat. Ando was accompanied by his second-in-command, the maverick Intelligence operative Staff Officer Major Asaeda.[10] Both men had reputations in Japanese military circles for being equally ruthless, and sharing inherent abilities to think quickly on their feet in the heat of battle. That was why in the lead up to this particular deployment, Ando and Asaeda's respective troop divisions had been merged into the newly established 42nd Infantry Regiment. Ando retained command; Asaeda remained responsible for operational intelligence.

Singora Beach
0200

Even though the seas were choppy, Saeki's Detachment's approach to Singora Beach was relatively straightforward. Once the Singora lighthouse's flashing beacon position had been determined, it was just a matter of heading the vessels towards the easily discernible coastline laying immediately before them. As the Japanese troop transports finally came to anchor in two columns running parallel to the coast, the weather turned worse, with higher winds strengthening the rolling waves now crashing up to three metres high. The heavy squalls and heaving seas were not making the landing an easy job, especially because weeks of heavy surf had already created problematic sandbanks at the highwater point. As the rolling and pitching that was causing some of the light armoured vehicles to smash into one another or the boats continued, in the crashing momentum it was soon realised it was going to be impossible to land any of the tanks at this particular place, at this particular time, and in this particular weather. But for now the rain had stopped, and in the brief lull the moon was slowly emerging from behind the darkened, stormy clouds, helping light up the beach even more as several other of the landing boats arrived.

Among the scattered Japanese infantry troops coming ashore on Singora's smooth beachfront this morning was Tsuji. He was accompanied by two Staff officers, Lieutenant Colonel Hongo Takeshi and Major Tadahiko Hayashi.[11] Hongo was tasked with leading the railway and railway transport spearhead detachment.[12] His primary mission was in securing the Singora railway yards, and immediately thereafter commandeering the train line to Haad Yai as soon as possible after landing. That was because Haad Yai was going to become Japan's main forward transit hub for the oncoming Malayan invasion.[13] Hayashi remained responsible for operational intelligence. Following closely behind them were the wireless section, signallers, orderlies, medical, and the remainder of Yamashita's headquarters staff. As they were openly coalescing on the beach without cover and no resistance was forthcoming, Tsuji surmised his plan was working. He had ensured copious amounts of Thai money was freely available to help smooth their arrival through financial 'donations' if needed, and it seemed the Japanese Consul, Katsuno Toshio, and the rest of his staff, had obviously done their jobs.[14] But where was the expected warm welcome waiting for them supposedly to have been put in place by the Japanese Consulate?[15] It was Hayashi who volunteered to make his way to the Consul, wake up the occupants, and get the next phase of Singora's landings up and running.

Pattani Shoreline

0300

Further south, Ando's Detachment was having a harder time in just trying to get close inshore. In the early hours of Monday morning, 8 December 1941, they were still attempting to land further south at Pattani, but it had been a stormy night as the Japanese troopships approached, and the choppy seas continued tossing their flat-bottomed landing barges around as though they were nothing more than toys.[16] In the shallower and heavier muddied waters of Pattani Bay, the accompanying sharp, rocky outcrops hugging the jagged shoreline were not helping their forward advance, and time was still of the essence for the Japanese invasion. Ando's Detachment did not want to be left behind in the push south for Singapore. As the inclement monsoonal weather continued doing its utmost to throw their incursion timeline off track, the time lost was weighing heavily on the shoulders of Lieutenant General Takuro Matsui. He had been given the great honour of leading Japan's 5th Division ashore in Pattani, but soon he like several others was realising any planned amphibious landings, at least for now, were impossible. Ando's more experienced forward reconnaissance troops also realised the situation, and after jumping overboard, were sloshing about in waist-deep murky waters and heading for the shoreline. Eventually gaining footholds on some of Pattani's shifting coastal sands, it probably felt more like walking through a pit of writhing vipers than anything else. But they too, like their colleagues further north, were proving a monsoonal landing on this part of Southern Thailand's east coast was not impossible.

As the bitter piercing winds stung their eyes and lashed their ears, Ando's troops continued struggling against the raging seas and tides that went with them. To these battle-hardened men, this little bit of saltwater discomfort meant nothing in the greater scheme of things because the men wading ashore on this particularly nasty monsoonal morning were highly experienced, veteran troops redeployed from the Sino-Japanese theatre of war. They were the Japanese soldiers who had broken through the Great Wall of China, and who had been honing their skills over the past few years while defeating Chinese and Communist guerrilla forces in Mukden, Nanjing, and Russia.[17] As they approached the town's outskirts, they were met by pockets of localised armed Thai resistance, but that did not last long once the news from Bangkok arrived at 0730 telling them to immediately cease hostilities against Japan. By now, the rain had stopped, the heavy winds were subsiding, and a steady stream of Japanese troops and hardware was being brought ashore, including Ando's artillery battery, engineering company, and a bicycle infantry division. His troops then wasted little time in securing their first primary objective, which was establishing occupying control of Pattani, and establishing tight perimeter security along with the usual controlled access chokepoints. Within hours the second objective of securing a makeshift headquarters in the centre of town along with a forward operating base had been set up, and it was now that Ando and Asaeda turned their attentions to the next part of the invasion, and that was to start heading west and inland. Their orders, it seemed, did not include taking prisoners.

Chapter 16

Cavalry And Chaos

Saeki's Detachment

It had not been as smooth sailing as the Japanese had hoped for after landing earlier in the day. Despite Bangkok having despatched orders that all Thais were to cease hostilities against Japan, that communiqué did not quite reach all of Thailand's outlying fighting forces.[1] That was something Saeki had found out first hand in Singora, when as his detachment began moving out and were departing the outer approaches of town, they were confronted by a barrage of concentrated fire that forced them to an immediate halt. Apparently a unit of Thai troops from nearby Camp Suantun had set up positions on the higher ground of Rūp Chang Hill, which had prime position overlooking Singora's road approaches.[2] They were firing on the column as it was advancing, and despite the Japanese column leader's pleas that Bangkok had given them permission to be in Thailand, it was not until further confirmation arrived from Bangkok to cease and desist that the firing stopped. That showed that Japan's occupation of Singora was not a *fait accompli*, and the Japanese were put on notice that they were not going to have it all their own way, although they did have the element of time and surprise on their side.

Within hours of landing, all of Southern Thailand's railways were under Hongo's control, and the first train full of Japanese troops and equipment was already enroute to Haad Yai. The local power station, wireless telegraph transmitter and post office were under Japanese authority, as was the harbour and port. The latter were integral entry points to incoming Japanese military support for the Malayan invasion. The Singora Governor's residence had been taken over and was now functioning as Yamashita's temporary headquarters, and Singora jail was under Japanese occupation. One side was allocated as a three-hundred strong accommodation barracks for Japanese troops, while the other half was divided between enemy detention cells and interrogation spaces.[3] It would not be long before arrests were starting to be made, not only of British or Allied enemies, but also of those suspected of possessing alleged pro-British, or at the very least, anti-Japanese sympathies. Anyone possessing weapons, ammunition or even any types of radio would be summarily arrested and thrown into jail. The only exception to these rules, seemingly, was Yamashita's later actions over Singora's British Consul, Alan Trevor Oldham. As soon as he had set up his 25th Division headquarters, Yamashita had confined Oldham and his local staff to the British Consulate, after which the British Consul was almost immediately put on a train under Japanese armed guard, and within hours was heading for incarceration in Bangkok.[4] Much to the Japanese Consul's displeasure, Yamashita had done so without even consulting him on his actions. The only other known European was a long-time Singora resident, a Dane by the name of Captain Vosbein whom everybody seemingly ignored.[5] Other than that, Singora Jail was now ready and waiting for whatever new prisoners of war would eventuate.

As part of the Japanese Army's spearhead mechanical division, Saeki's Detachment had been originally tasked with protecting the disembarkation of the main forces, but after not facing any real opposition to the landings, other than from the inclement weather, Saeki was keen to take the fighting to the British. Once Tsuji had joined him as Staff Officer, both men were keen to get under way and head west. They already knew that earlier Japanese air surveillance was reporting that a large enemy mechanised force of motor transport, and possibly Bren gun carriers, was heading in the general direction of the Thai–Malay frontier area near Sadao, so they wasted little time in deploying from Singora as soon as practicable.[6] They took with them some of Hongo's fighting engineers; that was at least until they reached Haad Yai, when Hongo's men would break off and finalise setting up Japan's transit railway hub.

About seventeen kilometres (roughly ten miles) out from Haad Yai's northern approaches, Saeki suddenly halted his detachment. On the side of the road was a Thai policeman standing in shock at the sight of the vast Japanese column bearing down upon him. Sub-Lieutenant Swat Kamsuriya had been attending to some local police business, and was now making his way back into town.[7] He was not prepared for what happened next when a Japanese Officer pointed his loaded pistol at him and ordered him to accompany the detachment and show them the way to Penang.[8] With little choice but to comply or lose his life, the hapless policeman did as he was ordered and Saeki's Detachment continued on their way.

They made good time, because Saeki and his troops arrived in Haad Yai by mid-afternoon. Here they stopped at the Railway Hotel, which was the only place in town that would provide an adequate rest stop, and eventually a makeshift barracks for the Japanese Army and later Kempetai personnel. Already waiting in town to greet them was Sub-Lieutenant Kikuchi Segana, who up until now had been running a goods shop in the centre of town. Others, including a former civilian employee now Army major named Minamai, also welcomed the detachment as they arrived.[9] The nearby Mitsubishi and Dainan Koshi commercial offices had already been set up as a makeshift headquarters, and Saeki and Tsuji wasted little time in visiting them.[10] While both men were availing themselves of the hospitality, Hongo's troops were already swarming over the rail yards, and were busying themselves with taking over the railway station.

Also staying at the Railway Hotel were three Europeans. Heinz F Langfeldt was a long-time Danish resident of Bangkok and had been living at the hotel since October. He had been spending the past few months buying up as much rubber ready for manufacture as he could, and shipping it out of Thailand as fast as possible for what he described as a British denial scheme.[11] Antonin Vererka was a Czech national who was an engineer and manager of Skoda Works in Bangkok. He had been in transit and was merely stopping over in Haad Yai awaiting the next train back to Bangkok. The third European was an Australian tin miner named AJ King, who worked at the Ronpibon tin mine. King was desperate to get out of Haad Yai and head back to Ronpibon, and when he and Vererka heard the news that a large Japanese Naval convoy was seen approaching Thailand, and that the Japanese had actually landed and were making their way inland, both men had immediately made their way to the train station to try and get out on whatever next train might be passing through. Once they reached the railway station, however, they were turned away by startled Thai railway officials, who informed the two men that Japan was now in control of all of Thailand's railways, all railway movement into and out of Haad Yai was cut, and they had no idea what was happening or when the trains might be running again. King and Vererka had little choice but to return to the Railway Hotel and try to work out what to do next.

When they arrived back a short time later, a plethora of Japanese soldiers had magically appeared, and the hotel was practically being overrun. What was peculiar was that it was only yesterday that some of those now appearing in full Japanese Army uniforms had previously been local shopkeepers, barbers, and bicycle goods sellers, and were now stepping out as Japanese Army officers. It was not just the sudden appearance of this and the arrival of the heavily armed troops that put the men on edge, it was the sights, sounds and smells of tanks and other armoured vehicles pulling up just outside the hotel. Not long afterwards a handful of Japanese soldiers were searching inside the hotel, and on finding the three European men together had separated them, confined each man to his respective room and then started questioning them. As armed Japanese soldiers maintained guard on their doors, each man's identity papers were confiscated, and they were individually and repeatedly questioned about their nationalities, their movements, where they had come from, why they were in Haad Yai and when did they get there. They seemed particularly interested in King. Shortly after dusk, and as the last of Saeki's Detachment thundered away from Haad Yai heading towards Sadao, the three men were not quite sure just what it was the Japanese were looking for in their questioning, especially when there seemed to be some fixation about their whereabouts throughout 1940 and 1941. It would be the same ongoing questioning until they were later transported by cattle train under Japanese armed guard, and taken to Singora Jail a few days later.[12]

Chapter 17

Rapid Advance

Ando's Detachment

Ando's Detachment
Pattani Harbour Town
Afternoon

In Pattani, the same type of Japanese occupation as Singora's was already in play, but on a much smaller scale. Although the landings further south had taken a bit more time than planned, Ando's Detachment was making up time in getting on land. With the rains subsiding, and the rest of the troops streaming ashore, it did not take long for Ando to establish occupying control of Pattani, and secure tight perimeter security around the town. He had already despatched some of his front-line reconnaissance troops west. They were heading for the railway hub town of Yala. He had wanted them there as soon as possible because Ando's mission was to secure the geostrategically important The Ledge. Now that he had taken over the town, Ando probably confirmed how the town's main road was barely suitable for the movement of troops, let alone the movement of military hardware. That had been part of the logic as to why some of Japan's earliest tank landings had also happened further north in Singora, and further south of his position in Kota Bharu, and why he and Asaeda would commandeer vehicles and anything else they wanted to use along the way.

Pattani's terrain was not as well known as Singora's, and he probably also scanned the immediate terrain, taking note of how the town's landscape aside from the beach was one of surrounding thick jungle undergrowth interspersed by claustrophobic rubber plantations, as well as insect-infested tropical marshes and swamps that suggested other threats of tropical disease. The one bright light was that there seemed to be a lot of rubber plantations in and around Pattani and along the roads leading out, which meant he might have the tactical advantage of line of sight. By later in the morning, as his troops were busy confiscating buses, trucks, lorries, cars and anything else that could be used to transport troops, he and Asaeda and along with their newly appointed Japanese driver had already requisitioned the Pattani Mayor's car for their use, the Mayor's residence becoming their makeshift headquarters. Ando's next thoughts were probably those of the immediate tactical kind. Even though Pattani was a relatively insignificant coastal backwater, he would still need to set up operational command and control of Pattani's outskirt approaches.

As a professional soldier, and noting the type of terrain he was possibly going to be facing ahead, he was probably already determining how best to get his troops to exploit any battlefield advantages from this tiny, remote position astride the Malay Peninsula. But Japan's substantial pre-war Japanese intelligence had done its job well. Unlike up in Singora, this part of Southern Thailand, and this eastern side of Yala, had little infrastructure development to speak of. He also knew that at this monsoonal time of year communications were haphazard, flooding was common, and roads, bridges, godowns (warehouses), shops and supplies of anything including food or petrol were routinely washed away. A precarious situation, given that part of Ando's blitzkrieg success relied heavily upon travelling light and, once deployed, exploiting whatever local resources were available *in situ* to meet his war-fighting demands. Thanks in large part to Asaeda's pre-war 'tourist' intelligence sojourns across the Singora Line area, Ando already knew where some of the more important ones were located.

Tin mines were important because they often had fuel and fresh water supplies; rubber plantations were useful because they usually had well-maintained roads within and interlinking with other rubber estates, and more often than not were also criss-crossed by jungle tracks. Both would be good for Japanese troop movements, but not good enough for constant heavy vehicles; a combination that might provide Ando with the offensive edge he needed. If he could establish Japanese command and control across these lesser-known roads, he might be able to set up networks of narrow battle frontages, and that could give him a chokepoint advantage, either by forcing any Allied actions to engage within the only accessible road networks, or doing the opposite. With these under Japanese control, it could also prove effective in reducing any potential Allied offensives the further westwards and southwards he advanced. These were battlefield advantages that played directly into what he probably suspected was his numerically inferior troop strength.

If that were the case then a combination of naked dense jungle and equally claustrophobic plantation vegetations, could offer ideal fighting conditions for what his troops excelled at, and that was guerrilla-style combat. Which was probably why Ando's immediate focus may have centred around using hit-the-ground-running type of planning, especially around ways and means of breaking deep into the flank of whatever unknown enemy forces might lay before him. On the east side of Yala, however, he need not have worried about that because there did not seem to be any evidence of British, Allied, Thai or any other military presence that might be blocking his route. There was no British military presence anywhere across this part of the interior, and nothing of any real threat anywhere along the Thai–Malay border. Aside from that, as Ando's Detachment were making their way down through the Yala District, the other key advantage in their favour was that any and all potential Thai opposition would be practically non-existent. The ceasefire imperative from Bangkok earlier in the day had seen to that problem, but the other thing that put Ando's confidence in good stead, was that he was already aware that with all British military strategising still myopically focusing on the Fortress Singapore analogy, and all major defence resources centred around protecting airfields located either on the extreme western or eastern coastlines, his job in immediately heading inland and away from either already gave him a strategic upper hand.

By the time his forward troops had arrived near Yala, probably by lunchtime, they had wasted little time in taking control of the ferry crossing. After transporting a few more troops over to the other side of the river, they very soon after occupied and took full control of Yala and all of its approaches. Similar to what had happened up in Singora, it appeared some local businesses, including the newly established Japanese company offices of Dainan Koshi MBK and Hai Nam and Company, were warmly welcoming them. Dr Sam Thomas, on the other hand, was not. He was continuing on going about his daily business when by lunchtime his dispensary was commandeered by an 'elderly Kempetai man' who spoke English very well.[1] What unnerved him more was that the Japanese officer had then shown him some of the books he carried with him, and they were compiled lists of names of European and potentially pro-British sympathisers living and working across the entire Yala to Betong area. Thomas was quickly taken into Japanese custody and was soon heading to Singora Jail.

Elsewhere in and around Yala, and much to the Japanese soldiers' relief, not a single bridge had been readied for destruction, all the roadways were clear and intact, and taking control of the ferry had not proved an arduous task. Neither had they seen any indications whatsoever of any potential British military presence. After having secured that particularly important river crossing, the next goal was setting up bridge guards and checkpoints on The Ledge's approaches, which it seemed Ando's Detachment had managed to achieve without any problem. As the Japanese troops made their way across The Ledge without incident, and were advancing down the Yala to Betong road, by early afternoon checkpoints and roadblocks were soon in place. They had even gone a little bit further and also set up roadblocks not far from what was the turn off inland to the Pinyok Mine. The Japanese troops did not have to wait too long for them to be effective. Within a few hours the first vehicle that reached the checkpoint was a lorry carrying three European tin miners, and they were barrelling down the highway at full speed heading directly towards them.

Chapter 18

Laycol, Krohcol

And the Singora Line Battle Begins

Inland
North Malaya
Sungei Patani
11th Division Headquarters
8 December 1941
0600

While Japanese forces had spent the day meandering their way west across Southern Thailand, British forces were still playing catch-up. By the time news of Japan's landings was reaching Major General DM Murray-Lyon's advanced headquarters further inland in North Malaya, his 11th Division had already lost hours of precious time. The 4/15th Punjabi Battalion under Brigadier Lay's command was already in Padang Besar and had moved up to the border, as had the 3/16th Punjabis under Lieutenant Colonel Moorhead in Kroh. Laycol and Krohcol, as they were respectively known, had already been given their mission goals.[1] Laycol's 4/15th Officer Commanding, Major Andrews, was tasked with delaying any Japanese advance from Singora, and he was to stop them at the Sadao and Haad Yai approaches; Krohcol's 3/16th Officer Commanding, Robinson, was to head to and hold The Ledge, and Yala's southern approaches, as well as delaying any Japanese advance anywhere west from Pattani.[2] By lunchtime both men were already receiving further reports that two vast Japanese troop movements were on the move and heading west at speed from Singora and Pattani, and heading in their respective directions. If they kept on at this pace, Laycol and Krohcol would in all probability be engaging the Japanese before nightfall. Both men knew they needed to move sooner rather than later if they were going to meet the Japanese Army, especially if they remained hopeful of cutting off the Japanese as planned across Southern Thailand, but everyone was still awaiting orders to commence operations. It was twelve hours after the Japanese had landed, and both Laycol and Krohcol were stuck on the Malay side of the border.

Laycol's positioning was problematic, because even though it had its full complement of one section of the 273rd Anti-Tank Battery under Lieutenant May, and two sections of the 17th Field Company, none of the expected outposts were in place, and no clearing work had started anywhere along the frontier approaches.[3] That suggested potential forward positions were still covered by marsh, quagmires and dense jungle undergrowth, and bridges, railways and roads that were supposed to have already been identified as possible disruption targets had not even been prepared for demolition.[4] Even the three main bridges linking this part of the border with the Thai frontier town of Sadao, for example, remained intact. With Saeki's Detachment already mobilised and on the road heading west, Laycol was already hours behind schedule and nowhere near where they needed to be further eastwards and into Southern Thailand. When the orders did finally arrive at 1330 to commence operations, Andrews knew he was already going to have to attempt to stop the Japanese not in Southern Thailand, but practically on top of the Thai–Malay border. That scenario was made even worse when some British aerial reconnaissance reports began trickling through that a mechanised column of Japanese infantry, and possibly ten or more tanks, had been seen leaving Singora, and they were on a direct course heading towards Sadao.

Andrews' orders were clear, however, that he and the rest of Laycol were to immediately head over the border to Sadao and engage with the Japanese as soon as possible. They had made good time up from Padang Besar, and now as they were finally heading over the border, the latest aerial reconnaissance was confirming that Japanese troops had already reached Haad Yai, which meant the Japanese were far closer than Andrews would have liked.[5] By the time he and the rest of Laycol had crossed the main railway crossing over the trunk frontier road to Sadao's western approaches, it was already late afternoon. As predicted, they were practically sitting on top of the border, and he was probably silently hoping that Operation Cleeves had been able to hold up their end of the operation.

If they had been successful, then that might mean communications with Singora had already been disrupted, or at least hopefully the northern railway line link had been cut. The last thing Laycol or anyone else wanted was to have a train full of Japanese soldiers heading south towards them from Bangkok. That was because a large part of Laycol's tasking was in laying the groundwork for the arrival of a British armoured train, and it was being readied to be deployed from Padang Besar to Haad Yai as soon as possible. The plan was that the train would be carrying one of the 2/16th Punjabi Platoons under Lieutenant Burns, and a detachment of the 3rd Field Company under Lieutenant Poyser, and they would meet up with Andrews in Haad Yai before heading up together in convoy to Singora.[6] But for now, the latest torrential downpour was not helping with visual identification of anything in front of them, let alone potentially around them, and Andrews ordered his troops to stop roughly fourteen kilometres (nine miles) just outside the western outskirts of town.

From there, it looked as though all was quiet in Sadao. So far, they had not seen any Japanese nor faced any resistance, other than somebody had driven a car and left it blocking the road as they were approaching, but the unknown driver had departed in quick haste.[7] After deploying forward reconnaissance troops to do a quick communications check, much to Andrews' annoyance he soon discovered that none of the telephone or telegraph lines had been cut, to which he quickly despatched another handful of troops to sort that out. He then began positioning his forces and, keeping the main road on his left flank, sent his carriers over to the other side of the road. He was aiming to form a northward-facing arc covering his anti-tank guns, because they were sited to shoot straight ahead down the road that led directly into the centre of Sadao. He kept one platoon in reserve, and readied his combat raw recruits as best he could, because he had no idea of where or how close the Japanese were, let alone any confirmation as to what troop strength or firepower lay before him. All Andrews knew was that it was inevitable that at some time over the next few hours the Japanese Army would be advancing at speed towards him, and all he could do for the present was lay in wait.

Chapter 19

Krohcol

Guerrilla Fighting in Betong's Mist

Although Laycol had their own set of difficulties in terms of battlefield unpreparedness, it was worse for Krohcol further south because they had not yet been fully formed. Their 5/14th Punjabis under Lieutenant Colonel Stokes were still back on Penang Island, and their Light Battery Federated Malay States Volunteer Force (FMSVF) 10th Mountain Battery under Major Cowie, were likewise also down south in Kuala Lumpur. That meant Krohcol's 3/16th Punjabis were the only troops with any state of adequate readiness for their main mission, to advance and occupy The Ledge.[1] The only thing the 3/16th had going in its favour was that over the past few months Moorhead had undertaken his own personal reconnaissance of the Betong to Yala terrain, and after hearing that morning's dire news he was already re-strategising his approach into a more broader defensive one.[2] When he finally received the order to commence operations in the afternoon, Moorhead immediately despatched his 3/16th Punjabi Regiment's forward scouts to the Betong frontier border.[3]

Unlike Andrews' orders to engage with the Japanese and hold Sadao, Robinson's troops were to cross through the usually undefended and unlocked Thai–Malay frontier barrier gate, and march in defile over the next two or so short kilometres, where the next part of the operational plan was to occupy the Thai border town of Betong before nightfall. After Betong was secured, Krohcol was then to advance up the Betong to Yala road toward Pinyok's general area, set up a base camp, and finally occupy The Ledge. Their presumption too was that Pinyok's Operation Cleeves cell would have already commenced their various small-scale sabotage and other designated taskings. Hopefully that included taking control of the ferry, rounding up all the local vehicles, putting in place the information blackout, and securing the southern approaches to Yala. All were actions aimed at laying the pathways for the 3/16th and others to rendezvous with Operation Cleeves in the Pinyok vicinity. On reaching the border, however, and for the first time in recent memory, the large, heavy steel gate was firmly closed and heavily padlocked. Even more peculiar was that a man was standing next to his car on the Thai side of the border, trying to figure a way to get out. He identified himself as an English tin miner named Skryne.

Skryne and his wife had apparently driven down from Banang Sta, a small area just outside of Yala, and had arrived in Betong just before sunrise.[4] He advised the scouts the drive south had been uneventful, and they had not met with any unusual interference anywhere along the road until reaching Betong. On arrival there they had met with unfamiliar customs and immigration officials, who were uncharacteristically obstructive in actively preventing them from continuing on with their journey, and now he and his wife were trapped in Southern Thailand. The 3/16th troops still had their orders to cross the border, so Skryne and the troops agreed to work together to open the gate, which they did using a combination of axes and brute strength. An hour or so later it was smashed enough to allow the troops access. As the first lead scout stepped through and on to Thai territory, he was immediately fired upon and instantly killed. The unexpected hostile reaction took the troops by surprise, and they immediately withdrew to reassess the situation. Skryne took cover in his car.

When news reached Moorhead, he immediately deployed Lieutenant Thatcher's carrier platoon to recommence the advance. Coming under rapid fire as they crossed the border, this time two flanking companies were also accompanying them and cutting their way through the densely cloistered jungle on either side of the road. Slowly but surely as they progressed, they seemed to be eliminating enemy fire as they inched ever forwards, but as they made their tentative way around the first sharp bend, the road was now fully blocked with felled trees and other detritus strewn across the road. Skryne was puzzled, because it had not been there when he had driven through a few hours earlier. As the forward scouts advanced around each snaking bend, progress was continually hampered by alternating sniper activity from the jungle canopy, and heavy rifle as well as light automatic fire emanating from the rubber plantation areas. That meant flanking operations would need to take precedence before the main force could even attempt any advance. It was slow and heavy going for Robinson's men, and keep going they did, as they continued flanking operations over undulating terrain, alternating between dense jungle and rubber plantations, and always around never-ending, snaking S-bends. They were measuring their forward advance incrementally in metres, but at least the rain had stopped for a while, and even though they could not see around corners, it had given them some much-needed visibility of the soldiering country around them.

Literally hours later, Krohcol's carriers were still creeping along, still navigating heavily jungled S-bends, clearing the road of blockages every few metres, while at the same time continuing to evade sniper, heavy and light automatic fire. That continued until sometime just around dusk when the enemy's tactics abruptly changed. Just as Krohcol was clearing the third corner, all firing stopped, and they were met by a series of Pathan-style fanatical charges, not seemingly by Japanese soldiers, but reportedly by hundreds of uniformed Thai policemen wielding fixed bayonets.[5] In the fierce and bloodied fighting that followed, Robinson's troops repelled the attack but at great cost and it did not stop there. The more they advanced, it seemed the more ferocious the hand-to-hand combat became. After repeating the same tense operations and securing the first three block areas around the next two treacherous bends, it had been a long, tedious and hard day of fighting. As night fell, Krohcol had only managed to advance just over six kilometres (roughly four miles) over the frontier. This latest abrupt change of the enemy's battlefield tactics had caught them off guard, and when they were only a few kilometres (almost a mile) short of Betong, Moorhead immediately halted the carrier advance.

The reach back reporting he was receiving was perplexing because it seemed the 3/16th was facing literally hundreds of what appeared to be well-armed, cohesively organised, and uniformed enemy combatants. Even more problematic was that the enemy also seemed to be consistently being reinforced around each bend; not only with what seemed incomparable supplies of fresh reinforcements, also weapons and reammunitioning readily available, and all magically appearing from somewhere into this remote, wild frontier region. The other unsettling observation being made by Moorhead's field commanders, was that although the enemy they were engaging may have been dressed as Thai police, they were carrying state-of-the-art Japanese weapons and using Japanese ammunition. They also seemed to know exactly what they were doing in this jungle fighting terrain, and how to effectively exploit that to their full advantage. To Moorhead it was increasingly apparent that these were not ordinary infantry troops, and probably not even Thai policemen. He realised these were soldiers who were highly trained in jungle warfare operations, and guerrilla war-fighting tactics, neither of which were specialisations in which any of his Krohcol troops had been trained.[6]

Based on these assumptions, Moorhead had already reasoned that any Krohcol advance would be literally stepping into the tactical unknown. But it was also thanks to his first-hand knowledge of this area that when their reinforcements of the 5/14th Punjabis had arrived in Kroh earlier that morning, he had made the command decision to hold them back. Firstly and foremostly, he knew the relatively narrow and congested terrain ahead of them could not sustain another battalion, and neither was there anywhere that could provide safe havens for any battery activities, especially when it looked like all gun positions would have little choice but to remain located out on open exposed road. They were still facing constant sniping attacks throughout the night, and they had already lost at least one runner, but when the battalion had gone into 'company jungle perimeters' on both road-flanking positions by nightfall, Moorhead was spending the night again changing his battle tactics.[7] It might have helped him if he had known that the entire area they had been fighting through since deploying from Kroh earlier in the day, was actually the convergence of the three largest rubber plantations in this part of Southern Thailand. It might have helped him even more if he had known that they were all owned and operated by the Japanese.

Chapter 20

Singora Line North

Ronpibon, Phuket and Indecision

For Singora Line North operatives, it was sometime before lunch 1100 that 'Abide With Me' was finally played over the radio, signalling it was time for all Operation Cleeves personnel to get ready.[1] According to all the information coming out of Singapore and being reported back to London, everyone in Southern Thailand was purportedly on standby and ready to go. Apparently the only thing they were all waiting on was the next signal tune, 'Keep the Home Fires Burning', and that was to let them know that now was the time to commence operations.

In Phuket, WJ Parsons and his team, on hearing the news of Japan's landings over MBC English language breakfast radio that morning, were on edge. They had heard 'Abide With Me' over the radio the previous Friday night, and the pre-arranged 'Alert' signal on Saturday, and now all were waiting with bated breath for their next set of instructions to be broadcast. Parsons had then spent the rest of the day preparing mobilisation plans, and drawing up complete instructions for the other mines under his responsibility, including the Takuapa Tin Mine dredge down in Ban Pru.[2] Like everyone else, he could do nothing but wait for the appropriate signal tune to be played, as well as the other one indicating which objectives were to be undertaken and in what order. Parsons knew that aside from tin mine denial, the Ronpibon, Phuket and other Operation Cleeves cells in the Singora Line North area had other taskings including enlisting local Thai help, gathering all Europeans around the district to Phuket's aerodrome, and if possible defending the aerodrome from Thai or Japanese attack. The only problem was that at this particular time, Parsons had not yet visited the aerodrome, was not up to speed with the area in question, and was still working on the precept that once the operational order was broadcast, they would have at least two to three days to begin mounting operations.

As the day progressed and the order to commence operations finally came through at 1330, Parsons immediately informed his scattered Operation Cleeves operatives to start denying their tin mines, their dredges and all the other operations that had been planned. By the time they heard the objectives to attack being broadcast from Singapore, no one had any idea where the Japanese were or what was going on further south because there was no connectivity between any of the sabotage cells. Parsons at least had managed to get some instructions out to the Kumunting Tin Mine dredge, and they were removing a few vital parts of their diesel engines located in the mine's powerhouses.[3] He had planned for that to be a quick, ten-minute job, after which the rest of the operatives could then get on with some of the more intensive work including destroying the north–south train lines and rail bridges.

Yet for reasons that remain unclear, especially given there would be no Japanese in their immediate vicinity until the next day, no railway lines were cut, no bridges readied for demolition, and no telephone or telegraph lines disrupted, and most of the tin mines in Singora Line North remained in working order. That may have been in part a consequence of Parsons and his team having trouble decoding the follow-up news report of the lost missing files, the one giving different cells their objectives, and the order in which they were to be undertaken. In his own later reporting of events, Parsons admits that they had heard the news broadcast, and had also received the additional transmission of a further sequence of numbers including via the W/T set, but it had taken him and the others at least two and a half hours to decode, which meant they had lost even more hours to get the job done. In essence, the wasted time meant their Operation Cleeves actions had been literally and figuratively overtaken by events. Others however, did not have the same degree of difficulty in understanding their tasks. The two newest tin miners who had only recently arrived a week or so earlier knew exactly what they were doing. When the operational orders came through, Misselbrook quietly packed up his W/T set and went to ground heading for the Burma border.[4] His orders were to head for the northern Shan town of Lashio, because this was a major terminus of the Burma Road.[5] Wright did the same thing but was heading in the other direction.

One half of Parsons' combined Ronpibon and Phuket cell divided itself between organising evacuees, while the other half ostensibly was working on operations against potential hostile Thai or Japanese forces, including any parachute threats. They were supposed to defend the airfield at least until the British arrived. Those not involved with either were to travel by vehicles in convoy to the pick-up point on the west coast near Phuket Island, where a Royal Navy vessel would be waiting for them. Because Parsons already had a well-established and good working relationship with the local Phuket Governor, he had rung through his intentions that tin mining Europeans would be leaving soon, they would be armed but would only be using them if needed for defence, and could they please have smooth passage along the way. The Governor and everybody else including the police and customs officials were more than happy to oblige. They were so keen to get the Europeans out of the district that every assistance was given in helping the scattered European enclaves reach the agreed pre-evacuation point, and helping them get on board the evacuation ship. Phuket aerodrome's defence failed dismally because Parsons was still working under the erroneous assumption that they would have days to organise, and news of imminent Japanese arrival took everyone by surprise. Despite a half-hearted and unmatched attempt at protecting Phuket's airfield, what was left of Operation Cleeves' Singora Line North soon began scrambling to the west coast and head for safety in Singapore.

It was a different approach further south at the Takuapah Tin Mine's Ban Pru Dredge near Haad Yai. Tin Mine worker TB Snow had just come off night duty when he heard the news that the Japanese had landed in Singora and elsewhere.[6] As he listened in disbelief to the late breakfast news broadcast, he quickly jotted down a note to that effect, and then tasked his houseboy with running it over to the acting mine manager's office. The mine's accountant, Albert Bentley, had only been in the job for a few weeks, and was the temporary replacement for the usual mine manager, a Mr Heimrich, who had left for Australia a few weeks earlier. Roughly half an hour or so later, Bentley arrived on Snow's bungalow doorstep and he too was in disbelief upon hearing the news. They then quickly dispatched a runner to take the news down to the Ban Pru Dredge, which was only a few kilometres down the track, where English mining engineer James Rigby and Dutch dredge master John Tebbers had just taken up the day shift. Upon receiving the worrying message, both men immediately returned and made their way directly to Bentley's office.

For the next hour or so, Bentley, Tebbers, Snow and Rigby remained huddled together in Bentley's bungalow. They were still listening closely to the wireless radio but there was no news of the expected arrival of British forces, nor any of the signal tunes. All the broadcasts kept repeating was that the Japanese had landed, and although Parsons had telephoned earlier with the unhelpful news that nobody had received any instructions to commence denial operations, that line had gone dead and was still not working.[7] With no other news forthcoming, Bentley dispatched one of the mine's bicycle couriers in the direction of Haad Yai on a fact-finding mission. When the courier returned sometime later, he reported that the Japanese Army was closing fast and that they were only about seven or so kilometres (four miles) north of the mine. His other news was that the Japanese had already set up roadblocks and guard posts along the main Singora to Haad Yai road, and were now seemingly in complete control of Haad Yai. On approaching the blockade, he had been stopped by a group of armed Japanese soldiers who refused to let him pass, and immediately ordered him to turn around and go away.[8] More troubling was the fact that the mine's courier had not seen anyone else other than Japanese soldiers throughout his travels.

On hearing how close the Japanese were, Bentley made the decision to release the non-European mine staff. He then instructed the others to load up the mine lorry with cash and luggage. The plan was to head to Sadao and cross over the border to Malaya as quickly as possible. The three Europeans had asked Snow to join them but he had chosen to stay behind, just in case they somehow received word about Operation Cleeves. His other reasoning was that as a Eurasian with extensive local knowledge, he would be better placed to evade the Japanese than his European-looking cohorts if that was to happen.[9] As the three men were driving out, Bentley made the point of asking Snow to look after the place because they all thought they would only be gone a few days before returning, and besides he was sure the British would be arriving from the other direction any time soon. Not long after Bentley and the others had left, a unit of Japanese soldiers pulled up close to the mine. They probably paid little attention to the half-naked man wearing a sarong, who was barefoot and sauntering along on the opposite side of the road. As Snow continued walking away from the tin mine and in the opposite direction of the soldiers, he was confident he had managed to destroy at least a couple of the mechanical bits that would stop the dredges working, and was secure in the knowledge that he had already thrown the offending parts deep into the dense jungle undergrowth. At least Ban Pru Tin Mine's Dredge would not be working again for anybody any time soon.

Around the same time Snow was disappearing into the jungle, his three Ban Pru Tin Mine co-workers had made it to the Thai–Malay border in the mine's lorry, but they could not get through. On arrival they had been stopped by Thai customs officials, who informed them that the border had been closed since 0730 that morning.[10] As the men protested the local Thai District Officer waded into the argument, reiterating that they could not cross the border, and neither could they return to their tin mine. Stuck in limbo, he informed the men they were to be taken into Thai protective custody for their own safety, and shortly afterwards all three were locked up in Sadao's police cells and the police left them alone.[11] Soon afterwards they could hear sounds of panic outside, and it seemed the local police were trying to clear Sadao's streets and advising everybody to go home, lock their doors, and stay inside their houses. From what they could make out, there were reports that the Japanese would soon be arriving in force on one side of town, while the British were going to be doing the same on the other.[12]

While this was going on outside the police station, inside Rigby was fiddling with the cell door and trying to find a way out, which he managed to do a short time after. Stepping out of the police station, there were no cars or people to be seen anywhere, no workers on the rubber plantation around them, and not a single Thai policeman in sight. In what seemed like minutes, Sadao had become a ghost town.[13] After a quick conversation between all three, it was decided Rigby, who was the fitter and younger one in the group, should make a run for it, try to see what was going on and, if possible, go for help. Pooling their monies now recovered from the previously locked police desk, they thought the best bet would be if Rigby paid one of the local smugglers to take him by jungle track over the border and into the British side.[14] Keeping to the wider outskirts of town, he eventually found a local man hunkered down on the western side of the surrounding rubber estate. He accepted Rigby's money, and the two men headed off into the jungle. Back in the cell, Bentley and Tebbers were confident that at any time soon British troops would be arriving and this ridiculous nightmare would be over. It would not take too long for all three men to learn that 'gentlemanly' warfare was a myth.

Chapter 21

Singora Line South

Pinyok Swings into Action

Meanwhile, on the other side of the Singora Line, things were taking a different turn. When the Pinyok Mine compound heard that the Japanese had landed, and more worryingly were already occupying Pattani, English mine manager Frank Butler-Jones and his team were also listening for the expected 'Keep the Home Fires Burning' to be played. He and his Australian assistant manager Thomas Donnelly, and Welsh mine superintendent Harding Thomas huddled around the radio listening to the grim news broadcast. The importance of Pinyok to Malaya's defence operations was not lost on anybody, especially as it had been impressed on their Operation Cleeves cell just how important their operations were going to be to Malaya's defence. Soon afterwards the three men were joined by the mine's recently arrived chief chemist, Danish-born Georg Laub, and English shift engineer Edward Valentine Peters. All five men, along with New Zealand mining engineer George A Ravenwood, formed the backbone of Operation Cleeves' Pinyok Mine denial team. But today the Pinyok Six were a man down because Ravenwood was away in Singapore. That was problematic because Pinyok's operational responsibilities were more complex than those further north.

They knew there was a lot riding on the Pinyok cell's success for two main reasons. The first was the mine's proximity to the geostrategically important The Ledge. That had placed Pinyok's Operation Cleeves cell directly in line with Operation Matador planning, and its general vicinity had become the planned main forward staging post for British troops in Southern Thailand.[1] Butler-Jones and his men were to hold the southern approaches to Yala because another British military component would be moving up through Betong, and from there would be planning on using that area as a base from which small mobile forces could operate into the

Pattani area. The second was the importance of other denial operations, including occupying the ferry and destroying the bridge closest to it, implementing communication blackouts from Betong to Yala, securing any and all transport vehicles, and then disrupting the Pattani approaches from one side of the river with the other. In between those operations, the Pinyok Six were also to disable their tin mines, and potentially the Ayer Weng Tin Mine Survey complex on the other side of the highway. The importance of Pinyok to British military planning for Malaya's defence had been made known only a few days earlier on 3 December 1941, when the War Office was again chasing the geographical co-ordinates from Malaya Command as to Pinyok's exact location.[2] But for now, Pinyok too was also playing the waiting game, and there was nothing anybody could do but wait.

Meanwhile, unlike the police who had disappeared up in Sadao, down at the Pinyok Mine the opposite was happening. Butler-Jones had received a peculiar visit from a local Yala policeman and he came bringing bad news. He informed all and sundry that the Japanese had landed in Pattani, all the borders were shut, all the railways had ceased running, and all local police had been given additional orders. Although they were not at war with the British, he had been given strict instructions to confiscate any weapons on the mine site. Quietly and quickly Butler-Jones and Australian mining accountant Malcolm Macfarlane, ushered the policeman away from the office, escorting him to the more comfortable mine manager's bungalow. They were hoping to stop panic from spreading but they were already too late. After chatting a few more minutes with the policeman, who very soon thereafter left emptyhanded, it was obvious that the jungle telegraph was in full swing. All of the outdoor staff had gone, and the entire Malay and Thai labour force had disappeared. So too had the tiny Chinese market gardening enclave living on the mine's edge. Within the hour the mine site's workings were totally deserted, and the Pinyok Mine was falling into a deathly unquiet of mechanical silence.

Shortly afterwards Butler-Jones despatched Thomas and a few of the others to retrieve the hidden weapons stashed around the mine site, and prepare the mine's two lorries for deployment. One was packed full of weapons and explosives, and the other was readied for evacuation. Both lorries were parked outside the main office. When the signal to commence operations finally arrived that afternoon Thomas, Laub and Peters swung into action and were heading out towards their first mission. They clambered on board their waiting explosives-laden lorry and sped off over the water-filled rutted tracks. Driving at speed over slippery slush and mud that passed for the mine's access road, they made it to the main highway in record time, after which they made an immediate left turn and were soon heading as fast as possible towards The Ledge, and then hopefully, on to the ferry. They did not get as far as they hoped when only a few kilometres down the road they were forced to come to a screeching halt. What appeared to be large numbers of Thai police and Thai soldiers had mysteriously appeared out of the jungle, and were busily blocking the road and setting up a cordon. Now surrounded, the three operatives were detained, disarmed, arrested, and almost immediately afterwards escorted under armed guard back to the mine. It was almost as if the enemy was waiting for them.

On hearing the news that it was time to get out and to get out now, the other lorry had also left but was heading in the opposite direction. On board was the mine's nineteen-year-old Eurasian stenographer Maureen Magness and her family: her father KM Magness, who was the mine's laboratory superintendent, and her mother.[3] Travelling with them was Englishwoman Mrs Elizabeth Jeavons, whose husband Leslie Jeavons was the senior mine accountant but today was away in Singapore; three shift engineers namely, South African Klaas de Boer, Danish engineer Ole Roschke and his Norwegian counterpart ST Larsen; the Polish on-site physician Dr Rosenberg; and Penang-based Welsh mining consultant Matthew Arnold Francis.[4] They were planning on crossing the border at Betong, but first they would be calling in at the Kampong Toh Tin Mine to pick up passengers.

The Kampong Toh Tin Mine, lying closer to the Thai–Malay border and the frontier town of Betong, was also at the vanguard of newly improved hydraulic dredge technologies, and had only recently purchased some state-of-the-art equipment, including the latest version of hydroelectric batteries capable of producing more reliable and stable forms of power. In charge of this new tin mining toy was electrical engineer Philip van der Straaten, who lived with his wife Doris in the mine's European compound. Kampong Toh's staff too, were paying closer attention to this morning's radio broadcasts than usual, because although they did not house a dedicated Operation Cleeves denial team, and none had been trained as operatives, their mine was one of the twenty-six or so tin mines in Southern Thailand co-operating with the denial scheme.[5] When the news reached them that the Japanese had landed in Pattani, they were probably breathing a sigh of relief that they were this far away from the east coast. Everyone knew it usually took a couple of days or so to drive from Pattani to Betong, but that it only took a few hours or so to cross the border along the Betong-link road and into Malaya.

Unlike the evacuation priorities established further north, there was nothing put in place for anyone in southernmost Thailand. Operational planning had presumed that because all of them were living and working with close access to the main road, everybody in Pinyok, Kampong Toh Mines and anyone else living close to the main road could probably make a ready getaway once the job was done. That meant the various European communities including Operation Cleeves operatives would have to look after themselves. So when the large, six-wheeled Pinyok Mine lorry pulled up outside Kampong Toh's main mine's office it was a welcome sight. As the van der Straatens climbed on board, they were joined by Englishman Charles Kitts.[6] Kitts was a winchman working at the Labu Tin Mine site that was closer to Pinyok, but today he just happened to be down on the Kampong Toh mine. With Betong and the border only being a few kilometres away, the promise of relative safety in British Malaya lay tantalisingly close for everybody.

As the lorry pulled away, and they had almost reached Betong's outskirts, whatever collective sigh of relief they may have had was cut short when they were immediately stopped by two Thai police officers.[7] The two men spent little time in letting the travellers know that there was heavy fighting up ahead, and that the border was a raging and bloodied battlefield.[8] The group were strongly advised to turn around and return to the mine. Finding themselves unsure of what to do next and uncertain what to believe, it was probably only the fact that the two Thais quickly became increasingly agitated, almost to the point of threatening to commandeer the lorry, that spurred the group into action.[9] With little other option, they turned the lorry around and headed back to the Kampong Toh mine.

Chapter 22

8 December 1941

Singora Line Dancing

On the evening of Japan's invasion, most of Southern Thailand was in disarray. Singora remained a hive of activity because of its pivotal role as the essential transit gateway for the ongoing Japanese troop landings. Any break in the weather meant a welcome chance to get more of their mechanised units offloaded. Hongo and his railway engineering troops in particular had been more than concerned about that, especially in trying to get their specialised railway carriages ashore, not only in the face of violent monsoonal wind and rain, but increasingly, potential Allied air strafing attacks. Down in Pattani, on the other hand, the job was less hectic because Pattani's only importance had been as serving as the gateway for Ando's Detachment. Now they had departed, the small town would soon fall back into its rhythm as a remote coastal backwater. All the Japanese left behind was a small rear support unit. The real action would soon be starting further west, and not just between two imperial armies officially going to war.

Saeki's Detachment had continued making good time despite the blustering monsoonal wind and rain, and on arrival at Sadao's eastern outskirts at dusk he was glad to see their advance party had already set up camp. It was located on the edge of a vast rubber estate, and close by the town's only police station. Not long after taking a short rest break, Saeki and Tsuji had then set down to the business of war-fighting. The detachment's forward scouts had information that the British had been sighted on the other side of town, and they too had some sort of mechanised capabilities. It also looked as though they had dug in on the western approaches on the other side of town. As Saeki and Tsuji went about their forward planning, they seemed to have little use for the Thai policeman they had kidnapped at gunpoint earlier on in the day, other than making sure he too did not slip away. Much to his horror, as the detachment slowly came to a halt, he caught sight of two bloodied and beaten European men each tied separately to individual rubber trees. He knew the men well. They were locals, they were tin miners and one of them was his friend.

Sometime between when Rigby had left the Sadao cells and Saeki's advance reconnaissance troops had arrived in Sadao, a small contingent of Japanese soldiers had found Tebbers and Bentley. The two men had been taken out of their cells, and each tied to a rubber tree on the Ah Toe Rubber Estate that bordered the back of the police station.[1] Some of the residents were forced to witness the horror of the two men being horrendously tortured by Japanese soldiers, including being disembowelled with fixed bayonets, slashed with knives, and disfigured with hammers. By early evening, when Saeki ordered his detachment, tanks, and his heavy guns to head out, nobody it seemed paid any attention to the two men. Because now was the time to advance and engage the British on the other side of town, the two men were left for dead and still tied up against the trees. Their bodies were still tied there when Laycol arrived on the other side of town.

Andrews had little idea what was happening in Sadao and his mission goal had changed. Now he was going to be trying to hold this west side of Sadao, at least until the sappers had time to prepare the three bridges separating the town from the border for demolition. He knew it was going to be a very wet, nerve-wracking and uncomfortable night. As night fell and the regular torrential downpour only got heavier, the noise of tracked vehicles could be heard somewhere off in the distance. Soon after, his spotters could just make out a series of undulating headlights heading towards them through the piercing rain, and they counted roughly thirty-five vehicles in all. Andrews' troops lay in silent wait, using the cover of the heavy rain to their advantage. As soon as the Japanese lead tank came into range, British anti-tank weapons immediately opened fire, hitting their target, and the tank slew to the side of the road. As that happened the carriers also opened fire, taking out the two tanks following behind. It was then that all hell broke loose as the rear Japanese tanks immediately began blazing away indiscriminately at anything and everything before them. Within minutes they were returning rapid mortar fire back at the British troops.

Saeki's mortars too found their mark, and at least one of Andrews' carriers took a direct hit, but it was only now that it was ablaze and burning brightly against the pitch black darkness that he could make out how many Japanese infantry troops he was actually facing, and what firepower lay before him. The attrition rate was so devastatingly quick and high that Andrews was only now realising just how woefully under-gunned, undermanned and under-reinforced he was. He had little choice but to order the withdrawal and head back over the border as quickly as possible to avoid an impossible bloodbath. Just as Laycol's remnants were limping back over the three frontier bridges, a man dashed out of the jungle and into their western flank. He was waving his arms around and shouting at them in English. He said his name was Rigby, he was a British tin mine manager, and he had been taken prisoner and locked up in Sadao police station along with two of his mining colleagues earlier in the day.[2] He had escaped, but now he was pleading with Andrews to let some of his soldiers come and help him rescue them. Andrews' response was that nobody could be spared to go back into Sadao, let alone go and get Bentley and Tebbers, but Rigby could come with them as they headed back into Malaya if he wanted to.[3]

Not long after midnight, and while Laycol was in rapid retreat, the expected Japanese pursuit did not happen, and for whatever reason it seemed they had little interest in chasing the British all the way to the border, let alone over it. That was some good news for Andrews as what was left of his troops and machines continued limping back over the even, flat and straight road stretching across the border. At least they had managed to destroy two of the three major bridges along the way. Disheartened, Rigby was soon realising that this was not the mighty British Army coming to save them. The now former Ban Pru tin miner ended up travelling with Laycol, and on reaching Padang Besar later the next day wasted little time in taking the next train to Penang. Along the way he had stopped at Murray-Lyon's 11th Division headquarters in Alor Setar to try and raise the alarm, but they were too busy dealing with their own ongoing Japanese aerial strafing and bombing attacks to pay any attention to the man. Rigby had no idea about the fate of Bentley and Tebbers, other than that he presumed they were probably still locked up in Sadao's police cells.

Chapter 23

Singora Line South

Battle Lines Being Drawn

Sometime after Thomas' three-man Pinyok team were heading east towards the Japanese, and the evacuation lorry was heading west in the opposite direction away from them, the Assistant District Nai Amphur and some of his staff had arrived at Pinyok.[1] While his staff began sealing up the mine's main offices, he was informing the rest of Pinyok's European staff that they were all now under house arrest, and confined to the immediate European bungalow compound. He warned them that if any of them tried to go anywhere else outside of the confines of the compound, they faced the threat of being shot by the armed guards that were now placed around them. Shortly afterwards the Labu Tin Mine's accountant, Australian Norman Holt, and his fellow Australian dredge master Reginald Stratford arrived, and they too were promptly placed under house arrest and confined to the bungalow area. Their fellow Labu surveyor, New Zealander Harold James Edmonds, followed soon after.

By the early evening, another local police official arrived with a number of armed Thai civilians, but they were more concerned with what happened to the mine's money, and were keen to have Macfarlane show them the combination safe, which he did and then left them to it. While that was happening, Butler-Jones somehow managed to grab one of the mine's cars and the company books and slip away. Sometime later in the evening, after Thomas and the others returned, they spent little time in letting everybody know that they had been stopped earlier in the afternoon, arrested by what they thought were Thai officials, and escorted back to Pinyok under armed guard. That probably also meant all of Pinyok's Operation Cleeves' weapons, ammunition and demolition stores were now in enemy hands. When Australian mill superintendent David Bailey returned to the mine, he too was promptly placed under armed guard and house arrest. Later in the evening, Labu Mine's winchman, Scotsman Henry Moore arrived by bicycle to find out what was going on, but he was refused permission to return to his mine, and under much protesting to no avail also found himself confined with the others.

The lack of communication infrastructure between themselves, and the general lack of connectivity both with Singapore and the rest of Operation Cleeves, meant Butler-Jones had no idea about what was happening towards Yala, around Pattani or Singora, in Betong, on the border or anywhere else for that matter. The radio was not helping, because it seemed MBC's transmissions had been cut. But as Kampong Toh Tin Mine had signed on to the tin denial scheme and was closer to the border, he may have thought they might have a little bit more information about what was going on. The last thing he knew was that Thomas, Laub and Peters were heading to the ferry, Donnelly was more than capable of sorting out whatever was needed in any of Pinyok's additional on-site denial operations, and Macfarlane would keep the mine running smoothly in one way or another. The only thing left for Butler-Jones to do was to try and garner whatever information he might find as quickly as he could and get back. But on arrival at Kampong Toh after taking a trip over one of the old back tracks, he soon found out that they knew even less than he did.

While Krohcol was still engaging with the enemy on the border side of Betong, Ando's Detachment was occupying Yala and beyond, and with Pinyok's Operation Cleeves cell incarcerated, it seemed obvious that something was very wrong, but nobody knew about any of that. Once Butler-Jones was informed about the earlier group having been turned back from the border, everyone was in a quandary because that was their only way out. None of them had to wait too much longer to try and find out what was going on because not long after Butler-Jones' arrival, a group of what appeared to be Thai civilian militia armed with long swords and knives had descended on Kampong Toh's European bungalow compound. In no uncertain terms they informed the scattered European occupants now milling about outside that they were all under armed guard, and were to be confined inside the No. 4 bungalow until further notice. Luckily for the now-incarcerated group, however, that was the van der Straatens' house, and their house staff were still hanging around. Their cook managed to provide them all with dinner, which was warmly welcomed by one and all. That is until nature began calling later on in the evening, and they were abruptly told that they could not go outside, nor use any of the ablutions, and that any and all of their movements were now severely restricted. Now, none of the Europeans were allowed to leave the van der Straatens' bungalow for any reason whatsoever.

There was not much anyone could do at that moment other than attempt to reconcile the events of the day, and try to work out what to do. All that anybody could be sure of was that there were now thirteen Europeans ensconced in a small bungalow designed to house two adults, and that the Kampong Toh Tin Mine, like Pinyok, was now some sort of makeshift prison.[2] As far as anybody knew, that also included the last four European women left in the Yala District, namely Maureen Magness and her mother, Mrs Jeavons, and Mrs van der Straaten, and they were all scared because everyone had heard all the horror stories of the Japanese atrocities coming out of Nanjing.[3]

As these events were unfolding up in Southern Thailand, down in Singapore Brooke-Popham was communicating to the War Office what he thought about the current situation, and the news was not good. He confirmed that the Japanese had landed in Singora, Pattani and Kota Bharu just after midnight, and that it had been a combination of merchant and military vessels that had been involved.[4] The only fighting involving British forces, so he reported, was that around the Kota Bharu aerodrome. He had no news to report from Thailand, other than the aerial reconnaissance units that had been sent out earlier had not as yet reported back. The only other snippet of intelligence offered was that some sort of aerial dogfight had taken place over Singora sometime in the morning. Unconfirmed news had filtered in from unknown sources that an aged Buffalo aircraft had valiantly taken on six Japanese Zero fighters, but the outcome was vague. Other than that, there was no other news available about whatever else was going on in Southern Thailand.

Percival's later reporting was a different assessment. He was praising Laycol's actions, but was doing the opposite for Krohcol. In his disingenuous reporting back to London, he had described how Krohcol had only encountered slight opposition, was not fighting Japanese soldiers but purportedly Thai police, and were making nothing but a minimal advance over territory.[5] He made no mention of Laycol's retreat.

Nobody was reporting that within the space of half a day the Imperial Japanese Army had set up two makeshift headquarters in Singora and Pattani; organised Haad Yai as Japan's main railway transit hub in Southern Thailand; set up two inland staging posts in Yala and Sadao; and now occupied The Ledge. Nothing was said about the possible fate of any Europeans still present in Southern Thailand, and no mention was made about Operation Cleeves.

Killery's reporting was more sombre. He had no information whatsoever about whether anything had been achieved under Operation Cleeves, or what the fate of any of the Oriental Mission's operatives might have been. He advised London the best they could do right now was wait.

Chapter 24

The Singora Lines Falter

Two Steps Forward, No Steps Back

On Tuesday, 9 December 1941, the day after the Japanese had arrived, the Japanese Consul in Singora was waking up to a new and different local power dynamic. A steady and growing stream of local complaints had started showing up on his doorstep about the actions and behaviour of the Japanese troops.[1] Reports were being made that all local forms of transport including vehicles, bicycles and even horses, bullocks and carts were being commandeered.[2] Various foodstuffs including fruits and vegetables and other supplies including clothing were being taken without payment from shops and market stalls. Widescale looting of other merchandise including precious items such as watches was ongoing. All types of personal and business property was getting damaged or being broken. Some local workers were being pressganged into positions, such as working as drivers for the Japanese. Even street beggars and poor street peddlers did not escape the Japanese wrath. It seemed to everybody that the Japanese were assuming it was their inherent right to take any and everything they wanted, let alone needed, as time progressed, and it did not seem it was going to stop any time soon. Those complaints were only being matched by allegations that Katsuno was receiving directly from Yamashita's headquarters, that some Thai police had been taking reprisal actions against Japanese civilians living elsewhere.[3]

Later in the day, as some of Yamashita's staff headquarters were moving down to Haad Yai and beginning their preparatory moves to enter Malaya, they had left behind the Toyohisa Garrison Unit to guard Singora town.[4] Singora Jail had its own group of allocated Japanese enforcers, possibly under command of a Lieutenant Hanada, who would ultimately be responsible for identifying, arresting, imprisoning and interrogating potential enemy threats. A separate maritime and other logistics unit remained responsible for ensuring the continued and unfettered flow of all port and harbour trade. Hongo's railway enforcers already had command and control of Southern Thailand's rail networks. As the Japanese continued securing strategic locations in and around the town, it was also now that arrests began taking place.

By now Singora Jail had been formally set up as a centralised holding centre for suspected enemy personnel across the district, and throughout the day civilian prisoners were constantly arriving. That included not only Allied military or civilian European populations, but also suspected pro-British, or at the very least anti-Japanese, sympathisers as well. Among some of the first to arrive were King, Vererka and Langfeldt, who had been brought up by rail car from Haad Yai. Later that evening they were joined by some downed British airmen brought in under Japanese armed guard from Wat Kanoon, a small coastal area roughly eight kilometres (five or so miles) north of Singora.[5] Apparently a British plane was involved in a dogfight and had been shot down somewhere close to Singora's east coast. King saw two of the seriously wounded British airmen being brought in on stretchers. One was in a semi-conscious and delirious state, but he had managed to have a brief conversation with the other airman, who seemed relatively fine.[6] After that, neither he nor any of the other European prisoners had any knowledge about what happened to the airmen next.

Local gossip was that reportedly a handful of British 'operatives' had been picked up by the Japanese somewhere in some frontier region of the Thai–Malay border.[7] Just where exactly was vague, but it seems others were picked up further north not far from Kantang, which was in the general vicinity of several working tin mines, including Ronpibon's offshoot Tongkah Dredge. Among the tin miners picked up were Roderick Gordon, Daniel Regan and Herbert Charles Wright, all from the Anglo-Thailand Tin Syndicate, who all, up until the Japanese had landed, had been rotating between and working on smaller tin mining sites in and around Singora and Pattani including Tah Seh. For the time being they were all being held in local Thai police stations far removed from Singora.

Not long after King and the others had arrived, two Indian men were also thrown in with them charged with aiding and abetting the enemy. The allegations being made against Hazarath Yusuf Khan and Santoch Singh, who were two long-standing members of the local Indian population, was that they had allegedly been using mirrors to somehow signal directions of Japanese positions to British reconnaissance planes flying overhead.[8] They were followed soon after by Dr Sam Thomas, who had been brought up under Japanese armed guard from the Yala district. It was curious that how, just over a day after landing, all the men incarcerated on 9 December 1941 had been profiled as potential threats to Japan. But there were other arrivals that evening, and they were neither airmen nor tin miners.

Further south and closer to Pattani, the entire crew of the Norwegian cargo steamer SS *Hafthor* had been detained by Japanese soldiers. The ship's captain, named Andersen, first engineer Birgid Røstad, second mate Henry Fredheim, thirty-nine Chinese seaman and the ship's dog had been found on a beach north of Pattani and promptly arrested.[9] The *Hafthor* was a cargo steamship with a top speed of nine knots, and had left Singapore the Friday before heading for Bangkok. Two days later, in the Gulf of Thailand, the Imperial Japanese Navy's warship *Uranami* had hijacked the vessel. It was Sunday, 7 December, and the same day Yamashita's forces were coalescing off Southern Thailand's east coast. After swarming on to the defenceless vessel, the Japanese had forced the crew into three lifeboats and set them adrift into the monsoonal squalls, abandoning them roughly halfway between east coast Kra Isthmus and west coast Vichy French Indochina. The boats were separated by inclement weather, and in the aftermath they lost sight of one another.[10] They eventually made their way back ashore and on to Pattani's northernmost coast, where they were taken into custody and sent to Singora. By the end of the day, Singora Jail's inmate population had exploded by forty-three.

While the Singora Line South populations were being rounded up, detained, arrested, incarcerated, and some of them interrogated, further north the Singora Line North cells were having better luck. In Ronpibon and Phuket, Parsons' teams had now gathered as many Europeans in the district as possible at the Phuket aerodrome, and by mid-morning half of Parsons' team were getting ready for evacuation, while the other half were supposedly focusing on securing the airfield. He and some of the others had rushed to the aerodrome ahead of the evacuee convoy, mainly because nobody including himself had actually done any reconnaissance of any kind, and he was trying to get there in daylight to get some sort of visual comprehension of just what it was they might be defending.

In his viewpoint, this short window of opportunity would allow them plenty of time to adopt defensive positions, because Parsons was still working on the assumption that although the Japanese had already landed, and the orders to commence operations had arrived almost twelve hours later, they were too far away from either landing site. When they did finally arrive and set up a few counterattacking positions at either end of the landing strip, later that evening Parsons and his cell found themselves unprepared when a handful of what seemed to be armed Thai police began shooting at them. They were too professional, too well organised, and had too much knowledge for Parsons and his crew to be effective, so the motley remnants of Operation Cleeves rapidly piled into their escape cars and headed west as fast as they could to the other side of the island towards the rendezvous site, and were soon on board ship heading for the relative safety of Singapore.[11] That effectively ended Operation Cleeves' Singora Line North operations, which had amounted to practically nothing. But it was not over yet for those in and around Singora Line South.

Saeki had only this morning left Sadao and crossed into Malaya. His engineers had been busy through the night, rebuilding the two bridges Laycol had destroyed, leaving behind a small garrison unit to keep an eye on the place. As his detachment rumbled away into the distance, it was only now that some of Sadao's local population were tentatively returning to their town. Here they found a similar sight of carnage as had happened in Singora, Yala and elsewhere. Shops and markets were stripped bare, anything of any use had been looted, wanton destruction was everywhere, and most of the local transport including livestock were gone. What was more horrific for some of the Chinese rubber plantation workers returning to the Ah Toe rubber estate that day was that the bloodied, battered and crumpled bodies of two European men were each tied to a rubber tree. In the searing hot sun and souring humidity, the workers quickly cut the two tin mining men down and, respectfully covering their bodies in blankets, buried them as quickly as they could in separate graves close by.

Chapter 25

Singora Line South

With Laycol now gone, it was left to Krohcol further south to continue on with the fight against the Japanese. As day two of Japanese occupation dawned, in Betong, Moorhead's sappers had continued clearing several blocks throughout the day, but by the afternoon all enemy firing stopped as quickly as it had started yesterday. It seemed as though the Japanese were withdrawing from Betong and heading further up the road towards the direction of Yala. Whatever their reasons were, the abrupt change of pace allowed the British to make better, albeit more cautious, progress along the road, and by later that afternoon Krohcol had finally reached Betong.[1] The town was awash with white flags hanging in windows and on poles, and on arrival they were greeted by the tin miner's wife, Mrs Skryne, alongside a minor Thai Government official. The Thai official kept apologising profusely for the opposition they had faced, which he described as a 'mistake', and he also did the same for the absence of the District Officer, whose car it was later reported had been found facing northwards in a ditch.[2] Now having secured Betong with a cordon overnight, some much-needed rest and food and water was had by all the troops. It was the first overnight rest Krohcol's men had had after weeks of being on standby, and two solid days of fighting.

There was no similar rest for those up at the Pinyok Tin Mine, however. They remained under house arrest and confined inside Donnelly and also the vacant Ravenwood's bungalows. The Thai guards had not interfered with them in anyway throughout the previous night and were still leaving them alone this morning. At least some of the various house staff including Donnelly's cook and houseboy were still here, and they had been allowed to bring the prisoners some food earlier on in the day. The Pinyok prisoners still had not engaged directly with the armed Thai guards outside, when by the afternoon the electricity and water sources connected to the bungalows began alternatively turning off, and on, and off again, as the powerhouse continued losing its electricity supply. Whether that was deliberate on the guards' part and a type of mind game, or a result of Pinyok's Operation Cleeves' cell successfully undertaking some of their small-scale sabotage responsibilities, remains unknown.

As dusk fell, the Pinyok situation changed again, when a different batch of what looked like Thai police arrived out the front of the bungalow compound, and in short order tempers started to flare. Now everyone could hear the sounds of raised voices quarrelling, and heated discussions and arguing going on outside. It seemed as though there was some vehement disagreement between the Thai militia, who had been guarding them since late last night, and the newly arrived Thai police, who were now taking that role over. Whatever the contentious opposition was, the terse engagement ended when the Thai militia very quickly dispersed and vanished into the jungle's black darkness. Everyone was anxious and getting worried because Butler-Jones had not returned, and after what Thomas and the others had experienced yesterday they were fearing not only for his safety, but their own. The best they could all do was try and settle down for the night and face the next day as best they could.

Down at Kampong Toh, the same argumentative change out of guards was also happening in the evening. Only this time their new jailors were accompanied by a large bus that had also pulled up outside. It looked as though it had been retrofitted with side-screens blocking out the windows, and not long afterwards all of the Europeans were being forced out of the bungalow and on to it. They had no idea what was going on or where they were being taken, until three hours later when, much to everybody's surprise, they found themselves up at the Pinyok Tin Mine's bungalow compound.

As they were being forced off the bus, the Kampong Toh's Polish medical doctor, Dr Rosenberg, called out to Macfarlane, who replied that they were inside Donnelly and Ravenwood's bungalows. The new guards wasted little time in cajoling the Kampong Toh prisoners into either one or the other. Much to Macfarlane's and the others' relief, Butler-Jones and the rest of the Pinyok Mine staff who had left for Penang earlier yesterday afternoon were with him. They were now accompanied by the van der Straatens and Kitts. Inside were also a few new arrivals, including Horace Cummins, SOE operative and estate manager of the sprawling Yala Rubber Estate just down the road, who not long before had been arrested and brought in, and was also now under house arrest with the rest of them. They were now in total twenty-seven adults crammed into two small bungalows; at least five of them were Operation Cleeves operatives and one was an undercover operative working for SOE London.

Down in Singapore, Killery was still waiting with bated breath for any information about Operation Cleeves to emerge. He had already let London know that commencement instructions had not gone out until practically twelve hours after the Japanese had landed yesterday, and he was worried.[3] The lack of communication meant it was going to be impossible to ascertain how effective his operatives had been, or whether or not any of the tin mine denial schemes had actually got off the ground. Trying to find out any information about either was going to take some time, not only because there had not been enough W/T sets to go around, but neither did they have enough operators either. He, like everybody else, was hoping they may at least have made it out, but Killery was also realising that time had been against them. Because the actual order to start operations had been given so late out of CICFE's headquarters, that meant the Japanese already had at least half a day's worth of soldiering time and effort to exploit. He also knew that while everybody including Laycol, Krohcol and Operation Cleeves had been sitting around and waiting, the Japanese would probably have been implementing their own scorched earth policy, which if Manchuria and elsewhere was anything to go by, meant disaster for his operatives.

Curiously, the anticipated pushback Killery was waiting on from Crosby, too, had not arrived. That was compounded by an even more interesting communiqué Killery had received earlier from the Foreign Office. He was given immediate notice that Crosby, and by default the Foreign Office, no longer had any objections to raise over any Oriental Mission, Operation Cleeves or any other SOE-related activities in Thailand.[4] As sheepish as it sounds, it seems to be that it was only the morning after the Japanese had landed, when Crosby had been confined to quarters under armed guard and Oldham had arrived from Singora, that the British Legation Head began to fully appreciate the gravity of the situation. Crosby had also gone on to ask whether Killery might consider informing him, from time to time, about how Operation Cleeves and other things were progressing. It was a complete about face to say the least after having fought hard against Killery, the Oriental Mission and Operation Cleeves over these past few months. In the end it would mean very little in the scheme of things, especially when Crosby would soon be incarcerated as nothing more than another civilian internee of the Japanese himself, and the reality of wartime occupation hit home.

The brutal reality was that while most Operation Cleeves operatives and Europeans around Singora Line North had managed to get out, practically every European around Singora Line South, from Singora to Sadao, Pattani to Yala, and Yala to Betong, had either been or were in the process of being rounded up, incarcerated, and in Bentley's and Tebbers' cases, executed. In just over two days of Japanese occupation, practically every European civilian in Southernmost Thailand was in Japanese hands. That was not going to change any time soon, even as the British Army was slowly edging its way towards them.

Chapter 26

Battles Lost

Battles Won

On Wednesday, 10 December 1941, the day after Yamashita's headquarters had left for Haad Yai, Japanese Consul Katsuno had received an urgent message from the Japanese Embassy in Bangkok. Allegations had again been made of the killing of Japanese nationals this time at a place called Nakhon Si Thammarat.[1] It was similar information Yamashita had passed on yesterday. The town in question lay roughly 160 kilometres (100 miles) north of Singora, and reports had arrived that on the same day Japan had landed in Southern Thailand, Thai police had killed eight Japanese who had been working with the Eikō Group. This was ostensibly a Japanese civil engineering company that had been set up as a joint Thai–Japan venture focused on road surveying and construction work. Katsuno's masters in Bangkok wanted him to travel to the town and elsewhere including into Sadao and Yala on a fact-finding mission. The rumour mill had gone into overdrive, not only over the suspected retribution killings against Japanese, but of other atrocities alleged to have been committed by the Japanese. While he was busy making plans, more tin miners were arriving at Singora Jail.

Another Takuapa mine employee named Kemp had arrived under armed guard from Sadao by mid-morning. On the day Japan had invaded, he had been travelling further north up country closer to the small harbour area of Kantang near Trang, when he heard the news that the Japanese had landed and that all Europeans of whatever nationality were being taken into protective custody by the Thai police.[2] Within an hour he too had found himself placed under arrest by Thai police, until being relocated first to Sadao Police Station, and then this morning to Singora. He had little choice but to leave his five bags of worldly goods in the Sadao cells, where he was placed under house arrest. The cell, it seemed, was unable to be locked, and after depositing him in the police station, his Thai police guards promptly left. Kemp was puzzled because there were no other Thai police to be found either in the station or anywhere else that he could see, and although there was a Japanese presence, it was minimal.

It was a half-hearted attempt at best by his Thai captors, because not long after Kemp's arrival, some of his local Thai friends appeared and quickly spirited him away into the jungle. They were moving slowly west through the jungle tracks, and had crossed over the Thai–Malay border by late afternoon, when they were met by heavily armed Japanese first-line troops coming towards them from the Malay side. This time at the end of a fixed bayonet, Kemp was taken into Japanese custody, and immediately taken under Japanese armed guard to Singora Jail. He probably had no inkling as to what had happened to his fellow Takuapah Tin Mine employees in Sadao just a day or so earlier, nor did he have any clue that they were buried close by.

By lunchtime, Ando's Detachment had covered roughly 113km (seventy miles) from Pattani, and had easily occupied all that lay before them, from Pattani to Yala and including The Ledge, in less than two days. Now they were going to be heading out further south along the road to Betong and the border. They had made good time because Ando's Detachment had not faced any ongoing denial and delaying tactics Robinson and Moorhead's men had been facing near Betong. There the British had been bogged down not only by bad terrain, but a paucity of tactical let alone any other useful battlefield intelligence. In comparison, Ando's run had been practically smooth sailing. He had faced no opposition anywhere, even when taking control of the ferry. By now Saeki's Detachment was already over the border and heading deeper into Northern Malaya, and Ando was probably equally quietly confident that his detachment would be doing the same very soon. If today was going to be the British Army's final push to try and make some ground towards The Ledge, Ando was already lying in wait for them.

Just after daybreak, the 3/16th had started moving out of Betong. Nearly six hours later they stopped just under ten kilometres (six miles) south of The Ledge. Curiously, they had not faced any harassment on that leg of the journey. It was here they debussed from their Australian transports, because Moorhead knew there were no useful turning circles anywhere further ahead. As they were debussing, two Japanese planes buzzed overhead and dropped four bombs but did no damage. They had only advanced 1,800 metres (2,000 yards) when they encountered some light opposition, but that did not hinder their advance. It was only after continuing a few more metres ahead that stronger opposition was met. This time there were no police uniforms in sight, only Japanese Army ones, and Krohcol was still five kilometres (three miles) short of The Ledge. Now, however, Moorhead could confirm the Japanese had well and truly beaten him to it.

That obviously meant both road and bridges were in working order either side of the main railway town of Yala, and the ferry had either been replaced or supplanted, which also meant here at least that Operation Cleeves had failed. Faced with Japanese opposition head on, and with the potential that the enemy might already be covering Krohcol's withdrawal route, Moorhead implemented a series of flanking manoeuvres. Heading back towards Betong, B Company, under Palmer, headed offroad west and vanished, and no more communication was received from them for hours. D Company, under Second Lieutenant Mohammed Zarif Khan, later followed and they had better luck, reporting their occupation of 'Jungle Hill' located at the rear of the Japanese Army's right flank. Once that was achieved with minimal casualties, it seemed the Japanese once again had withdrawn. It was only then that A Company, under Subedar Sher Khan, began resuming their forward advance along the road.

By late afternoon, Robinson was back in Betong, and reporting to Moorhead he had now lost communications with all three companies. Moorhead then deployed his Adjutant Lieutenant Charlton forward, to at least try and find A Company, who should have been somewhere directly ahead. Charlton soon found them but they were divided into two sections straddling either side forward over the flimsy wooden and rope bridge near the Kampong Toh stream, the stream that almost marked the turning intersection into the Kampong Toh Tin Mine. Almost as soon as Charlton had arrived, he spotted two Japanese light tanks coming around the bend towards them from the north, and roughly 360 metres (400 yards) ahead. How the tanks had managed to navigate the badly potholed roads on the Pattani to Yala side, the various flimsy bridges that criss-crossed that side of the district, cross over to this side of the Pattani River on a small, single car ferry, travel over the precarious road on The Ledge, and make their way to the outskirts of Betong in such a short amount of time was unknown. All Charlton and the now divided A Company knew was that the logical thing to do was to immediately withdraw back over the bridge towards Betong, which by now the sappers were hard at work demolishing. Once that was destroyed, the Japanese tanks were then met with accurate firing of British anti-tank rifles, after which they hurriedly retreated back around the corner.

Later that evening Palmer's B Company returned, explaining how they had been held up by the precipitous country west of the road, but had suffered no casualties. Now that it was A company, Charlton and D Company that were missing, Moorhead thought it prudent to send his two remaining companies to this lower end of the Kampong Toh stream. B Company took the right flank and C Company, who had up until now remained in reserve, took the left. Owing to the run of the stream and its steep banks bordering jungle-clad hills, their positions were salient to the apex of where vehicles and troops could not forge across, which would give them some sort of line of sight advantage. Behind them, about nine miles north of Betong, Moorhead had also moved up his long-awaited reinforcements of the 5/14th Punjabis and 10th Mountain Battery. He had chosen not to bring them any further forward because as with the earlier gun placement problems, there were no protective positions anywhere to be found. They had little choice but to remain out in the open and exposed on the road itself, and it was not a welcome thought that their dispositions would give the Japanese significant tactical advantage.

Just after dusk, and much to their relief, the bloodied and beaten survivors of A Company found their way back to Moorhead's makeshift Betong headquarters.[3] Only nine of them survived. They reported how not long after they moved out, they had encountered tanks approaching and immediately deployed east into the jungle offroad. Here they observed how the Japanese were advancing one company led by two tanks, with a few hundred metre intervals in between. They had allowed the first two tank groups to pass by, and then the company had charged the rear Japanese group. Many of the troops were severely wounded or killed outright by short-range fire, but A Company had continued despatching the enemy with some survivors heading into the jungle. By this time, however, the lead tanks had turned around and had started firing into the fighting melee. Despite being fatally wounded, the commander of the Bren gun section, Havildar Pabadur Khan, and Sepoy Muzaffar Khan, continued firing on the enemy tank positions until both succumbed to their injuries. A Company had tried to battle on against these overwhelming odds but essentially almost all of the troops had been wiped out, and the remaining badly wounded survivors opted to try and make it back to base through jungle tracks.

With D Company still missing and A Company wiped out, and the 3/16th casualty lists increasing rapidly, Moorhead messaged Murray-Lyon that withdrawal was likely. Murray-Lyon, some 240 kilometres (150 miles) or so from the battlefront replied, reminding Moorhead that his job was now to stop the enemy, and besides he still had the 5/14th Punjabis on hand.[4] Murray-Lyon's other reply made note that at this stage Moorhead only had concrete information of at most six Japanese tanks, and what he considered were three badly mauled companies, and they still did not have any real indications as to Japan's strength. Basically, he was telling Moorhead to get on with the job and stop whining.

Chapter 27

A Short (Operational) Life

The Death of Cleeves

While Krohcol was engaging in its own bloody battles further south, changes were happening in Pinyok. The prisoners had been noticing how, although the Japanese planes had been increasing over the past day or so, more worrying was that nobody was seeing any British or Allied ones chasing them down.[1] Every now and again a few Japanese seaplanes would fly lower and sweep over the compound, and using field glasses seemed to be looking for something. The flyovers seemed to be unnerving the new Thai police guards, who had only yesterday taken over from their earlier Thai militia captors. Now their dispositions had softened and they were going out of their way to convince the Europeans to stay in the bungalow, lock all the doors and windows, and stay out of sight. The head policeman in particular was making sure everybody knew and understood that even though they were all now under Thai protective custody, they had to be careful to stay out of sight of any Japanese who might see them. He did not give any reasons as to why.

Although the Pinyok Tin Mine proper sat higher up in the mountain, the bungalow compound sat lower and was nestled in the foot of the hill. Standing in the garden area, it was possible to see the main Betong to Yala road in the distance, and today it was crammed with bus, lorry and car loads of Japanese troops heading in both directions. While this was going on, the head of the Thai police group then set about dividing the Pinyok prisoners into two parties. One group including Mr and Mrs Magness, the van der Straatens, Macfarlane and a few of the others were sent out the back to the separate kitchen annex located behind the house, and they were to prepare breakfast. The others, including Maureen Magness and Peters, were to remain in the living room. There was no contact to be made between either group.

Not long after the prisoners had been divided into two groups, another loud argument broke out somewhere in front of the bungalow. Shots were fired and a short while later there was a sudden knock at the door, followed by someone calling out 'hello' in English. It was Peters who answered it, and on opening the door he was pushed back inside into the living room at the end of a fixed bayonet.[2] Three other Japanese soldiers soon joined them inside, two with fixed bayonets at the ready, and the third holding a loaded pistol in each hand. The group was immediately ordered to put their hands up in the air, and they were marched down the front steps and made to line up in front of the bungalow. Here they were aggressively bodily searched, the men more so than the women, which seemed at odds with all the horror stories about the Japanese treatment of women. Having relieved the prisoners of all their passports, papers and anything else of value, they were then force-marched down the road for roughly two or so hours, when they reached the small village lying at the edge of the mine's turn-off road. The Japanese soldiers continued poking and prodding them and threatening them with shooting if they paused to catch their breath, dropped their hands, or did anything else that might have held them up. Around midday, they arrived at and were corralled into the centre of the mining village of Tengading, and forced to sit under the blazing hot sun, without shade or water.[3]

While this had been going on for the living room group, the kitchen group were being treated very differently. While they were busy trying to sort out what type of food they could improvise, they seemed unaware that their Thai guards had been replaced by armed Japanese soldiers, and had not realised what was going on in the main bungalow. That is until a short while later when a group of soldiers battered down the back door of the kitchen bungalow and promptly left, after which they heard shots fired and glass breaking from the main bungalow, and then no other sounds.[4] Everyone was wondering anxiously about what might have happened to the living room group. Soon after, someone knocked at the front door of the kitchen bungalow and it was Philip van der Straaten who opened it. It surprised the young Thai youth, who was startled by seeing the Europeans inside, so much so that he managed to trip over his feet several times as he ran away as fast as possible into the jungle. Within seconds new voices appeared outside, and one of them, speaking in perfect English, asked the occupants to come out. They did so, cautiously, and found themselves facing two neatly turned out Japanese Army officers, accompanied by a Thai driver, and a handful of heavily armed Japanese soldiers around them.[5] The two officers shook all the prisoners by the hand, and informed them that due to the fortunes of war, they were all now prisoners of the Japanese. Nobody could see or hear what had happened to the living room group.

The senior Japanese officer, who spoke very good English, was asked by someone in the group, if some of those who had been living on Pinyok could go to their own bungalows and grab some important personal items. He agreed, but only two of them could go, and they would be under armed guard. It was Macfarlane and Philip van der Straaten who went, and they had to be quick about it. It was a fruitless trip, however, because all of the other bungalows' front doors had been kicked in, clothing had been scattered all over the place, furniture broken, and anything of value was gone. At least both men managed to grab a few necessary items of clothing including hats and other sensible coverings they might need to combat sandfleas, flies, mosquitos and tropical hot sun. By the time the men arrived back, the Thai driver was overheard telling the two Japanese officers in English that Thailand was not at war with Britain, and these actions were not legal. To which both of the officers merely laughed, and one of them, again using flawless English, said that as there were no Thai officials anywhere around them to raise any objections or protect the prisoners, then they were now all in Japanese custody. As that conversation was finishing, a bus pulled up and all the remaining kitchen Pinyok prisoners were ordered on board.

An hour or so later they pulled up in the same village where Pinyok's living room group had been sitting for hours. Following close behind them was an impressive car being driven by a Thai national, and two Japanese officers. Much to the relief of those who had been sitting under the midday sun, being ordered off the bus were the others who had been left behind at Pinyok, including Maureen Magness' parents, and they soon rejoined the others. So too did the two Japanese officers. Both men were tall, looked fit and healthy, and wore neatly pressed uniforms. Their entire demeanour was one of professional soldiering. One of them seemed quite amenable and was speaking perfect Malay in conversation with Mrs Magness. Maureen thought his name sounded like 'Ando'.[6] In later conversations with her mother, Maureen had found out that apparently this officer had allowed the prisoners who lived on Pinyok to return to their bungalows and get some of their possessions. But it was of little use because all of them had been looted or their furniture taken, drawers and luggage had been emptied, and anything of intrinsic personal value such as Klaas de Boer's silver-framed photographs of his beloved family, or Harding Thomas' gold lighter his wife Iris had given him for good luck, were gone. After returning from this wasted trip, and unlike the living room group, Pinyok's kitchen group had not been searched, threatened with shooting, or made to put their hands in the air, before being placed on the bus and sent down to the village; actions that were in stark contrast to how the living room group were treated. While the English-speaking officer seemed more amenable, the other officer, who did not interact with the prisoners, remained more aloof, preferring to keep his distance.

By the late afternoon another bus had arrived, and now everybody was put back on to it, only this time they were being escorted under armed Japanese guard, and were going to be travelling in the vanguard of a Japanese Army advancing convoy. Following behind them was the same car with the same two Japanese officers they had met in the village. Enroute south the whole group had stopped at the Tanicom Penal Settlement, where the Japanese officers took some light refreshment. The Japanese had prevented some of the local Thai officials from providing the majority of the bus occupants with drinking water, and it seemed the only ones allowed to have any were the Eurasian Magness family. Soon after, the officer Maureen thought was called Ando was in conversation with Macfarlane. He was advising that all twenty-seven prisoners were going to be interned at Kampong Toh's bungalow compound, to which Macfarlane had complained it was too small to accommodate all of them. The officer again laughed and said the war would soon be over, as Japan would be in control of Singapore within three months, to which Macfarlane later recalled that he had tried not to laugh.

An hour or so later, just after dusk, the prisoner convoy returned to the road and arrived back at the Kampong Toh Tin Mine by early evening. They were all ordered back into the home of Philip and Doris van der Straaten, No. 4 Bungalow in the European compound. One of the Japanese officers then addressed the prisoners, informing them that this was to be their place of detention for the war's duration, and if any one of the party attempted to escape, the entire group would be executed.[7] Having said that, the two Japanese officers returned to their car, and along with the buses loaded with Japanese troops, set off towards Betong. They left behind four unkempt Japanese soldiers to guard them. A short while later the screeching of a heavy truck's tyres coming to an abrupt stop shattered the night, and pairs of heard but unseen heavy boots were now stomping up the front steps. Seconds later the front door was violently flung open by another group of scruffy Japanese soldiers in ill-fitting, dirty and somewhat haphazard uniforms, who began tossing in a variety of mattresses in all shapes and sizes at the prisoners.

The bedraggled, unshaven and wild-eyed Japanese leader, using a combination of broken English and almost slapstick miming and gesturing that would have been laughable in other circumstances, began indicating to the prisoners he wanted them to start overlapping the mattresses on to the living room floor. Complying with the request at gunpoint, they were then all forced to sit down on top of them and were warned not to move. Once that job was done, these Japanese soldiers then abruptly left through the front entranceway, slamming what was left of the door on its hinges just for good measure. It was strange that they were all being left alone again. It was more unnerving that this time the Japanese were leaving without any yelling, or making any other sounds at all, and all inside the bungalow listened in stillness as the truck rattled away. Once these soldiers were gone, inside the small, claustrophobic space a new deathly silence prevailed. The sounds of panicked breathing pricked the air around the bungalow's occupants, as they all braced themselves for the fearful unknown of what might be soon coming, and that came shortly after, when one of the four Japanese guards placed a small oil lamp in the room. Sleep did not come to anybody that night. The twenty-seven prisoners were all confined to the living room, and had been made to lie prostrate on the floor. Throughout the night, two of the guards would take it in turns to walk around them with rifles and fixed bayonets, and every now again sweep the bayonets over them as they lay in rows alongside the walls.

Chapter 28

The Singora Line Defeat

Retreat is not Always an Option

It had been three days since the Japanese had landed, and for the existing prisoners in Singora Jail today was their first day of relative quiet. Food was scarce and of dubious health benefit, and other things had become unnerving as the day progressed. There seemed fewer guards, and it may have been because, just before daybreak, a rapid mass deployment of Japanese troops was being undertaken. The jail, along with the town, was practically emptied out of Japanese military uniforms well before midday. It was the same down in Pattani, where a mere skeleton garrison crew had now assumed responsibility for its security and control. In both cases, local buses, trucks, lorries, cars and practically anything else that ran on four wheels, were being used as troop transports. Ando's bicycle battalion had already confiscated all the pushbikes, and they too were now heading out in numbers. It seemed the larger majority of the Japanese troops were heading west.

Down in the van der Straatens' bungalow in Kampong Toh, they too were having what appeared to be a relatively quiet, undisturbed day, albeit in captivity. That is until mid-morning, when another Japanese officer accompanied by an interpreter arrived. His demeanour was exactly the opposite of the two Japanese officers the group had encountered yesterday, and his appearance did fit the stereotypical cartoonish Japanese characterisations most Western propaganda had been promulgating for months.[1] He was short, heavy set, clean shaven with protruding teeth and a large round face, but he was not wearing glasses. His tunic was having trouble buttoning at the front, and the Japanese soldiers with him were not faring any better. After making much ado about his arrival, one of his troop then entered the bungalow, and was busying himself with lining up the prisoners against one of the bungalow walls. After that was done, the officer made a grotesquely grandiose entrance, and then proceeded to give a very long, animated speech in Japanese. What he was offering to the prisoners in this lengthy soliloquy, nobody could really be certain about, because none of them spoke Japanese. Once that had been done, his next rant seemed to be more of an officious kind. This time the interpreter, who seemed to be a very scared Japanese civilian, and who spoke very poor English but with a clipped English accent, informed the group that 'all Britishers were to be executed…'.[2] After that statement was made, he and his entourage immediately turned on their heels and left abruptly, jumped in their waiting vehicles and drove off. The group stayed frozen in place for an instant, but the statement elicited the desired result.

Many in the bungalow crumpled with the shock. Some of the women cried. Holt collapsed. Everybody was scared out of their wits that death could come at any time. Fully expecting they were all going to be killed sooner rather than later, the emotional trauma took its toll, and everyone continued waiting anxiously and nervously for whatever horrendous fate may lie before them. Some sat in shock for hours, but when nothing had happened by midnight, a small sense of relief washed over the bungalow. It seemed at least for now, that the situation was returning to what over the past few days had been passing for relatively normal. The same four Japanese guards were back at their posts outside. The night-time jungle sounds, smells and songs were becoming their deafening selves, and the hot humidity of the night was slightly being dampened down by the evening monsoonal rains. Some were wondering whether it had been a case of bad mistranslation on the part of the interpreter, or whether it had been his lack of translation skills, that might have been wrong. The best they could all do for now was to try and hold on to both potential scenarios, and grab some sort of rest to try and face whatever was coming the next day.

While it was all quiet in Singora, Pattani and Kampong Toh mine, further west it was a very different and bloody story. From dawn onwards Japanese mortar bombardment had increased on what was left of the 3/16th's position near the Kampong Toh stream, but with little damage. By mid-morning that had dissipated, and the seeming absence of a dedicated Japanese offensive was confusing, especially when both Japanese mortar and sporadic rifle fire attacks appeared as an almost half-hearted offensive attempt. The situation for the British was dire without reserves let alone replacements should the Japanese take the initiative, and hopes lifted later that morning when D Company survivors arrived back in Betong camp, but they were short-lived. Although they had managed to rout the Japanese from the Jungle Hill summit and occupy the position yesterday, the fighting had been so ferocious and intense that there were several dead and at least eight or so of the 3/16th Punjabis had been taken captive.[3] They had tried to hold on overnight, but as a seemingly never-ending parade of Japanese reinforcements arrived and surrounded them, there was no other option other than using the cover of darkness to extricate themselves and attempt to disappear into the jungle. At least that way some of D Company might be successful in making their way back to Betong's outskirts.

After this skirmish, there had been little Japanese activity for the British Army for the rest of the day until late afternoon, when a series of right and left flank Japanese grenade attacks shattered the peace. Accurate Japanese sniper attack and rifle fire then ensued until the British counterattacked. They managed to dislodge some of the Japanese from their grenade-range nests, but even with the bringing forward of infantry guns and mortars, the lack of ammunition was taking its toll. Just on dusk, as the various company remnants reformed and the carriers were brought up closer and placed in position, Moorhead managed some sort of co-ordinated battalion-strength attack against the Japanese. But as the evening wore on, it seemed Japanese mortar bombardments of their positions were deliberately doing little damage, and it seemed the Japanese were now more on the offensive and advancing within grenade range. In response, Moorhead's infantry guns and three inch mortars successfully found their targets, effectively concentrating on the Japanese carriers and literally blowing several of them out of the ground. It still did not explain why the Japanese seemed to be deliberately trying to miss British targets on the ground.

Chapter 29

There is Always a Calm Before the Storm

The next day, Thursday, was no different for those in Singora Jail. More tin miners were coming in, and some of them had been arrested in Kantang. They included CW Billinghurst, WEJ Bird and George Powell. Shortly after their arrival, another Anglo-Thai Tin employee, GS Settle, who had only yesterday been scooped up by Japanese soldiers near Huey Moot, joined them.[1] On arrival at Singora, all the tin mining men were placed into separate cells downstairs. Only some of them were taken for questioning upstairs and at different intervals throughout the day, but that did not seem to last very long. As this was going on, an aerial dogfight over Singora was under way between Japanese and British planes, and it seemed the aging British Blenheims were being resoundingly beaten by the Japanese Zeros. Today, news was filtering in that a second British plane had reportedly crashed near Ban Pru.

Three aircrew survivors had been found by locals, given medical treatment, and had been placed into the nearby Haad Yai Police Station. They were all dressed in tropical clothing, wearing khaki shorts and shirts. One man who wore a black leather zip-fastened jacket had injured his right shoulder and his arm was in a sling. After entering their names in the station's prison registration book, the Haad Yai police then supplied them with dinner and fresh water, after which the three airmen tried their best to settle down for the night in their cell. The men probably thought it best to get as much rest as they could, because there was every probability they were going to be taken as prisoners of war. Later that evening orders arrived from Singora Police headquarters that Thai police Sergeant Major, Chamnarn, would be driving down the next morning from Singora to pick them up, and then take them all directly to Singora Jail.[2] Other than routine interactions, there was no major contact made with any Japanese by either locals or the prisoners.

It was the same type of unnerving Japanese silence that was going on down in Kampong Toh. For this disparate group of twenty-seven European

Yala Town c1940.

Haad Yai Railway Station c1941.

Unknown Tin Mine Southern Thailand near Yala c1941.

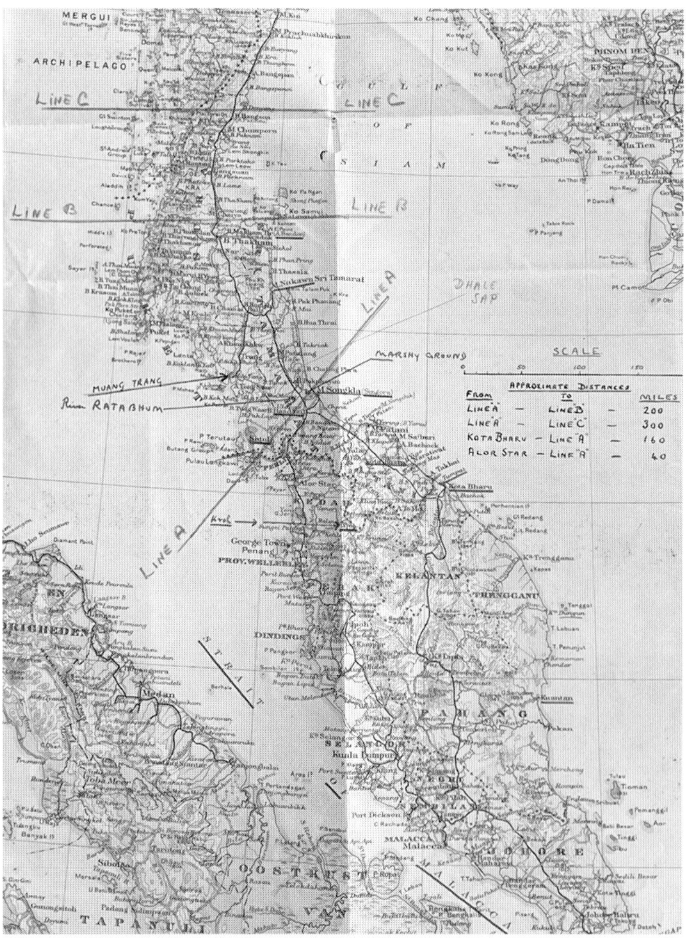

Original Singora Line Map 1941.

The Ledge c1940.

Singora Beach c1930.

Pattani Waterfront c1941.

Road to Pattani c1941.

Yala Ferry c1940.

Ban Pru Dredge.

Ban Pru Tin Mine c1940.

No 4 Kampong Toh Bungalow c1946. (Courtesy Wright Collection)

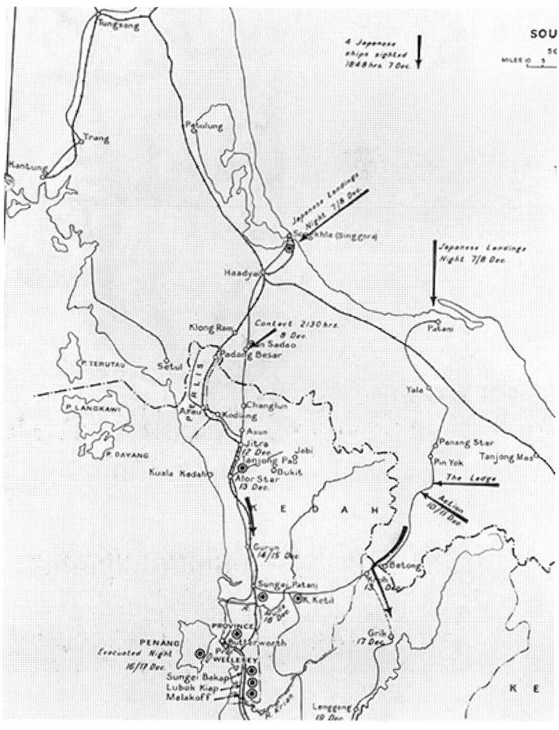

Krohol and Laycol Area of Operations 8 to 10 December 1941.

Kampong Toh Gravesite c1947. (Courtesy Wright Collection)

civilians in Southern Thailand, the events of the previous few days had been an emotional roller coaster. After tumultuous days in captivity, firstly in the hands of Thai armed militia guards, Thai police and now under the Imperial Japanese Army, the relative calm of the past few days seemed surreal. Everybody in the bungalow had been complying with their captors' requests, no one had tried to escape, and there had not been any violent or any other bad interactions between any of the two groups. It was even more bewildering for some of those in the group, especially the women, that none of them had seen any evidence of the types of Japanese atrocities they were all expecting, aside from that last Japanese officer and his badly translated threats bordering on the comical. Today four new Japanese guards had arrived, and the well-disciplined and polite manner of these four had been a welcome respite from the chaotic disarray and intemperance of their earlier captors.

Despite the callousness of the matter-of-fact execution statement made previously, nothing unspeakable had as yet happened. Since these four Japanese soldiers had taken over, and although the prisoners had remained confined to the bungalow under house arrest, they had not been interfered with in any way, shape or form, and had been pretty much left alone. For some in the group these actions were just that little bit too disconcerting, especially when some thought they could smell and hear the sounds of battle in the distance, and suspicions arose about where the guards were and what they were doing. For others, not seeing the soldiers had the opposite reaction, lulling them into a false sense of security. Most were probably still clinging to the forlorn hope that help was just over the horizon, and at any time now a British Army advance would be arriving sooner rather than later. The simplest argument among the majority was that if they continued to co-operate with their Japanese jailors, and carried on just as they had been over the past few days, then they may actually have a good chance of surviving Japanese internment until the British arrived. But for now a new and more immediate threat loomed on the horizon, and that was because there was not enough food to go around.

That problem had been a direct result of one of the Imperial Japanese Army's major flaws in their invasion planning. Although their strategic masters had mapped out the military occupation in fine detail, it was not detailed enough. There had been limited strategising over their own support and supply lines as it was, by adopting the principle that once in-country they could then exploit whatever resources were found *in situ* and along the way. But the real problem was in dealing with any enemy combatants. That had not been addressed at all, and perhaps mainly due to the influences of Japan's peculiar Bushido-stylised soldiering code. What to do with civilian enemy non-combatant populations the Japanese Army might come across, let alone house, feed or imprison them, was not even contemplated.

But for now at No. 4 Kampong Toh bungalow, at least everyone had easy access to clean drinking water again, but the already meagre food rationing was so bad that something had to be done, and it was Peters who took the lead. After lengthy amicable conversations with the four Japanese guards, he had managed to convince them that he needed to go out – under armed escort of course – and seek provisions for everybody.[3] That his brash proposal was tolerated was remarkable. That it was accepted, exceptional. How it came about was even more extraordinary. When one of the guards who spoke good English had casually remarked that there was no food left on the mine site, he had also let it slip that the Army had not provided them with any ongoing rations either. As these four seemed to be very young, and among some of the lowest-ranked recent recruits in the Japanese Army, none of them had any idea where to go to find food. More to the point they did not know what to do next, but they, like the prisoners, were hungry.

The guard went on to tell Peters that he had already personally tried to get food for both himself, the prisoners and his fellow guards from the nearby Tanicom penal settlement earlier, but had been rebuffed. He also revealed that despite repeated requests even from the smaller makeshift 25th Division headquarters in Pattani, the Governor of the Thai convict establishment had again refused. His argument was that although the prison was supposedly self-sufficient according to Bangkok, the reality was that without ready access to locally grown produce or the black market, they too did not have enough rice and water to go around for themselves. The last thing he wanted was to have a jail full of hungry criminals on his hands.

Given that Tanicom had only recently been built to house the overflow from Bangkok's overcrowded prison system, and that the Japanese were terrified of facing hordes of marauding hardened criminals should they escape, the Governor had played up Tanicom's limitations to the occupying Japanese. It may have been the threat of cut-throats and murderers rampaging anywhere within Southern Thailand's countryside that was more of a worry to the ordinary Japanese soldiers than it was in facing the British. When Peters heard the Japanese guard's accounts of food scarcity, it only seemed to fuel his foraging initiative. The end result was that after the mining engineer had taken the news back to the group, Peters along with his two-member armed Japanese escort, would be setting off the next morning in the remaining mine's car on a dedicated rummaging expedition around the countryside.

While Peters' food hunting expedition was away for most of Friday, 12 December 1941, the rest of the prisoners and the remaining two Japanese guards spent what could only be described as a peculiarly benign day in each other's company. All the remaining prisoners were still supposed to stay corralled within the main living room, and even though they were presumedly still under the watchful eyes of their jailors, some like Butler-Jones, Thomas and the van der Straatens (after all it was their house), were tentatively fanning out into other areas of the bungalow. Others like the Magness family and Mrs Jeavons remained firmly seated in the living room. Yet despite these openly defiant actions, the two remaining guards seemed even more relaxed than before. One of them opened up the back door and sat himself down at the top of the backstairs. The other guard did the same thing at the front. Both of their rifles, everyone noted, were still full of live ammunition and with fixed bayonets, but for now they were not pointed towards the prisoners' general direction.

A while later things took an even stranger turn when the Japanese guard sitting at the back wandered off, only to return a short time later with a supply of cigarettes. He spared little time in sharing them around with the eagerly awaiting smokers in the group, before once again taking up his backstep-seated guarding position and he too began enjoying a long, drawn out smoke. By now the other guard, the one who had been sitting on the front steps, and who had showed no interest in the cigarettes, had also begun fraternising with the prisoners. After some light banter with the women, he even ended up playing a few rounds of makeshift ping-pong with the older mining man, CF Chambers.[4] As the day progressed, the overall mood within the bungalow was one more of peaceful resignation than forceful retaliation on either side. Hopes were high among the disparate group of civilians that if this was what being a prisoner of the Japanese was going to be like, then being a civilian prisoner of war in a Japanese-run civilian internee camp for the war's duration might just be bearable until the war's end.

By later that afternoon when the foraging mission returned, it was nothing but bad news. The only supplies they had found were a few cigarettes and some potatoes, and a sack of what Peters had thought was rice flour.[5] Whatever it was, it was neither rice nor flour, and was deemed to be totally inedible. All the tinned provisions from Pinyok, Yala and other shops were gone, and so were any of the dry rations that were usually carried during the wet season. The group's hopes were dashed, and their mood fell further until once the Japanese guards were again outside and out of earshot. Now Peters began letting everyone know what the situation was outside of the Kampong Toh Tin Mine, and that was even more disheartening than the possibility of not having any supper.

Everywhere they had gone throughout the day was in turmoil. Wanton destruction was everywhere, and it seemed large-scale looting had taken place of anything and everything that had not been nailed down. There were no vehicles, no horses, bullocks and no carts, but even more perplexing was that when they had driven out heading to Yala, the checkpoint guards that had arrested himself, Thomas and Laub a few days earlier, were gone. In fact, he had not seen any large-scale presence of Japanese anywhere, other than one or two armed guards at other ad hoc checkpoints, and they were closer to the ferry, and not the town itself. But then, neither had he seen any indications of any British, let alone Allied troops, anywhere else either. Even the usual town beggars, roadway pedlars and always hovering blackmarketeers were nowhere to be found, and others including Thai police or local officials were equally missing. When they had visited the Pinyok compound, he had made the point of checking for certain items on behalf of some of the former residents, but he had nothing but bad news on that front as well. There was literally, practically, nothing left. Even the furniture was gone. The market garden had been stripped bare, and whatever was left of the drying sheds had been pulled down.

It seemed to Peters as if nearly every living thing had just melted away into the jungle, but he did have a bit of good news, and that was, unlike the first two days or so following the Japanese invasion, there were no roving bands of armed Thai bandits and militias roaming the countryside and seemingly doing Japan's bidding. After hearing all of this bad news, however, there was some silver lining to the cloud that was hanging over them. Paradoxically, it was precisely because they were all confined to Doris and Phillip van der Straaten's bungalow, and because their bungalow had become the group's makeshift prison, that the van der Straatens' residence was probably the only European home still left intact across Southern Thailand. By that evening, it was also perhaps more fortuitous that the van der Straatens' usual house staff reappeared.

It was a testament to their scavenging and procurement skills that somewhere and somehow later that evening, the Thai houseboy had been able to catch one of the geese that belonged to one of the former Kampong Toh residents, rustle up some rice and manage to find a few other vegetables.[6]

In an almost turning 'water into wine' moment, their long-term Malay cook then managed to produce an amazing meal of something out of nothing, not only for more than two dozen hungry adults inside the bungalow, but four equally hungry Japanese soldiers outside as well. Once the meal was completed, and after spending time chatting with Mrs van der Straaten, the two house staff once again vanished away into the night. Their Japanese captors, it seemed, remained unfazed by events.

Given the situation about the only thing anybody could do was make the best of the worst of conditions by trying to keep calm and carry on. That was what would see them through. The hopeful logic remaining premised on the fact that any salvation was just around the corner, and it would only be a matter of days or even maybe another week or so at most, that they would have to wait until being rescued. That meant the best they could collectively do for now was try to settle down for what they thought was going to be yet another quiet night, and worry about tomorrow when tomorrow came. For others including Butler-Jones, Thomas and the rest of the Operation Cleeves operatives, it was debatable as to whether anyone knew what was going on in Southern Thailand. For the SOE London operative Cummins, he very much doubted any news was being reported anywhere about what was going on in this remote part of the Thai–Malay border. As long as all of them stuck to their cover, it was hoped the Japanese just might brush them all off as nothing more than 'Britishers', or annoying civilian internees, and leave it at that.

As the bungalow occupants settled down for the evening, some listening to the comforting embrace of the sounds of the night-time jungle, nobody gave a second thought as to where their captors might be sleeping. It was enough for this motley group that at least they were going to bed with some food in their bellies, a roof over their heads, walls and mosquito-wired windows to keep out creatures, and the most reassuring of all, no guns pointed at them. In what had once been the van der Straatens' living room they slept head to toe, stranger next to stranger, unknown woman next to unknown man, and all within eyesight of the only light source they had left, the same single, small, oil lamp that had been placed in the bungalow a few days ago. As its flickering cadence of shadows danced up and down the wall, each in perfect rhythmic movement with the song of the evening breezes attempting to swirl around them through the windows, it brought a touch of light relief to most, while lulling others into a fitful sleep. Even some sort of broken rest was welcomed, because that was about the only thing any of them had any control over.

Chapter 30

All is Not Quiet on the Western Front

While it was quiet in Southern Thailand's east and on the Kampong Toh Tin Mine in the early morning of Saturday, 13 December 1941, all hell was breaking out on the western front. Today the Japanese began mounting their strongest attack yet on Krohcol, and it was going to be the heaviest and most lethal day of fighting for Moorhead and his men. As dawn approached, Krohcol's situation was getting even more precarious. Under cover of darkness the Japanese had begun mounting a heavy attack against the centre of Moorhead's Betong outskirts position, rapidly following that up with more bloodied and vicious hand-to-hand fighting. The only thing Moorhead knew with some assurance was that nobody had any information on Japan's troop strength, but he thought they were facing at least a full regiment.[1] From what he had seen over the past few days, his troops were facing more than a battalion, and with what seemed to be never-ending reinforcements and resupply of all kinds coming from somewhere. He also knew that Krohcol was being hit hard and bad, and it was almost as if the Japanese had some sort of sixth sense about what his battle tactics were going to be, and that they had been planning this for some time. The dire realisation was that Moorhead and his troops were facing an almost 'last man standing' scenario, and it was already beginning today just before daybreak.

Japanese light automatic fire from the jungle canopy was making short work of encircling the British troops, and they were threatening to cut off Krohcol's escape route back to Betong. In some of the fiercest hand-to-hand fighting yet seen, and led by D Company's Second Lieutenant Zarif Khan, the British counterattack continued. The 3/16th Punjabis were holding their own at least until sunrise, when line of sight revealed that the main Japanese attack force were actually bypassing their Kampong Toh bridge position. An hour later the Japanese launched their strongest attack, again using their preferred jungle fighting tactics of using their outflanking troops, supported by light automatic fire from the surrounding jungle tree canopies, and both tactics were proving exceptional in containing Moorhead's men. Now his troops were being backed into a single withdrawal corridor, and the hand-to-hand combat intensified as the Japanese attempted to stop the British Indian troops leaving, while the 3/16th Punjabis in turn were fighting back equally determined to achieve the opposite. By now even more disconcerting news had reached Moorhead that all of Britain's entire air force capabilities had been wiped out, there was not going to be any aerial support of any kind, nor was there any promised naval bombardment coming, because both HMS *Repulse* and HMS *Prince of Wales* had been sunk. It was in the heat of fierce battle that Moorhead finally gave the orders to withdraw.

Amid increasingly heavy Japanese fire from both flanks, Moorhead ordered D Company to occupy a lay-back position nearly a kilometre or so to the south. They were to be followed as soon as possible by the withdrawal of the remnants of the two flanking companies of B and C. Following up the rear to protect the companies were to be the last of the carriers. For the rest of the day, intense close combat between the 3/16th and the Japanese continued as the troops kept trying to withdraw. B Company suffered severe casualties but managed to make it back to D Company's position. C Company had found itself completely surrounded. With little choice but to take the Japanese head on, most of C Company, including the tin miner now field commissioned Second Lieutenant Skryne, had been fighting for hours until by early afternoon most, including Skryne, had fallen in combat.[2] But the 3/16th troops had not given any quarter in the ferocious, bloody fighting, and they had also managed to inflict equally major casualties on the Japanese. Only ten men from C Company survived, and as they were limping back to D Company's position, Moorhead was already making his way forward heading in the other direction towards the four remaining carriers to help protect his withdrawing troops. Taking his place in the firing line, and setting himself up on the last carrier's gun, he and the carriers began covering the withdrawal of the rest of Krohcol as best they could.

As they started moving out, the four remaining carriers were now coming under accurate Japanese shellfire. Heavy Japanese bombardment increased as one received a direct hit, another was knocked sideways and immobilised, and the third narrowly avoided suffering the same fate. The remaining carrier remained fully intact, and with Moorhead still mounting the gun in the rear vehicle, they continued edging their way back over the last standing Kampong Toh stream suspension bridge, laying just over thirteen kilometres (eight miles) north of Betong. As they sped towards Betong under continued heavy fire, behind Krohcol lay a heavily shell-bloated and bullet-swept road, strewn with disproportionate numbers of Japanese casualties and even more wounded. As they reached closer to the border, Moorhead and his men were more than glad to see the 2/3rd Australian Reserve Motor Transport Company waiting for them on the other side.

More than two thirds of Krohcol's troops had been killed in battle, but it seemed as though Moorhead and his men might have done their job in denying the Japanese advance, at least for a little while. Similar to what had happened up with Laycol's withdrawal up in Sadao, however, none of the Japanese followed, and what was left of Krohcol limped back over the border by three o'clock that afternoon. Southern Thailand was lost, Operation Matador was over, and nobody had any idea what was happening with Operation Cleeves.[3] Anyone left in Southern Thailand around what was once the Singora Line was on their own.

Chapter 31

Blood in the Darkness

My Prison, My Home, My Grave

While Krohcol was taking its last stand down the road, just before daybreak on Saturday, 13 December, there was a notable change in the air for the prisoners of No. 4 Kampong Toh bungalow. Loud knocking and crashing commotions along with roaring engines and screeching brakes had abruptly shaken the bungalow's occupants awake. It seemed as if within seconds a plethora of Japanese soldiers armed to the teeth had magically appeared and were surrounding the bungalow. Peters thought he heard the voices of their four jailors arguing with another Japanese voice somewhere in the din. Cummins thought he heard similar Japanese voices increasingly arguing over something or other, but nobody knew what they were arguing about. Macfarlane stole a few quick glances outside, but now it seemed their previous four guards were nowhere to be seen. What everyone including Maureen could make out was that the place was now swarming with all sorts of Japanese soldiers, trucks, buses, bicycles and other transports heading in both directions along the roadway below them. Everybody inside the bungalow was trying to catch a glimpse of whatever all the commotion was going on outside.

Because the bungalow sat on a higher ridge overlooking the edge of the Kampong Toh Mine entrance road, they could see how the area below them was being turned into a major staging point for Japanese troop movements. That was obviously not by accident, because unlike the secluded and hard to access Pinyok Tin Mine up the road, the Kampong Toh Tin Mine had easy access alongside and adjacent to the main Yala–Betong highway. Not only that, it did not flood from the nearby Kampong Toh creek, and was the only flattened patch of dirt off the Betong to Yala road that was wide enough to be used as a turning circle for vehicles of all shapes and sizes. Even in the dire monsoon season, this part of Southern Thailand was always drier than compared to the coast, and less prone to the whims of the swollen Pattani River near Pinyok and Yala, which made Kampong Toh a perfect area to be used as an operational staging post.

As the cloistered prisoners watched with intense interest, at what appeared to be more and more convoys of buses, trucks, and carts or anything else capable of carrying people travelling in both directions along the road. Maureen Magness thought that some of them looked like Thai civilians fleeing east from wherever the fighting had been. Speeding past them in the opposite direction also seemed to be literally hundreds of Japanese troops crammed into buses, lorries and other types of people carriers heading to the west. One of the older men, possibly Francis, thought he had heard the rumbling of engines, and maybe tanks somewhere in the distance, but everyone was sure they heard planes screaming overhead again. As the occupants continued trying to listen intently as to what was going on outside the bungalow, it soon became obvious that there could only be one place the Japanese were heading, and that had to be Betong, or at the very least the Betong–Kroh border crossing. At that point in time a glimmer of hope crept into the place that maybe just around the corner the British Army was on its way.

What also soon became glaringly apparent was that at differing intervals one of the convoy's trucks carrying Japanese troops would veer off up the road towards the bungalow, drop a batch of battle-worn Japanese troops off on one side, and then pick up another batch of fresh troops that had been waiting on the other. After that the truck would merge back into the convoy and continue on westwards. It seemed to indicate that although the prisoners were not being guarded, the never-ending and non-stop stream of heavily armed Japanese troops mulling around them made any ideas about attempting to escape severely limited. It would be a suicide mission if any of them attempted to escape, and besides they had already been warned on several occasions if one of them even tried to get away, everyone else would be executed on the spot. It was the latter that was driven home over the next few hours, when the constant noise, clatter and loud commotion of buses, trucks, cars and other types of transport including bicycles were only matched by the pervading smell of diesel, dust and gasoline. This was accompanied by what continued to be an incessant yelling of what appeared to be hundreds of Japanese voices echoing across the compound, and a combination of all these threatening noises continued to fuel the prisoners' collective sense of fear.

As tyres continuously screeched alongside the audible sound of gears crunching and the incessant stench of fumes, the frightened prisoners huddled together inside the bungalow. They had agreed among themselves that due to the pandemonium outside, and since they had not seen any Japanese guards inside since yesterday, as long as they did not draw attention to themselves the Japanese might even forget they were there. After all, everybody knew that had already happened to the separate kitchen group a few days earlier, that is before Ando and the other Japanese officer, probably Asaeda, had stumbled upon them. It might have been a vain hope to cling to but it was better than nothing; however by the time the suffocating humidity and heat of the day was at its zenith by the early afternoon, their relative calm was shattered when yet another different group of four dishevelled but heavily armed Japanese soldiers barged their way into the makeshift prison.

Once again the group was corralled into the centre of the living room, only this time they were aggressively pushed and pulled into position at the end of lethally sharp fixed bayonets. One of the loudest of the Japanese voices, the one who seemed to be the leader of this particular unkempt Japanese troop, continued shouting incoherently at them. Again, whether anybody understood what he was saying or not is unknown, but Laub was singled out. This particular soldier was getting so up close and personal into his face that Laub had little chance of escaping the guard's panted breath and spittle. It was while doing this the soldier then pointed both of his readied pistols directly at Laub's chest, gesturing for him to go outside. While Laub reluctantly did as he was ordered, other soldiers entered and rounded up four other men. Within minutes, four other mine employees namely Olsen, Larsen, Rosenberg and Roschke were also promptly marched out of the van der Straatens' bungalow at gunpoint, and along with Laub taken away.

There was obviously some logic to this latest Japanese activity because the five men all had something in common, insomuch as they were all nationals of neutral countries. After Japan had joined the Axis powers only a few months earlier, it too had adhered, at least nominally speaking, to the ideal of respecting citizens of neutral nations including Denmark and so on. How these guards knew to identify them from the rest of the Europeans in the bungalow remains unknown, but that might be surmised as having been a result of the bungalows being ransacked for paperwork such as passports, or perhaps the outcomes of the previous body searches confiscating personal papers, that aided in their identification. More worryingly for any of the SOE operatives, including Operation Cleeves personnel, was that if the Japanese had that knowledge at hand, the next question asked might be did they also have some other knowledge about them as well? The dire consequences if they were identified suggested they might be more at risk of torture, or worse summary execution, than others. That Laub was one of them only confused things, but also suggested that as all the other neutral nationals had also been taken away, perhaps the Japanese only knew he was from a neutral country and nothing else.

No one was sure what had happened to the five men until roughly half an hour or so later, when Maureen caught sight of them being shoved into the bungalow diagonally opposite. It was hard to tell if they had armed guards inside with them or not, but it was glaringly obvious that less attention was being paid to them than it was to the remaining prisoners inside the van der Straatens' bungalow. The next few hours progressed more or less the same as it had been going on since daybreak, with various trucks, buses, cars and what seemed like literally thousands of Japanese soldiers riding bicycles coming and going. There were even some riding on horseback, which only added to the frenetic confusion. But still, there were no armed guards being placed inside with them. As more loud voices and Japanese shouting happened at what became decreasingly regular intervals, over the next few hours the commotion seemed to be trickling down to only a handful of constantly changing, but always heavily armed, Japanese guards milling around here and there outside.

While this was going on, nobody was aware that the other peculiar noise that was mixing in among the ear-shattering din, was that the Japanese had started nailing shut all the bungalow windows from the outside. Amidst the loud cacophony of hammering and banging, and as the striking sounds of steel upon iron drowned out the mechanical sounds, whatever inner sanctuary of calm the prisoners thought they had was completely gone. By late afternoon, all of the bungalow's external windows had been nailed shut, the rays of daylight were locked out, and they were now in stifling darkness. As had happened before, now it seemed the mind games began again, with electricity and water supply to the bungalow being variously turned off, then on, then off again. No food or water was given. No medical attention was offered, and there was no interaction between the prisoners across the road, nor with any other Japanese or anyone else. The only thing the now twenty-two European prisoners shared was the same small oil lamp, the same sweat-drenched mattresses, and since yesterday, the same single ablutions bucket still shoved into the living room's corner.

Outside it seemed as though the noise of heavy transports and all other vehicles carrying Japanese troops was now rumbling away into the distance.

In which direction nobody could be sure, but by late afternoon the status quo was more or less the same as it had been over the past few days. In what was passing for relative normality under Japanese occupation, an anxious silence pervaded the bungalow. The same hopeful assumptions remained as before, that because all the Japanese troops had almost disappeared, perhaps their regular four Japanese guards would again return. The real hope, however, was that British forces were fighting through and pushing the Japanese back, and that meant help was probably just around one of the Betong to Yala road's notorious corners.

In what had been an unsettling and fretful day, and as the noise of the last of the convoys seemingly rattled away into the dark night, it was the relative familiarity of the jungle night being heard again that was probably comforting. None of the prisoners knew if or where any armed Japanese guards may have been stationed outside, but there were certainly none of them inside. Still cloistered together in the hot, repressive humidity, they soon heard a handful of Japanese soldiers mingling and chatting in low tones somewhere close to the bungalow, but they could not be sure that if they tried to go outside, or even tried to take a peek, how many of them would be shot. To their collective welcome relief, the van der Straatens' cook suddenly made another brief appearance at the bungalow's backdoor in the dying heat of the evening.

He had brought with him the last of their food rations, which was a watery soup he had managed to scrape together from the past few days of leftovers, including what was now the several day old remnants of a goose carcass. Whether he made it with or without the blessing of the Japanese remains unknown, but by roughly six o'clock that evening the cook had been allowed to pass the pot of broth through the edge of a broken flyscreened window the Japanese had missed when they were boarding the place up. Macfarlane took note of its position. This time the cook did not hang around, and disappeared as quickly as he had reappeared and was never seen again. When what had passed for dinner was over, the group were once more in an uncertain state of what might happen next. Nobody had any idea about what was going on with their neutral neighbours across the road, nothing was now being heard outside, and the blackness of night had fallen.

It seemed whatever this latest Japanese kneejerk reaction had been was over. In the pitch blackness it was the reassuring sounds of the jungle dominating the night that offered some emotional respite, and it seemed to be bringing nature's soothing sounds of music to everyone's ears. At least for a brief moment, the familiarity of the nightly wilderness was helping create a semblance of the familiar. They listened to the mournfully wailing gibbons somewhere out in the blackened distance; the rhythmic pulsing cadence of singing cicadas; and as the night progressed the 'click-click-click' sounds of the little gecko-like Chi Chis running across the roof. It was like visiting old friends; well-known rhythms that each in their own way were helping ease some of the pent up tension pervading the bungalow. Despite all that had gone on during the day, and in spite of not knowing the plight of their friends and colleagues across the road, there was another shared comfort for the group because at least they still had the shadow of a single oil lamp. Although it was a tiny little light in the blackened darkness of night, it helped calm the fraying nerves. It was hard to relax down again, but at least whispered banters and quiet intimate chatters among some were in their own peculiar way reassuring to the group. It was a deceptively brief lull before the storm, because it was only a few hours later when more screeching brakes and truck tyres, and the aggressively loud shouting of a different set of Japanese voices, fractured the night-time spell.

This time the next sudden flurry of activity was erupting at the bungalow's back door. A loud ruckus was going on somewhere outside the back of the bungalow, and accompanied by what sounded like heavy metallic doors opening, shutting and then opening again. The usual feverishly loud Japanese voices were back, only this time they were accompanied by a tumultuous frenzy of half-stomping boots dragging something heavy along the ground. Before anybody had any time to move or work out what was going on, the same heavy sounds were thumping up the backstairs and the back door was being ripped open by another armed Japanese soldier. His demeanour was somewhat more crazed than any of the other Japanese soldiers the group had experienced up until now. Following close behind him were at least eight dazed and bloodied British Indian Army soldiers being forced up the stairs.

Some were carrying significant and untreated wounds, but still they were being beaten, bayonet-prodded and pistol-whipped by three other Japanese troops behind them, continually pushing them upwards and into the bungalow. Each was trying to help the other as they were being thrust violently into the centre of the room. It was blatantly obvious that these men had just come from a battlefront somewhere, and they were hurt. As the Indian soldiers tumbled over themselves, the European prisoners already inside tried moving to the living room's outer edges to make room for obviously badly wounded men. The Japanese soldiers began gesturing to the European occupants with their fixed bayonets that they were to stay away from them. Once again, the Japanese soldiers departed as abruptly as they had arrived, rushing out the back entrance and slamming what was left of the back door just for good measure along the way. This time, nobody heard the truck drive away.

The actions of these latest Japanese soldiers were in stark contrast to the other Japanese the group had encountered earlier in the week. They were unkempt and not clean shaven, and their collective demeanour appeared to everybody as nothing short of bad-tempered revenge. From the smells emanating from some of them, their state of mind was seemingly fuelled by alcoholic rage. At the time, a couple of the engineers in the group thought they had heard the sound of something heavy and mechanical being moved around throughout the commotion. It might have been something with wheels, but it was puzzling what it could have been. None of them were to know that undercover of the tumultuous events surrounding the Indian soldiers' arrival, the sound that they were hearing were the Japanese dragging a machine gun into the space that lay directly beneath the bungalow's living room. Neither did anyone have any idea that the machine gun was loaded with live ammunition, and was pointing directly upwards at them from beneath the wooden floor.

With the van der Straatens' living room now an even further cramped, makeshift holding cell for thirty or so people, nervous chatter broke out among the prisoners. Panic stricken, the unspoken quiet inside was juxtaposed against the increasingly loud chaos being repeated outside, bringing with it a lingering uneasiness. That was only broken when Chambers, who spoke a little Hindi, tried breaking the uncomfortable silence by attempting to talk with the newly arrived British Indian soldiers. His attempts were unsuccessful, however, and the only communication made was from the Indian soldiers, who had kept repeating in broken English that that they were British. It was not Chambers fault, at least he had tried, and in all probability these men were among a mere handful of survivors of the 3/16th Punjabi troops who had been valiantly holding out against all odds against the Japanese. They may have been the same soldiers who had in the past few days been involved in days of combat anywhere ranging from the outskirts of The Ledge to the Pattani Road, near Betong, or closer to home in the violent and ferocious hand-to-hand combat yesterday at the

Kampong Toh stream. None of that mattered now, because whether civilian or military they were all now prisoners of the Japanese.

Huddling together for safety and comfort, the Indian soldiers had remained almost statue-like in the tiny central space in the middle of the living room. The rest of the Europeans merely fanned out around them. Some, such as Stratford, Peters, and de Boer found positions close to the shuttered windows. Others including all three of the Magness family and Mrs Jeavons, crouched together and situated themselves close next to a wall. Butler-Jones and Thomas positioned themselves either side of one of the living room's interior doorways, while Laub and Cummins did the same opposite them. Everyone else made a space for themselves wherever best they could in the hot, humid, and stifling conditions.

Nobody had bathed in days, no one was allowed to go outside to use the bathroom, and the incessant mosquitoes as well as sandfleas only contributed to making everybody's life even more miserable than it already was. But now, as the deathly jungle silence once again prevailed outside, it was no longer welcomed by those inside. The expectations of what was going to happen was worse than living on a knife edge in the claustrophobic atmosphere. With a deathly, unseen skeletal hand gripping them around the throat, it was more like waiting for the executioner's hatchet to randomly fall than anything else. Inside the bungalow, it was the unspoken silence between them all that was only deafened by their collective uncertainty as to what had just happened, and what might happen next. They did not have to wait too long for either unwelcomed answer to arrive. Soon afterwards the same back door was again violently thrust open and one of the Japanese soldiers lobbed a hand grenade straight into the middle of the Indian soldiers. Seconds later came two more, followed almost immediately by strafing gun fire shooting up at all of them from beneath the living room's floorboards below.

Chapter 32

Black Bloody Saturday

The devastating blast was loud, fast and deafening, and the deadly impact wreaked absolute destruction as bullets and debris flew everywhere in the frenzied black night carnage. There was no escaping the bloodlust that followed. Most of the Indian soldiers, who were probably from the 3/16th Punjabis, were killed outright. Others screamed as limbs and other body parts were torn apart. Mrs Jeavons, or what was left of her, was literally blown to bits.[1] Mr and Mrs Magness, as well as their teenage daughter Maureen, were all slammed backwards against the wall as the shockwave of the blast hit them. Shrapnel splintered Maureen's thigh and leg bones, while shards of glass splintered her mother's heart and slashed her body to ribbons. Her father lay askew on the other side of the room, still breathing, barely, with his body riddled with multiple bullet wounds. Next to them lay Harding Thomas, who had also been caught by the wave and had been smashed against the door frame; he too had been fatally hit, with a gaping chest wound. Butler-Jones gasped for air, suffering from a massive gunshot wound to the stomach. Then, as abruptly as the firing had started, it stopped. A dangerous peace descended on the bungalow. In the immediate aftermath the only other sounds that could be heard were the screams, moans and groans of those writhing around in dying agony on the floor.

For some who had escaped relatively unhurt, including Macfarlane, Stratford, Moore and Cummins, taking advantage of the darkness was the catalyst for heading towards any open window, and getting away as fast as possible from the bloodied carnage.[2] For others injured but still unable to move, including Maureen Magness, all that mattered was trying to crawl to a safer and more protected position as soon as possible.[3] Chaos and confusion reigned in the blackened darkness of the dying, compounded only by the panicked sobbing of the living. The only certainty for the trapped prisoners now swamped by the utter annihilation all around them was that they were alone. But before anyone had time to even try and process what had happened, within minutes Japanese soldiers were again stomping up the back stairs. Ripping the back door off its hinges, one of the soldiers stood in the doorway carrying a flashlight and began sweeping it around the room, lighting up the proceedings. Two others entered and began dragging out any Indian soldiers they thought were still alive. One by one each badly injured soldier was being kicked and pulled out of the bloodbath, while another Japanese soldier who had positioned himself on the landing just outside the doorway was busily bayonetting each soldier that came out through the door. Each man finally tumbled downwards and collapsed into a sprawling heaped mess at the bottom of the stairs.

That job soon having been finished, two of the soldiers then re-entered the bungalow seemingly intent on killing any and all European survivors. One soldier shone the light of a single small torch around the room identifying anyone still alive or moving, while the other soldier fired his light automatic gun in the general direction towards them.[4] While this was going on, a third Japanese soldier then entered the room and, with his fixed bayonet at the ready, randomly started stabbing at what must have been a mishmash of bodies and corpses strewn across bloodied mattresses, his sharp blade intent on piercing whatever lay beneath him. Maureen Magness, Doris van der Straaten and Peters had managed to scramble under whatever mattress and body mayhem they could, hoping to hide from the frenzied slashing blade. Then almost in the blink of an eye, the murderous madness ended as abruptly as it had started, when all of a sudden the soldiers stopped their vicious attack and, running as fast as they could down the back stairs, jumped into the waiting truck and sped off into the distance. It was close to midnight, and Japan's first mass killing of unarmed European civilians in wartime Southeast Asia had taken place in Southern Thailand.

Chapter 33

Black Bloody Sunday

On the morning of Sunday, 14 December 1941, rumours were swirling around Singora Jail that all sorts of Japanese attacks were happening across the region. The jungle telegraph had been awash with stories of how Japan's air force had been bombing Penang for days, how thousands had been killed and how the British had been useless in the face of Japan's onslaught. Kuala Lumpur and Singapore and elsewhere on the Malay Peninsula had not fared much better. Other disturbing news was that the entirety of Britain's air fleet had been wiped out, and today it seemed Penang was still in disarray after the mass evacuations of British and other select European civilians yesterday.[1] For the prisoners it was not welcome news, any more than was the gossip passed on by local Chinese labourers working around the prison that Japan had chased the British Army out of Southern Thailand, and that a house full of Europeans had been executed. The hubbub surrounding the Japanese arrival had seemed to be dying down, and the majority of Japanese uniforms around town had practically dwindled overnight to being divided between the Japanese Consulate, the small 25th Headquarters' Garrison Unit, and the jail.

Meanwhile, the Japanese Consul Katsuno was becoming fed up with ongoing reporting of Japanese Army misbehaviours both near and afar, and he was less than pleased that he had again been tasked by the Japanese Embassy, this time directly from Tokyo, to find out immediately if there was any truth surrounding the again reported upcountry killings of Japanese civilians. Before the heat of the day was on the rise, Katsuno, accompanied by one of the Japanese interpreters named Iwasaki, begrudgingly headed out on a six-day fact-finding mission, beginning up north.[2] After that he was to head to Haad Yai, Sadao and Yala to address some of the complaints the Thai police had been making about Japanese Army activities over the past few days.

As soon as Katsuno left, several changes were being implemented across Singora town, which by now was turning into a military outpost that was more or less under imposed Japanese military rule. The small Lamsai Beach area, in particular, had for some reason taken on significant importance to the Japanese, and they had made a point of posting sentries at either end of the beach itself, and checkpoints on the road running alongside it. It seemed more attention was also being paid to the pine grove at one end of the beach than the other.[3] The Japanese had stopped short of cordoning off the Lamsai Beach police compound sitting almost directly opposite, but had also severely restricted Thai police access into and out of the area.

By lunchtime, Singora Jail too was becoming a hive of activity. The Australian tin miner King had been pulled out of his cell and unceremoniously dumped on to a Japanese transport. He was being immediately transferred to a civilian internee camp in Vichy Hanoi. The two Indian men who had been accused of using mirrors to signal the British, Hazarath Yusup Khan and Santoch Singh, were dragged out of their cells with their hands tied behind their backs, and shoved into the back of a waiting lorry. On the back of the lorry hung all sorts of tools, including shovels and ropes. A few hours after waiting in the stifling humidity and heat, they were later joined by three airmen from the Ban Pru air crash who had been brought up from Haad Yai, and two of them looked to be wearing RAF uniforms.[4] They too had their hands tied behind their backs. The lorry had driven out heading along Singora's northern coast road that ran towards Lamsai Beach. When it came back half an hour or so later, the Thai prison guards on the other side of the prison, some of the Thai policemen, and the Chinese labourers working on the nearby road, noticed it was empty.

Later that morning, another three men were likewise taken out of their cells with their hands also tied behind their backs. They were all tin miners and they had not long arrived in Singora Jail. All three men, namely Herbert C Wright, Daniel Regan and Roderick Gordon, were seen being escorted out of the prison and placed into the back of a lorry that also drove out and along the same road. All the remaining European prisoners still inside Singora Jail presumed all of the men had, like King, been transferred to different prisoner of war camps. In the afternoon, five more men were also seen leaving Singora Jail in a similar fashion. They had been kept in isolation from everybody except for an exclusive group of Japanese interrogators. Nobody knew who or what their nationalities were, but they all seemed to be dressed in black.[5]

It had been Sergeant Major Chamnarn of the Thai police who had days earlier driven the thirty-six kilometres (twenty-two miles) down to Haad Yai to pick up the three downed airmen. On arrival he noted they were dressed in British tropical uniforms, and he thought one was a sergeant and the other might have been a corporal. He was not sure about the rank of the third man, who was injured, because even in the heat of the day he was still wearing his black zip-fastened jacket.[6] His return journey had been intercepted around the halfway point, he was stopped at rifle point by the Japanese. He tried to argue with the head of the Japanese entourage, Dr Seto, that he was on official police business and the prisoners were in his custody, but after much duress, including having several Japanese rifles point in his general direction, he had little choice in the matter.[7] The British airmen were removed from his car, their hands tied behind their backs – even the injured man – and then all three were shoved back into the rear seat of his car. He was ordered to sit on the front passenger side, as an armed Japanese soldier was now the designated driver. The airmen were then driven straight to the 25th Headquarters in Singora, where they were interrogated for several hours until being taken to Singora Jail. It was only after the three British airmen had been placed into their cells in a separate part of the prison, that the Thai policemen himself was released from Japanese custody. Soon after, the three airmen too, were similarly placed into the lorry. All were actions that for whatever reasons, only occurred after Katsuno left Singora.

In a similar story, Thai Police Corporal Thepa had also been tasked by Singora Police Headquarters to head out early to Chinko, pick up three Europeans, and bring them back to Singora Jail.[8] Whether these three men were the tin miners Wright, Regan and Gordon remains unknown, but Thepa was to take the three Europeans into custody, and drive them directly to Singora Jail. In much the same story as Chamnarn, he too was intercepted by Seto and a small army of armed Japanese soldiers, whereby the three European prisoners were forcibly taken into Japanese custody, subsequently interrogated at the 25th Headquarters, and then afterwards placed into Singora Jail. It was only then that Thepa, as had happened to Chamnarn, was also released from custody, while the Japanese again assumed responsibility another three European prisoners.

By the end of the week, rumours were swirling around the community, and among the Thai police, that up to six Europeans and two Indian men had been executed on Lamsai Beach.[9] The two Indian men had reportedly been among the first to be shot and beheaded, and they had been followed closely by the three airman from Haad Yai.[10] In the afternoon on that same day, purportedly the three tin miners named Gordon, D Regan and HC Wright were shot, bayonetted and then beheaded in the same place.[11] The five men dressed in black suffered similar fates.[12] Among some of the varied descriptions, at least one of the Europeans was fair-haired and wearing a khaki uniform, with some sort of badge on his breast pocket. Another was described as tall and dark but dressed in civilian clothing, and it seemed one of them had a gold tooth.[13] There were other rumours coming in as well. Apparently some Europeans had been sighted roaming around the Thai–Malay frontier regions, and some of them had even been involved in skirmishes. One of them was reportedly a woman. When Katsuno arrived back in Singora a week later, it was an entirely different place.

Chapter 34

Survival of the Fastest

As horrendous as the massacre had been, there were survivors. After the strafing had stopped, in what seemed like an eternity later, the survivors dared neither to move nor make any noise, at least not until the noise of the truck's engine had well and truly disappeared far off into the distance.[1] Somehow, in the utter annihilation that surrounded them, Chambers and Australian mining engineer Alan Keith Craigie, had been slightly wounded but were still relatively mobile. They managed to find their co-worker Bailey, whose lower leg and ankle had been shattered by shrapnel, but he was still alive. Now, with the only light source smashed, all three men were doing their best to try and do a quick check around the room to see who might still be alive. Calling out names and not hearing any replies, they assumed that all the others had been killed outright until in the deathly quiet they heard the badly injured Maureen crying softly into the darkness searching for her mother and father.

As they pulled the teenager out from under the flesh, bones and blood-soaked mattresses laying on top of her, Chambers and Craigie then turned their attentions to some of the others. Butler-Jones was dead, and Thomas was barely clinging to life. Kitts' and Francis' lifeless bodies lay strewn to one side. Maureen's badly wounded mother was still alive and lying not too far from her, but unable to move. The two men then helped find her father, who all this time had been slowly crawling in the direction of his weeping daughter's voice. With all four of the survivors badly injured and already having lost large amounts of blood, the only imperative the three men had in the moment was to try and save those they had already found in the mayhem. With that in mind, Chambers and Craigie left the bungalow and headed out in different directions in search of help. Bailey, unable to stand upright for too long, stayed behind to see what he could do for the others.[2]

Sometime later he and Maureen heard a group of men chatting in the distance and heading their way. With the arrival of this group in the aftermath of the massacre, the remaining survivors thought it best to pretend that they were dead. This was mainly because Craigie had caught sight of the men as he was returning, and they were dressed similarly to the Thai militiamen who had first rounded them up days earlier. Whether these were the same men who had placed them under house arrest at the behest of the Japanese remains unknown, but they were casually chattering between themselves in Thai, when they started looting whatever jewellery or anything else of value they could find on the corpses strewn around the room. Rummaging around and between the dead in search of anything valuable did not take long and, once satisfied with their gains, the men then left the bungalow, vanishing into the blackness of the jungle.

One of them, however, stayed behind on catching sight of Maureen Magness. She did not look European. One of the looters had already stolen the gold watch she was wearing off her wrist but, approaching her, this man took her pulse. Just as it seemed he was busying himself and starting to check the rest of her wounds, Bailey and Craigie both now re-emerged back on the scene alone and without any help in tow. After a brief discussion in English between the Thai man and Craigie, both agreed that they were fearful for the young woman's safety should the Japanese soldiers return. The horrors of the Rape of Nanjing it seemed were even known in this remote part of Southern Thailand.[3] So much so that an evacuation plan of sorts was sorted out between them, one that for Maureen was probably the only thing that saved her life.[4]

With that plan in place, the Thai man carried Maureen, Craigie helped her mother, and Bailey and Mr Magness, helping each other, hobbled slowly behind. Leaving the hellish bloodbath behind, they headed across the road to another bungalow, where it was determined it might be best if they sought cover underneath the house, rather than in it. Craigie, who was wearing a white shirt, removed it in case its night-time reflection gave their position away. With all the Magness family now practically unable to be moved again, decisions were made that maybe some first aid kits or something else of use could be found on Kampong Toh's mine site. Soon afterwards Bailey limped out in search of whatever medical supplies might be around, while Craigie stayed behind to tend to the wounded. They agreed that keeping any noise down to a minimum would be safer. It helped that the Thai man who was still with them, and who was now helping Craigie as best he could, was just one of several escaped convicts from the Tanicom Penal Settlement, and as it turned out also just happened to be part of the place's medical staff. He again raised his concerns to Craigie about what might happen to Maureen should the Japanese return, and suggested it might be best if he removed her somewhere else for her own safety. Craigie agreed, and stayed behind with the other Magnesses. The Thai man and Maureen set off into the darkness. Chambers still had not returned. Thomas, barely clinging to life, was still in the van der Straatens' bungalow, because there was no way Craigie or the others could move him without killing him. All Craigie and the Magness family could do was wait in hope.

Over the next few hours, and unbeknown to them, other survivors had begun slowly emerging from out of the mine's jungle fringe but on the far side of the site. Several of them, including Cummins, de Boer, Stratford, Holt, Moore and Donnelly, had all taken advantage of the element of surprise when the first grenade had been thrown into the room, and in the melee had individually fled into the blackness of the jungle in any way and as fast as they could.[5] Van der Straaten and Edmonds too had managed to do the same but had taken off in opposite directions. Peters and Doris van der Straaten had survived the initial shooting, and then after hiding under the mattresses to avoid the bayonet attack had fled out of the bungalow almost as soon as the truck was driving away. They had eventually taken shelter together at the tin mine's dredge.

The five neutrals who had been separated from the group had also fled the compound. They had been watching on as events had been unfolding throughout the previous day, and had indeed been ignored by the Japanese. They had not been put under guard and had been left to their own devices, and as they watched the horrendous bloodshed unfold during the evening, they had all fled into the jungle after the first grenade attack. The man leading them into the darkness was chemical engineer turned Operation Cleeves operative Laub. Like the Magness group, they too each thought their group were the only survivors because nobody knew who was dead, who was injured or who else might have survived.

As dawn approached, Stratford and Moore caught sight of each other in the dense undergrowth. Elsewhere, Edmonds and Chambers had met up. It seemed Chambers had completely lost his bearings and was literally going around in circles until Edmonds stumbled upon him. They were later joined by the now badly limping Bailey, who could no longer stand for any length of time. The three men then found refuge in an old, deserted hut somewhere on the edge of the Kampong Toh stream that ran almost parallel to the mine's outskirts. Chambers went out in search of water and was never seen again. Edmonds and Bailey too thought they, along with Craigie's group back at the mine, were the only ones still left alive.

Just after sunrise, other massacre survivors were slowly, and cautiously, making their way back to the jungle clearing on the far edge of the Kampong Toh Tin Mine. Donnelly, Holt and de Boer were among some of the first to arrive, and as Sunday wore on, Cummins. Stratford and Moore soon made their way back as well. None of the men had any idea about what had happened to anyone else, and like the other disparate groups, all presumed they were the only ones left until later in the morning when Laub, Olsen, Larsen, Rosenberg and Roschke returned. By lunchtime, Peters and Doris van der Straaten, on hearing their familiar voices, had also emerged from their dredge hiding places and joined them. After a quick head count, the general consensus in the first instance was that those who could escape and go in search of help should head out and look for that wherever they could. All of their collective hopes were pinned on eventually meeting up with any British or Allied forces, mainly because some of the survivors still held the belief that somewhere nearby the might of the British Army were forcefully rebuffing the Japanese. With both these premises in mind the survivors decided to maximise their efforts, reasoning that they probably had a better chance of finding the troops if they covered a wider area.

Splitting up into two groups, the larger eleven-man group led by rubber planter and SOE operative Cummins, would travel overland and continue heading west and southwards through the jungle towards the Malay border. The smaller group of Peters and Doris van der Straaten would be heading in the other direction, sticking to the Pattani River routes and south-eastern-flowing tributaries if and where possible. Slipping away into the jungle ill prepared and without weapons was not a recommendation any of them would have welcomed, but faced with the choice of either being tortured or murdered by rampant Japanese soldiers they were left with little option. Heading for British Malaya through any means or ways available was their only viable chance of survival.

Meanwhile, there were other massacre survivors who had escaped into the night, but they had not met up with the initial Stratford group, nor had they remained with the bungalow survivors. Macfarlane had survived by clawing his way through the badly damaged mosquito-netted window he had seen earlier.[6] He had heaved himself through the small opening and had fallen head first on to the hard, concrete pathway nearly five metres (roughly sixteen feet) below. Dazed and with his head badly gashed and shrapnel in his thigh, he crawled away on all fours heading for the small swamp that lay just behind the bungalows. On hearing the sound of running feet coming towards him, one pair at first and then another two, he was trying to melt into the shadows in case it was the Japanese stalking him. Over the next few hours he painstakingly made his way down to the banks of the Kampong Toh stream and its now destroyed bridge, where he smeared himself with mud to try and stop the never-ending mosquitoes biting, and then crawled into a hollowed out tree stump. He had no sooner got himself into position when he heard the voices of a man and a woman whispering somewhere close by. He stayed silent, and still, until he could no longer hear them. Now he waited with bated breath, as he once again heard the sound of boots on boards echoing from the bungalow compound. Macfarlane knew that aside from the fireflies that kept lighting up his position, and the potential threat of Japanese soldiers on a murderous rampage, at that moment he was more scared of tigers than anything else.

Chapter 35

When Jungle Survival is the Only Option

After travelling about a week in the jungle without food, the larger eleven-man party was slowly making headway south until just before Christmas, when they were ambushed somewhere along the southernmost reaches of the Toh River by what a few thought were sword-wielding Thai militia. Holt, Laub and the other four neutrals were killed outright, and the remaining survivors of Moore, Stratford, de Boer, Donnelly and Cummins again dispersed their separate ways back into the jungle. Moore eventually found Stratford, and both men eventually stumbled upon the now badly injured de Boer. A day or so later, Moore, Stratford and de Boer fell in with six fleeing Chinese men and women also heading south. As an example of wartime collaboration in its more positive meaning, the group hastily built a raft and poled down the Muda River together, until they arrived at a small Chinese village named Kampong Sok. After resting and recuperating, Moore and Stratford then parted ways from their Chinese benefactors. By now de Boer was too ill to be moved and in the throes of a bad fever. He was left behind in the care of an elderly Chinese man and his fate remains unknown.

Moore and Stratford tried to make a go of it over the next month or so, eating bamboo shoots and insects, but neither man had any idea how to survive in the jungle, and they soon found themselves garnering unwanted attention among the locals. Most ignored them, but it was not too long after the heavy monsoon rains were starting to dissipate that the two men, severely lacking in resources and now both badly ill, surrendered themselves to Japanese authorities. The Japanese ensured that both men were told the glorious news that Singapore had fallen. Promptly interned first at Taiping and then Pudu Gaols, six months later both men would subsequently be taken to Changi civilian internee camp, where they remained until Japan's surrender.

After surviving the ambush, the last two remaining survivors of the Oriental Mission's Operation Cleeves, Cummins and Donnelly, had both become separated from the main group and each other in the aftermath of the ambush.

Not long after the new year of 1942, Cummins would subsequently be arrested by the Japanese and interned in Bangkok as a civilian rubber estate manager from Yala. There he found some familiar faces, not only from among his fellow Kampong Toh massacre survivors, but among fellow SOE operatives including tin miners ES Wright and Terence Coyne/Collins. Donnelly lived for another two years in the jungle in and around Ayer Weng tin survey fields. His last known contact was in a letter to the Meug-Sian and Company in Yala in 1943, asking for food and medicine. Apparently they had been in constant contact with him over the period and had helped conceal him from the Japanese, but he had reportedly died from an unknown disease in 1943, and some of the local Chinese had purportedly buried him near the survey site.

Macfarlane, Bailey, Edmonds and Maureen Magness' survival could not have been more different. Bailey and Edmonds had been arrested by Thai police a few days after the massacre, and were being kept in a small tin hut near Yala. The hut was being used by the Thai police as a makeshift holding cell outside of the main town area. Macfarlane, meanwhile, had managed to avoid the Japanese patrols in the days following the massacre, and had hidden himself in a small abandoned Chinese hut. He was pleased to find some tinned food, which he shared with a tiny kitten that had also been left to fend for itself. After a fitful night's sleep, he decided to head out the next morning, only to run into a startled Thai youth, who immediately ran off and later returned with an armed policeman. Macfarlane was promptly taken into custody and moved to a hut that was also functioning as a temporary police station that had been set up on the outskirts of Betong. Here he was given medical aid and other assistance, and whenever Japanese troops came near, the policeman and the villagers would usher him into the jungle until they had passed. That continued until late one afternoon roughly a week or so after the massacre, when Betong's new police captain arrived.

Macfarlane was next taken to a small labourers' camp situated next door to the Tanicom Penal Settlement further up the road. This was the same camp that provided a workforce not only for Tanicom, but had also been employed in cutting and supplying wood to the Kampong Toh Tin Mine powerhouse. Some time in the week before Christmas Eve, he was taken into Tanicom's superintendent's house, and offered food and clean clothes. Macfarlane was informed local Thai authorities had already heard of the massacre, and were hopeful he might help them in identifying the victims, which he agreed to do. On arrival back at Kampong Toh Tin Mine, he found a shallow grave in front of No. 4 Kampong Toh Bungalow. In it were the bodies of Butler-Jones, Thomas and Mrs Jeavons.[1] Over the road was another shallow grave and there lay Francis and Kitts. He was then taken to another bungalow further along the road, and here he identified the bodies of Mr and Mrs Magness. After this morbid task, he was then taken back to the temporary police station, and was more than glad to see inside the badly wounded Maureen, and she was being well looked after.

Over the next few days both he and Maureen remained under Thai police custody, until around Christmas Day, when they were both hidden under fruit and vegetables in the back of a local Thai market lorry and taken back inside Tanicom. Macfarlane was put into the general population; Maureen was left in the care of the superintendent's wife and other women. A few days after Christmas 1941, Macfarlane was again hidden in a similar fashion and driven to the makeshift Thai police holding cell near Yala. Curiously, and although there was hardly any Japanese presence outside of the main towns, for some reason the Japanese were still on the hunt for certain tin miners. Now Macfarlane's thigh shrapnel injuries were festering so badly that he could not walk, and after being carried inside, he soon found himself in the company of his fellow massacre survivors Edmonds and Bailey. Alongside them were two others from the Labu Mine, a New Zealander named LS Jones and another tin mining man named Wills, and three more Pattani tin workers named Young, Beasley and Haderup.[2] A day later two more tin miners named John Jupe and Gordon Dawson joined them. All of the men had been working at mines supporting tin mine denial operations.

That evening several armed Japanese arrived at the Yala hut unannounced, and immediately began a heated argument with the Thai police chief. It seemed the Japanese were demanding the immediate release of only five of the tin mining men, namely Young, Haderup, Beasley, Wills and Jones, and they were to accompany them to Singora.[3] All five, although not officially Operation Cleeves operatives, had worked at mines that were participating in the tin mine denial scheme. The Japanese soldiers were not interested in Macfarlane or the others, and ignored them. That might have been more as a result of the Japanese soldiers presuming the Pinyok and Kampong Toh tin mine denial problem had already been sorted out. The end result being that evening the soldiers drove off at speed with their five prisoners heading for Singora.

After Maureen arrived all the prisoners soon found themselves heading for Yala train station under Thai police guard. From there they were going by train to Bangkok and they were not alone. Accompanying them was the Governor of Yala along with his wife and daughter, and several other higher-ranking Thai police and their families. A close watch was kept on all the girls and women, including Maureen. On each of the three stops along the way to Bangkok, the Governor and the Thai police were confronted by Japanese soldiers, who continued demanding the Europeans be handed over, but the Thai officials had somehow managed to acquire an official-looking piece of paper giving them both Japanese permission and authority to take the prisoners to Bangkok. From there they were to be taken to a Thai-run civilian internee camp somewhere near the capital. Macfarlane, Edmonds, Bailey and Maureen Magness probably presumed they were the only survivors of the massacre until after they arrived, and found Philip van der Straaten was already incarcerated. For the rest of the war, the Prachand civilian internee camp was their home. Whatever they knew about Operation Cleeves, as Macfarlane and others undoubtedly did, stayed silently with them.

The last of the survivors to fall into Japanese custody in the months following the massacre would be Peters and Doris van der Straaten. It was not the first time either of them had been in a tropical jungle nor in the Far East, and they had a lot in common. Both had been born in Bengal, both hailed from an extensive elite Anglo-Indian pedigree, and both had spent most of their formative years growing up in the hot and humid Indian tropics. Now they too had been slowly making their way south, until somewhere in the mountainous region between Perak and Kelantan they reached a Sakai Indigenous area.[4] Here, the Sakai provided them with food and shelter, allowing them to rest up before heading onwards. Along the way, it had been the various Chinese enclaves they had come upon during their travels that had provided them with similar hospitality, that is until they reached the general vicinity further downriver of Kedah, Kelantan and Upper Perak, which for all intents and purposes, appeared to be actively pro-Japanese. However, appearances to European colonial eyes could be deceptive, and although many locals from the area were working as guides and informants for the Japanese military, several of them were also proactively supporting the only anti-Japanese fighters operating in the area at the time, and they were the Chinese Communist guerrilla groups.

Armed with this knowledge, the duo thought it prudent to head in the other direction, wandering back upriver and travelling almost to Belum and then down to Ulu Temengor, before heading to Ulu Piah.[5] The other information Peters had gleaned along the way was the jungle gossip that Ipoh had been retaken by the British, to which he and Doris then again altered course, heading for the outskirts. On arrival they surreptitiously noted that this was far from the case, and Peters put it down to a good piece of Japanese disinformation dissemination and probably a way for Japanese intelligence services to herd

European stragglers across the country by dangling hope. After the four-month deprivations of surviving in the jungle, and with Doris suffering badly from malaria and beriberi, by April 1942 they had given themselves up at Sungei Sipet in the hope of finding help. Neither would survive the war. Peters would later die of disease in Changi, and Doris would die after a later interrogation at the Kempetai headquarters in Kuala Lumpur in mid-1943.[6]

While Macfarlane and company were heading to Bangkok, his former tin mining prisoner cohorts were in Singora Jail. They included those that had been rounded up down in Yala, namely the aforementioned manager and accountant of Pattani Tin Ltd, Messrs Young and Haderup, along with Wills, Beasley and Jones. These were the five the Japanese had insisted be brought up from Yala. But by now it seemed any sense of urgency that had been around the prison in the weeks leading up to Christmas had dissipated. The prisoners were no longer put into isolation from one another, nor housed in separate buildings, and were now sharing a single building. Each man had his own separate cell that was now being supplied with beds and bedding. Their cell doors were left unlocked, and they were free to walk about in the corridor, to talk, and to play games. Even the quality and quantity of the food being offered was substantially higher than it had been previously.[7] Things remained more or less the same until the Allied bombing raids began in the first week of February, and the remaining prisoners were shipped out to Taiping Gaol.[8]

Now that the main forces of the Japanese Army had already left, Singora's only function now centred around morphing into a Japanese rear echelon support depot. One half of Singora Jail remained the soldiers' barracks. The other half returned to routine prison duties. There was no paperwork left behind as to the identity of many of those who had been arrested, including European, Chinese, Malayan or Indian, and absolutely no records kept of any of those executed. That brought Singora's initial role as interrogation, execution and centralised holding site to a close. It also drew the curtain not only on Southern Thailand's pivotal importance of bearing the first brutal brunt of Japan's invasion, but also the human collateral damage against tin mining communities and Operation Cleeves as well. By now, the Oriental Mission was also gone, its staff dispersed, and most paperwork related to either its Singapore or Penang personnel and activities along with it. That was until a few months later, when rumours started to emerge out of civilian internee and POW camps about certain gruesome incidents that had happened in Southern Thailand in the first few weeks after Japan invaded.

Chapter 36

Gossip, Rumour and Plausible Deniability

Around Easter 1942 there was further credence being given to Operation Cleeves and the fate of operatives in Southern Thailand, when stories were being passed around between prisoners that several tin miners, along with some British airmen, had been tortured, executed, bayonetted and shot on a beach somewhere in Southern Thailand. Others were reporting that a massacre had also occurred somewhere called Yala. Many spoke of how so many tin miners were missing, and nobody knew if they were alive or dead. Details were scant, but after the Japanese finally allowed International Red Cross (IRC) representatives into civilian internee camps near Bangkok, including Prachand, information was slowly being pieced together about the fate of all of those involved. With this new information to hand, SOE London and the War Office were getting nervous about the fate of their operatives, and what the Japanese might find out about British SOE operations under duress. That was part of the reasoning behind why both would find themselves at odds with the Foreign and Colonial Offices, when discussions over a prisoner swap with the Japanese began in earnest.

Not long after the fall of Singapore, proposals had been made to the Japanese by the British, Australian and United States governments, that a prisoner exchange of sick and wounded personnel might be open to negotiation. Earlier Allied negotiations with the Japanese for an exchange of sick and wounded military POWs had produced no result. Subsequent negotiations for similar exchanges of civilians proved more positive. As early as February 1942 proposals had been made to the Japanese by the British Commonwealth and United States governments for an exchange of civilian officials together with a certain number of non-officials. Interned Japanese from various parts of the Commonwealth were to be exchanged with interned Commonwealth civilians from China, Japan, Thailand, and Indo-China. Any discussions on Malaya were completely off the table. By

July 1942, the details of the agreement had been finalised and with processes and programmes mutually agreed upon, the first handover exchange was to take place in mid-1942 at Lourenço Marques, a port city located in what was ostensibly neutral Portuguese East Africa.[1]

In what was turning out to be a clash between competing wartime priorities as to whom should be considered for the proposed Anglo-Japanese Exchange, the Foreign Office had their preferred list, which generally included the former upper echelons of Bangkok including civil servants, politicians, businessmen and their families. The War Office and SOE's list, on the other hand, contained the names of several Operation Cleeves and other Oriental Mission-related personnel who had been in Southern Thailand.[2] The assumption was that because no information had been heard from any of them, then they must all, presumedly, be interned. ES Wright and Cummins were considered such high-value assets that they were specifically recommended in the top four the War Office wanted back, especially as both men had been arrested and imprisoned as civilians, and both of their covers remained intact.[3]

In early August, one of the appointed vessels, the Japanese cargo ship *Tatsura Maru*, was carrying among its 1,800 Allied passengers at least thirty-nine civilians repatriated from Thailand's Prachand internment camp.[4] Much to the dismay of SOE London and the War Office, however, none of them included any Operation Cleeves or Oriental Mission personnel, but they did include senior civil servants, bankers, businessmen, politicians, and other members of Bangkok's social elite, such as Crosby and his close friend AA Gentry, and their respective wives and offspring.[5] Among those also arriving was an Australian public servant named Bernard Kuskie. Kuskie was a former member of the Royal Australian Naval Volunteer Reserve and had been in Japan working with Australia's Department of External Affairs.[6] A fluent Japanese speaker, he was part of Australia's Japan Delegation previously based in Yokohama. His job prior to the war had been reporting back to Canberra on Japan's increasing militarisation and southern economic expansionist planning.[7] Kuskie was neither being repatriated, nor returning from internment. His presence on board ship was as a relatively minor Third Legation Officer, who just happened to have been tasked by the Department with gathering information about the Japanese from passengers on board the ship, including events in South Thailand.

Kuskie's job may have been associated with events that had occurred a few weeks earlier. Just before the exchange went ahead, Australia's External

Affairs Officer based in London had forwarded information back to Canberra of a disquieting report received from the Swiss Consul in Bangkok.[8] Three months earlier in May, the consul had visited Prachand civilian internment camp in Thailand, and had in secret held various conversations with some of the internees who had originated from the tin mining region of Southern Thailand. Some internees had reported that tin miners had been executed not long after Japan had landed, and that a large group of British subjects, including Australians, had been imprisoned near Yala and killed while attempting to escape from the Japanese. Other rumours were that another group of tin miners, including a man only known by the surname of Holt, were also believed to have died in South Thailand in December 1941, and that others including tin miners and airmen had been executed on a beach somewhere.[9]

Although not all were second-hand reports, especially among the five Kampong Toh massacre survivors now in Prachand Camp, to the Foreign Office their vagueness of details was unhelpful. The sticking point appeared to be that none of these allegations were being reported through what Foreign Office civil servants deemed official channels, which in their eyes was highly suspicious. It was just one of many problems the Foreign Office bureaucracy had continually stressed to the Australian Government about these or any other rumours, that there was a real need to treat information on these, or any other similar accusations, 'with reserve'.[10] Nonetheless, by later that month other information about the fate of some of the Operation Cleeves personnel was coming in not from the field, nor the newly set up SOE FE replacement India Mission, but from other sources.

In one routine intercept of a Thailand Tin communiqué with one of its extension offices in New York, for example, company representatives in London were advising the loss of their tin mining personnel in Southern Thailand. Similarly, in its shareholder reporting at the end of the year, it was reported that some of their staff from the Pinyok Mine were dead, and everyone else was missing. Intercepts of personal letters shed more light on some of the operatives' locations. Mrs Nancy Fitzgerald, who had recently been released from an internment camp in Bangkok under the Lourenço Marques exchange, had contacted the wife of Sergeant ES Wright when she arrived back in Britain. Fitzgerald had sent her a letter with news that she had been interned with her husband Wright in Bangkok.[11] Apparently he had arrived at the camp suffering badly from malaria in early 1942, but after spending time being treated and recovering in a local Thai Red Cross Hospital was now in very good health. Mrs Fitzgerald stressed to Wright's wife that if she was going to send any letters to her husband, he particularly asked she only address them to him as a Mr Wright.

In other cases it was through personal contacts that information about Southern Thailand's operatives was getting out. In one case a Mrs Wait, who had been secretary to the former Military Attaché in Bangkok, Major PD Barry, had also been part of the exchange, and returned with news of two tin miners named Collins and Pattullo. They had asked her to take a message to the War Office regarding their plight, in the hope that something could be done to obtain their release.[12] But still there was little formal confirmation about what had happened to Operation Cleeves personnel. Nobody, it seemed, had any conclusive lists of names, or any other relevant information about Singora Line operations, Southern Thailand SOE missions, or anything else to do with Thailand for that matter. It was not helping when some of the earliest misinformation surrounding Operation Cleeves and its personnel had started with the SOE (FE)'s latest incarnation in the India Mission.

Chapter 37

Misinformation, Disinformation

Bureaucracy Gone Mad

Sometime in late 1942, Colonel Basil Goodfellow, based out of the India Mission in Calcutta and heading up the Malay country desk, had informed London that problems in identifying Oriental Mission casualties appeared to be nothing more than a straightforward problem.[1] It was just a matter of getting the right person in place and getting an identity card index system up and running. He presumed it was an administrative oversight that could be easily fixed, just as Malaya's Oriental Mission operatives had been identified, found, tracked, and other information discovered, including where they were at the outbreak of war, any particular missions, their current fate if known and so on. That approach worked in part for most of the Malayan operatives because the larger majority of them were regular military, policemen, civil servants, game wardens, district officers and so on. There may not have been too many records left about them in Malaya and Singapore, but there were threads of information back in London and elsewhere.

The overwhelming majority of Thailand operatives, on the other hand, and more particularly those associated with Operation Cleeves, had nothing to do with government circles. They were civilian tin miners, working under contract, with civilian tin mining companies, and most of their records had been kept locally. As the British had destroyed large swathes of paperwork in the chaotic retreat, several civilian mining companies included, little was left about any Oriental Mission personnel or activities, especially in Southern Thailand.

It was a problem exacerbated by what had been the Oriental Mission's segregation of local recruitment and training practices, with Penang handling most of Operation Cleeves and Southern Thailand's requirements, and Singapore all the rest. Because both paperwork and paper trails were completely disrupted when Japan invaded, and any tangible documentation destroyed, the India Mission and others would have to rely heavily on individual personal knowledge and oral history to try and gather some information as best they could. The trouble was that although there was a plethora of those experienced with Malaya and more to the point, those who could be spared from the armed forces or essential war work, there was hardly anyone with the same type and level of experience regarding Thailand. Nonetheless, eventually one of Goodfellow's associates, a Mr AC Pointon, was put in charge of the Thai Country Section.[2] Although he had closer ties to the Bombay Burma Trading Corporation than Thailand, he did have several years' experience of living and working in the Far East. Besides, he would be just another one of the many civilians in the India Mission's expanding bureaucracy who would have to use on-the-job-training to learn about the intricacies and exigencies of Special Operations.

The bottom line was that nobody had any up-to-date records of anyone associated with the former Oriental Mission, and even less regarding Operation Cleeves. What was even more problematic in the aftermath of the fall of Singapore, was that not only were there competing lists of Oriental Mission-related casualties, such as one being compiled by the Foreign Office, another by SOE, and a third by the India Mission, all three were working off common presumptions of an SOE FE operative list that had been compiled prior to Singapore's capitulation. All three lists were not being helped in part because of the necessary compartmentalisation of mission tasking or field operations, or protection of certain individual identities due to operational security requirements associated with the former Oriental Mission activities. It also did not help that most Oriental Mission survivors, and others who had escaped before Malaya and Singapore had fallen, had little or no idea about each other let alone Operation Cleeves activities.

Most of those who had made their way to India, for example, including former policemen, game wardens and civil servants, had been recruited in Malaya and had been focused exclusively on Malayan-related operations, including stay-behind-parties. They knew more about one another and their particular areas of responsibilities, because they were all administered out of GOC Malaya and the Oriental Mission's headquarters in Singapore. For Operation Cleeves it was the opposite, with many of their operatives recruited, trained and administered by Heath's III Division headquarters in Kuala Lumpur, or by the Oriental Mission's Penang advanced headquarters. It seemed nothing could be done with anyone or anything to do with Singora Line operations because nobody knew anything about them. That was until a Major Benn on loan from the War Office visited the India Mission in late 1942, and he brought with him a more inclusive and comprehensive listing of Oriental Mission operatives. His list included the twenty-nine or so Operation Cleeves operatives known to have been in Southern Thailand when the Japanese invaded.[3]

The added confusion was due to the fact that although the majority of Operation Cleeves personnel were deemed civilians, some held Army service numbers, field commissions and other ranks, or had been given block Army numbers by virtue of GOC Malaya's arrangements with Killery.[4] That was another paperwork trail that seemingly disappeared in the aftermath of the fall of Singapore, but even then it was precarious. In some cases Japan's speedy attack had meant those records of personnel that had managed to survive the chaotic British retreat were either piecemeal or incomplete. Even other SOE operatives who had been commissioned and were on the Army's General List, such as other SOE operatives including the Irish 'tin miner' Terence Coyne/Collins, and Australian 'journalist' George Loftus Windred for example, were recognised as such but nobody could find their actual commissioning personal numbers.[5]

As the snippets of information kept creeping into the War Office, by November more requests were being sent out for any and all information on Oriental Mission personnel who may have been in Southern Thailand when the Japanese arrived. London was especially keen to find out anything about the tin mine denial schemes, and if any of them had been successful, but nothing was forthcoming. Without any hard intelligence, most of the fate of Operation Cleeves and its operatives remained based mainly around erroneous information, gossip, rumours and hearsay, and nothing was able to be confirmed or denied. Trying to find out what happened to any of them, let alone those civilians who had been executed by the Japanese as collateral damage, was at best fragmentary. The only thing that could be confirmed without any doubt was that there was an almost blanket silence over Operation Cleeves. Why that was the case seemed odd until roughly around the end of 1942, when SOE (FE) casualty statistics were starting to be counted across the Far East and disseminated back to London.

In all the areas of SOE operations ranging from China to the Dutch East Indies, Malaya held the most with forty-three missing operatives, and Thailand remained second with thirty-one still unaccounted for.[6] The contrast between the two being that forty-one of those missing in Malaya were considered Army personnel, and somewhat traceable. The majority (twenty nine) who were missing in Thailand were civilian operatives, and they had simply vanished. The contrast was obvious. More civilian personnel were missing under the auspices of the Oriental Mission in the Far East and specifically in Thailand than anywhere else.[7] Even more perplexing was that SOE London was reporting that only eleven Oriental Mission operatives were reported as missing in Southern Thailand, but they only really had any information on two of them, which was significant given the overall number was closer to thirty.[8] By early December, while there was little headway being made surrounding the fate of Operation Cleeves' civilian casualties by the India Mission, there was some movement in tracking them down back in SOE London, and they were following the money trail.

It seemed the Treasury and the Department of Finance had been advised that a number of tin miners in Southern Thailand had been recruited as far back as June 1941 by the Oriental Mission, specifically for some highly classified sabotage, tin mine denial and stay-behind-work. Most had been recruited through Heath's III Division headquarters in Kuala Lumpur, and a large majority of them believed they were working covertly for the British Army. Bearing this in mind, and noting how many civilian operatives were already missing especially in Southern Thailand, things were coming to a head when an increasing number of SOE operatives were disappearing on active service, in disparate enemy war zones, scattered around the world.

Many were either going missing, being interned or made prisoners of war, suffering extensive injuries or permanent disabilities, and even death, and this opened up the British Government to all sorts of unforeseen legal issues. This was especially if, for example, a widow might seek to sue the Government for compensation over the negligent death of a spouse who was at the time of death, undertaking some sort of covert mission on their behest. This was such a significant financial and legal realisation that both the Treasury and the War Office, thought it might be a situation best to get out in front of sooner rather than later. To address this possible scenario, the British Government began introducing a new set of rules to cover benefits, pensions or other compensatory payments that might arise from the rapidly escalating SOE civilian casualty lists.

The shift in practice was that certain financial obligations in these situations for SOE operatives, would now cover not only those given military commissions or non-commissioned field ranks, but also be extended to those not covered by either. That implied that civilians working for specific SOE covert operations and in the pay of local SOE coffers, such as many had been in Southern Thailand, might still be afforded some comparable compensation if needed. For unpaid personnel such as those who had committed to the small-scale tin mine sabotage operations under Operation Cleeves, but were not operatives, they too might also qualify for ex-gratia benefits on the recommendation of Head of Mission, or SOE London.[9] But that might only work if London actually had correct details and information about operatives, including their next of kin or marital status, and there were examples of that not being the case, such as Pinyok Mine's Operation Cleeves member Harding Thomas being erroneously described as not being married.

These were important bureaucratic oversights, especially because the Department of Finance, in agreement with the War Office, had also suggested the only standard way to calculate compensation for families of those Operation Cleeves' operatives that may have been killed or incarcerated, was to give them field ranks.[10] As compensation only applied to the married British Caucasian men of Operation Cleeves, giving them a field rank made it easier to offer lump sum payments to the men's widows as compensation for services rendered.[11] It was a neatly efficient and tidy way to not raise too many questions, especially ones the British Government might not be able to answer. Hence, by the end of 1942, most Operation Cleeves personnel relevant to the Singora Line area of operations, had been given ranks for the purpose of casualty benefits. Orton, Gordon, Omay and Butler-Jones were regarded as second lieutenants, while Peters, Powell, Daniel Regan, HC Wright, Belcher, Billinghurst, Bird, Redford, Turner, Pattullo, Brauchman, Sarrell, Donnelly, Ravenwood, Laub and Thomas were considered sergeants.[12]

That latter of which is probably why on 14 December 1942, Harding Thomas' widow received a letter from the Foreign Office offering condolences on her husband's demise, but no mention was made in it of compensation, the circumstances of his death, or whether he had been involved in way with some sort of classified operation.[13] She was also asked to refrain from making the news public, because the information had originated from those who were still in Japanese hands, and there was a very real threat of reprisals against them should the Japanese find out their identities. It was also a convenient way for SOE London and the War Office to shut down any information about Operation Cleeves until they had some themselves. It was not a lot to go on in trying to track down Operation Cleeves personnel, but at least for some including the War Office's Casualty Department it was somewhere to begin searching. It would not be until three years later, in early 1945, that any real progress would be made about the fate of Operation Cleeves operatives.

Chapter 38

Falling Down Through (Historical) Cracks in the Dark

In early 1945, and as the tide of war was turning against the Japanese, it seemed a bureaucratic flurry was also looming on the horizon. The attempts to identify and discover the fates of any of the civilian SOE operatives in Southern Thailand or anywhere else was gaining greater impetus. The trouble was there was still no overarching nominal roll for Oriental Mission operatives in 1941, and information that was now appearing was increasingly stemming from erroneous and competing organisational administrations. SOE London had started working on yet another list of names whom they thought had been working with the SOE in the Far East, including in Southern Thailand, to the War Office. The other problem was the new list only included the names of British Army commissioned men, and even then the list was incomplete, missing out some of those who were now imprisoned in Prachand, such as Omay.[1] That same list was then passed on to the Colonial Office Malaya desk, who expounded upon the information by only focusing on those missing SOE operatives who had been employed in local authorities or governance structures, such as police, politics or the civil service and so on.[2] The Foreign Office Casualties Department was also working from a different list of civilian SOE casualties. Where this list originated from is unknown, but it seemed the Foreign Office was presuming it was the same one that had been in place before the fall of Singapore.

Aside from the competing and ever-changing nominal lists over Oriental Mission operatives, especially those affiliated with Thailand, there were other problems in trying to pin down dates of any event, and at any given time. A major chronological problem was that often when anything to do with Japan's war on the Malay Peninsula involved casualties, it was usually based around an artificial start date of 15 February 1942, the day

Singapore capitulated. That was at least one of the reasons why several casualty records all shared the same casualty, missing or death date, even though the event might have occurred prior. It is also how in a similar way some Oriental Mission personnel were deemed as having separated from SOE in December 1941, that date being linked to when the Japanese started their invasion on 8 December 1941, and when all communications were lost with certain personnel. With a paucity of records in general, but covering those three interim months in particular, it was one suggestion as to why Operation Cleeves personnel and the Oriental Mission's Southern Thailand operations literally fell through the historical cracks.

A month after Japan had capitulated in August, there were more questions than answers being raised about SOE's missing operatives in Southern Thailand. As survivors were being repatriated home and journalists were covering their survival stories, some families were finally getting some news about their loved ones. On arrival back in Australia, the Kampong Toh massacre survivor Stratford, for example, had given several newspaper interviews recounting what the Japanese had done at the tin mine. He had also named those who had been with him, including those working for Operation Cleeves, and those who had lost their lives in general. One of them was Norman Holt, who had died in the ambush by purportedly Thai militia. Shortly afterwards an Australian Stock, Station and Real Estate Agent named WP Beahan had written to his local Federal Member of Parliament, advising that he had just read about what had happened to his son-in-law Norman R Holt, who had been missing in Southern Thailand since the Japanese had landed in December 1941. Beahan had been pressing the Australian Federal Government since at least 1944 to find out what had happened to him, only to be rebuffed with silence. He emphasised how he thought that the Department of External Affairs may have had some knowledge about certain events in Southern Thailand at that time, but it was information they were either unable or unwilling to share.[3] Beahan was like several of those families, including the de Boers in South Africa, who had no information given to them whatsoever about their missing relatives.

Beahan, however, had his own means available to pursue the problem, and had made that point in a letter to then Australian Prime Minister JB Chifley. He informed the Australian Government that he now had confirmation surrounding not only Holt's fate, but the fate of several others including Operation Cleeves personnel Laub and Donnelly.[4] Accompanying the letter was a signed witness statement by three of the Kampong Toh massacre survivors, namely Reginald Arthur Stratford, Henry Moore and London's SOE operative, Horace Travis Cummins. Noting the gravity of the allegations made, the Prime Minister replied to Beahan post haste, informing him that inquiries would be made into what he phrased was the Yala incident.[5] Less than a fortnight later the slow wheels of federal bureaucracy appear to have finally begun gaining momentum, when the Yala incident was now officially referred to war crimes research teams that were just starting investigations into potential war crimes in Southeast Asia. The Yala case was handed to the Australian war crime commission leader, Chief Justice Sir William Webb, for investigation.[6] That the Australian Government – or some portions thereof – may have known about the massacre as early as July 1942, as had the British, was probably the last thing anybody wanted made public. Nor would the failed catastrophe of Operation Cleeves, and the equally disastrous fates of Europeans in Southern Thailand be welcomed. Webb and other investigators, it seemed, never quite got around to it, but paradoxically in 1946, a small handful of British military investigators did.

The War Office had sent out an order that it was essential to make every endeavour to trace all members of the Oriental Mission including in Southern Thailand, because there were several members still unaccounted for.[7] The second was that every effort should also be made after tracing said personnel, to render any and all assistance possible to provide them with early repatriation back to their country of origin. These were practical aspirations even if they were improbable, and that was because nobody in London, including the War Office and SOE, still had any concise nominal roll of who had been recruited, let alone trained by the Oriental Mission, or for what operations they were given responsibilities.

The other sticking point was that most of Operation Cleeves' operatives had remained fully employed in their regular places of work, and some had only drawn small local SOE financial advances, which suggested any financial paper trail too was limited, especially if the requisite paperwork had not yet been filed or was still going through the administrative process at local Penang or Singapore headquarters levels as the Japanese advanced.[8] That was probably only exacerbated by timing problems, especially given that most operatives had only been undergoing training in the weeks and months before Japan invaded, and probably had not had enough time to lodge relevant Army forms, including the vitally important Army Family

Lodging Allowance Form for married men.[9] Things were getting even fuzzier when after the war, some tin miners who had been part of Operation Cleeves, and who thought they were attached to the British Army, such as AR Redford, sent letters to the British military authorities requesting their military discharge, only to be told they could not help them as they were not, and had never been, members of the British Army.[10]

Those who had survived such as Cummins were found and identified, as were some such as Peters, who had died in Japanese captivity. All of the soldiers, operatives and other European deaths at the Kampong Toh massacre were confirmed, although the wrong date of the event was given as January 1942. Donnelly's death in Ayer Weng in 1943 was also confirmed. The postwar joint statement made by Stratford, Moore and Cummins described what had happened to the five neutrals that had been in their survival group. Although there was a record of Peters' death and he was buried at Changi, it was only an unconfirmed account that suggested Doris van der Straaten's body had been taken to Kuala Lumpur's main hospital. Someone had also reported to one of the other British Army Liaison Officers in Bangkok, that Laub had been taken with Butler-Jones, Thomas and the others to a bungalow in Kampong Toh in Thailand, but that Laub had declared himself a neutral and had been taken away by the Japanese.[11] The others were reportedly killed by machine gun and his fate, and the fate of the other neutrals, remained unknown. It was also unknown where the final resting places of the Indian soldiers who had also been in No. 4 bungalow, Kampong Toh Tin Mine, may have been. That is until sometime in 1946, when one of Harding Thomas' former co-workers visited the massacre site. He had been told by locals that all of those who died in the bungalow, including the Indian soldiers, had been buried together in a mass grave, upon which he had laid flowers in commemoration. There are no indications that any of the bodies were recovered postwar.

The bodies of the Sadao atrocities and Singora executions were also tracked down. In December 1945, war crimes investigators recovered the remains of two bodies from a rubber plantation in Sadao. The Coroner's Report suggested the two in Sadao were European. Another eight were found on a beach north of Singora, and at least six were thought to have been European. One of them was still wearing the remains of what had once possibly been a leather zippered jacket. It seemed by 1946 at least, some of the fates of Southern Thailand's missing were finally being revealed, but trying to apportion blame or find those responsible for any atrocities committed was another problem entirely.

Chapter 39

The Hot War is Dead

Long Live the Cold War

One of those tasked with Southern Thailand's war crime investigations was British Army officer Captain J. Kennedy. In mid-1946, he and his team started off by tracing some of the Thai policemen and other members of the local population who had been in Sadao, Singora, Yala and Betong when the Japanese invaded. Despite several of them offering corroborating eyewitness testimonies of Japanese atrocities, including the executions of Bentley and Tebbers in Sadao, and the same of HC Wright, Gordon and Daniel Regan in Singora, as well as the three Ban Pru downed airmen, it seemed no further action could be taken. Although it was confirmed the actions had taken place, it was impossible to find out who was responsible. For others, including those potentially involved with missing Operation Cleeves tin miners such as Billinghurst and Bird, as well as those executed at Kampong Toh, Sadao, Singora or perhaps even elsewhere, their postwar fates as former Japanese military personnel remained unknown. But then Kennedy could only go on the information he had at hand, and none of the casualty lists he was working off seemed to correlate with what Japanese actions he was finding out in Southern Thailand. With written records at best scant, and the paucity of survivors of Southern Thailand not helping, any information was still piecemeal. Those who may have had any insights into Operation Cleeves or the small-scale tin mine sabotage scheme, including Cummins or Macfarlane, were still not talking.

One of the most significant problems for Kennedy and any war crime investigations, was that most Operation Cleeves personnel had been recruited at the eleventh hour, meaning almost immediately prior to Japan's invasion. Due to a variety of compounding issues including the destruction of any local paper trails handicapping the War Office Casualties Department, it meant taking any necessary actions in connection with casualties, whether in searching for their remains or in affording financial reparations to next of kin and so on, was even more compounded by the lack of information as to who was on which small-scale denial sabotage team, and in what Singora Line area of operations. Trying to trace them was more of an Abbott and Costello-style 'who's on first base' type of scenario, rather than anything else.

There was also not much hope for any information being gleaned through post-war interrogations of former Japanese military personnel either. Although the hunt was on for alleged Japanese war criminals who had been deployed within the Singora Line both north and south, especially those that had been attached to the Imperial Japanese Army's 25th Division, the focus was on capturing the big fish rather than the small fry. That would prove pointless, because almost immediately after capitulation several former Japanese military commanders and their senior ranking troops simply disappeared.

Some had been supposedly traced back to having returned to Manchuria before Japan had surrendered, but after the war it also seemed many had been arrested by the Soviets. Despite repeated requests from Britain and the USA as to their identities, no information was ever forthcoming and it remains that way at the time of writing. At war's end for example, Masanobu Tsuji was reportedly last seen in Bangkok, but had disappeared soon after, only to magically reappear in Tokyo in the 1950s. That destroyed some postwar assumptions that he may have committed suicide in keeping with the Bushido code that he often espoused.[1] Nothing conclusive was known about the whereabouts of Ando and Saeki or their detachments, but some thought that given that they were front-line troops, they may have perished in the Philippines or elsewhere. That in itself was an indication of one of the biggest hurdles in trying to pin down any of Japan's 25th Division in Southern Thailand, especially because it was a highly mobile force. Personnel were constantly being rotated and were routinely in transit on widely dispersed operational duties.

As one particular Kempetai officer, Lieutenant Murakami Shuji's wartime record showed, he went from being a member of the Kempetai's horse unit responsible for looking after the horses for Saeki's and other cavalry units in Haad Yai, to being part of Kuala Lumpur's Kempetai investigation unit tasked with interrogating prisoners. It was Murakami Shuji who had been the Kempetai officer accused of murdering Doris van der Straaten in August 1943, but at his war crime trial in 1946 he had been acquitted due to the fact that he was not even in Kuala Lumpur at the time.[2]

Trying to identify let alone locate any others of those guilty of Southern Thailand's wartime atrocities would literally be like looking for a blunt needle in a messy post-war haystack.

In Britain, too, things were different in the new post-war world, when internal recriminations and the finger pointing started over Operation Matador's, and by default Operation Cleeves' abject failure. It did not help that both Percival and Brooke-Popham's individual versions of events were equally as scathing of those who were around them at the time, as much as they were of each other, and Whitehall was more than concerned about the forthcoming publication of Percival's accounts of events.[3] His versions made sweeping generalisations that all Thais either before or during the war, should be considered as having been Japanese collaborators. In some of his more damning descriptions of the Thai government and other Thai officials, the War Office made it known that certain passages he had written about Thailand were to be left out altogether.[4] The Foreign Office concurred, and both were making it quite clear to all and sundry, that their collective preferences remained that anything of any kind related to Operation Matador not be given any publicity.[5] That also included no mention being made of Operation Cleeves, the Oriental Mission, Krohcol, Laycol or anything at all to do with Southern Thailand. Those orders effectively silenced acknowledgement of any official military or SOE-sanctioned operations that may or may not have occurred in Southern Thailand.

Without London and anyone else looking too closely into any operations in Thailand anyway, Kennedy was soon finding out that most of the information he was getting was equally confusing. Although the murders had purportedly started within a day or so of the Japanese landings, and had continued on until the main Japanese force deployed for Malaya a week or so later, and several eyewitness statements between Chinese, Thais, Malays and others had corroborated accounts of the Sadao, Singora and Kampong Toh massacre, they still had no agreed upon suspects to pursue.[6] The location of the 'grenade' incident, as the Kampong Toh massacre was now being referred to, was also being confused. The War Crimes Investigation Unit took it on face value that it had occurred in the Pinyok Mine, or at least somewhere close by including around Yala. In none of the reporting did the Kampong Toh Tin Mine appear as a potential site, other than in a later statement made by a Singora-based driver in mid-July 1946.

In his post-war statement made to British Investigators, Nai Kalai said he had been working just outside Singora when, almost immediately after the Japanese arrived, they had seized his and roughly seventeen other people's trucks, and he, like the other men, was made to become a driver for the Japanese. He testified that in the week after the Japanese had arrived, he had been forced to drive a lorry full of armed Japanese soldiers out west to a specific house on the Kampong Toh Tin Mine site near Betong.[7] Here he had witnessed a house with European men and women inside, and also the Japanese throwing in hand grenades and machine gunning the house. But there were problems with all the statements. Although various reports more or less carried the same threads, of a house full of Europeans being executed by grenade and machine gun fire, of tin miners across Southern Thailand seemingly being persecuted to the exclusion of all others, and a short two-week period in which at least six Europeans, two Indians and five men of unknown nationality were executed, nothing else matched.

In all these cases, the biggest problem the War Crimes Unit faced was in accurately fixing the date and exact locations of where Japan's alleged wartime atrocities occurred, and the gruesome details accompanying them. In the chaos of war, all three were often fluid, and that meant under British and Allied judicial rules none of what had been alleged could be proven beyond a reasonable doubt. But there again, there was no link analysis going on between all the statements being uncovered in Thailand, with those being made publicly by survivors in the media, and it seems not even a cross-matching was being done between the financial records the Treasury had at their fingertips, with any of the casualty listings being provided. That also suggested any post-war debriefing of now former SOE operatives including Cummins, Windred and the others was probably also quietly and permanently being filed away, that is if they were not destroyed in the first place. Nobody could investigate a war crime if nobody knew anything about it.

To compound the time restrictions, 1947 was looming as a potential cut-off date for beginning any new investigations into alleged Japanese war crimes, and 1948 was being put forward as the cut-off date for widows and survivors to claim compensation. By now, however, there was another worldwide threat coming into view, as the Cold War began marking a different emerging post-war world, and a new East versus West international stage was emerging out of the ashes of the Second World War. The Singora Line battlefront was forgotten, the Southern Thailand battlefield faded into obscurity, and the story of the Operation Cleeves operatives and their mission simply vanished.

Conclusion

History, so the old saying goes, is always written by the victors, but sometimes history is also unwritten to hide the vanquished. In the early days of the Second World War in Southeast Asia, that was the fate of a small handful of Europeans living and working in Southern Thailand, when in the days leading up to Japan's invasion on 8 December 1941, an ordinary group of mining engineers, rubber planters, accountants and housewives were all going about their daily business, and waiting in nervous anticipation for the all-important signal tunes to play over the radio. In their midst were a group of extraordinary tin mining men who had all volunteered to undertake dangerous, small-scale, enemy denial sabotage operations in their own places of work (Appendix A). Some had been formally recruited into the SOE Far East's Oriental Mission, and had undertaken training at STS101 down in Singapore and in Penang, while others were merely willing and unpaid volunteers who were also supporting the anti-Japanese tin mine denial scheme in their own way.

Whether Operation Cleeves would have been a success rather than a disastrous failure remains a moot historical point, but in the week leading up to Japan's invasion there had been warning signs coming in from all sorts of areas, and on all sorts of potential threats heading Southern Thailand's way. Just as time is an essential part of any operation, whether that be military, covert, or otherwise, it was something neither those involved with Operation Matador nor Operation Cleeves had on their side on 8 December 1941. Whatever the reasons were behind why the order to commence operations took so long, they matter little now in the grand scheme of things, but the delay does relay how disconnected Southern Thailand's SOE non-conventional operations were from Singapore's conventional military mindsets. It also highlights unrealistic expectations placed on Operation Cleeves personnel, especially on Pinyok Tin Mine's geostrategic proximity to The Ledge, which in and of itself places the bravery of the civilian operatives themselves under the spotlight. But that is not to detract from so many others who either lost their lives or were incarcerated through no fault of their own, other than being in the wrong place at the wrong time. That is all that can be said about the housewives, and several others including those in Sadao, Singora, the Kampong Toh Tin Mine, and probably other unknown places, who were massacred alongside them.

Neither should the bravery and determination of the British Indian soldiers in Southern Thailand be ignored. Despite facing horrendous tactical disadvantage and operational difficulties, and in Krohcol's case holding out for days against overwhelming odds in the aftermath of Japan's landings, these men of India's 11th Division should also be better recognised for what was undertaken in their concomitant field of battle. Noting how outstanding Japanese pre-war intelligence was in comparison to Britain's paltry attempts at covert craft, that alone highlights one of the colonial era's most significant weaknesses: the abject belief in European superiority. That is even more troubling when considering that Krohcol's troops in particular may have already been fighting through an essentially enemy-occupied corridor in Malaya from the outset; Laycol's plight was that they too seemed to have been expected, which suggested neither British military force had any element of surprise. Dismissing the atrocious outcomes of Operation Cleeves focus on Southern Thailand as a mere consequence of war, does not mean their sacrifices should remain as a footnote to history, but rather, should offer glimpses into what goes into all the best of the fighting traditions of professional soldiering.

The harsh reality was that Operation Cleeves was relying exclusively upon Operation Matador and vice versa. Neither was supposed to have been operating in isolation of the other, but lacking any communications, transport or supply between them in the first instance actually broke all the rules of conventional war fighting. The trouble was, however, conventional war fighting was not Operation Cleeves' mandate. Those recruited into Operation Cleeves were SOE operatives and they were given individually unique code names (Appendix B). They were recruited to undertake specific SOE-approved missions. They did undertake particular SOE training either in STS101 or Penang or both, and regardless of how it came about, they were given concomitant field ranks in accordance with the duties expected of them. As of November 2024, only three of them have been given any official recognition.

At Thailand's Kanchanaburi War Cemetery lie the headstones of Captain Roderick Gordon, Captain Henry C Wright and another bearing the name of

Captain E Regan.[1] All of the men are described as British Special Forces, and are noted as having served with SOE in Southern Thailand, and also that they died there on active duty. But they were not the only ones who were serving with SOE and Operation Cleeves who lost their lives after Japan invaded on 8 December 1941. That the majority of Operation Cleeves operatives literally fell through the cracks of history cannot be ignored, just as much as it can be argued they are not merely insignificant footnotes to Southeast Asia's wartime history, but rather the opposite. To address the latter this work does not in any way profess to be the definitive account of SOE in Southern Thailand in December 1941, nor about Operation Cleeves operatives or their missions, but it is a small attempt to bring some of Southeast Asia's hidden wartime history out of the shadows and into the light. To those who still rest somewhere in silent, mournful unknown graves in Southern Thailand, perhaps the only real historical lesson anybody can learn from the Operation Cleeves disaster is that no jungle, let alone unwritten history, is impenetrable.

Appendix A

Operation Cleeves

Small-Scale Tin Mine Sabotage: Southern Thailand 8 December 1941 (list not definitive)

Co-operating Tin Mines – Possible Locations

Name of Mine	**Location: Singora Line South**
Ayer Weng Level Co. Ltd	Kliam Weng (Betong-Yala)
Kampong Toh Tin Ltd	Kampong Toh (Betong-Yala)
Labu Mine	Labu (Betong-Yala)
Straits Consolidated Tin Dredging Ltd	Kumang (Betong-Yala)
Thailand Tin Mines Ltd	Pinyok Mine (Betong-Yala)
Pattani Tin Ltd	Lamphya (Betong-Yala)
	Location: Singora Line North
Nawang Pet Tin Ltd	Ronpibon
Takuapa Valley Tin Dredging Ltd	Ban Pru
Anglo Thai Syndicate Ltd	Bandinlan
Tongkah Harbour Tin Dredging Ltd	Ronpibon
Nawang Pet Ltd	Ronpibon
Ratrut Basin N.L.	Sichol
Peninsular Tin N.L.	Langsuan
Thai Tin Syndicate Ltd	Hooey Moot (Huey Moot)
Anglo Thai Tin Syndicate Ltd	Hooey Mot (Huey Mot/Yot)
Thai Tin Syndicate Ltd	Takuapa (Takuapah)
Kamunting Tin Dredging Ltd	Paggna
Takuapa Valley Tin	Takuapa (Takuapah)
Paggna River Tin Concession Ltd	Paggna
Pungah Tin Dredging Ltd	Paggna
Renong Consolidated Tin	Renong
Bangrin Tin Dredging Ltd	Renong
Thai Tin Syndicate Ltd	Renong
Katu Tin Dredging Ltd	Puket (Phuket)
Kamra Tin Dredging Ltd	Puket (Phuket)
Tongkah Harbour Tin Dredging Ltd	Puket (Phuket)

Source: After NAA: A1608 AC47/1/1

Appendix B

Operation Cleeves (OC) Personnel

8 December 1941

(Oriental Mission Thailand (not definitive) as at 30 November 2023)

SOE No.	Name	Codename	Rank/ Field Rank	Recruitment Place	Miscellaneous
O.2510	AITKEN, AF	Gloaming	NFI	NFI	NFI
O.2803	ARTHUR	Arthur	NFI	NFI	NFI
O.2630	BELCHER, HR	Scrooge	Civilian/sergeant	Recruited III Corps Malaya	Trained Penang. OC cell Huey Mot. Interned Bangkok. Recovered.
O.2614	BILLINGHURST, CW	Quilp	Civilian/sergeant	Recruited III Corps Malaya	Trained STS101. Cover: Nawng Pet Dredge, Ronpibon. OC cell Ronpibon/Ban Neang. MIA (Kantang 10/12/41). Death confirmed. Place unknown.
O.2615	BIRD, WEJ	Grimwig	Civilian/sergeant	Recruited III Corps Malaya	Trained STS101. Cover: Anglo-Oriental Tin Mining Assets, Ronpibon. MIA (Kantang 10/12/41). Death confirmed. Place unknown.

O.2608	BRAUCHMAN, Emil Franz	Twist	Civilian/reported as both sergeant and 2/LT	Recruited Thailand/ Malaya	Ronpibon Tin. AKA Brauckmann. MIA. Interned Bangkok. Recovered.
O.2009	BRYCE-SMITH, RB	NA	Nominal roll only	Inactive	MIA Bangkok. Reported KIA February 1942 Burma (British Forces).
O.2010	BYLES, DV	NA	Nominal roll only	Inactive	MIA. Interned Bangkok. Recovered.
O.2700	BUTLER-JONES, Frank	Walter	Civilian/2/LT	Recruited London	Trained London, MEW and STS101. Previous SOE Number 3499. Cover: Metallurgist/Mine Manager Pinyok Tin Mine. I/C OC cell Pinyok. Death confirmed Kampong Toh Tin Mine massacre 13/12/41.
O.2612	COLLINS, T	Doyle	A/2LT (237197)	Recruited London	See O.217. Local rank of Captain. Interned Bangkok. Tin miner cover intact. Recovered.
O.2001	CUMYN, AL	NA	Nominal roll only	Inactive	AKA AL McMyn. MIA (Kantang 10/12/41). Interned Bangkok. Recovered.
O.2004	DAVY, E Raymond	NA	Nominal roll only	Inactive	MIA. Interned Bangkok. Recovered.
O.2701	DONNELLY, TJB	Rob	Civilian/sergeant	Recruited Thailand	Trained Penang. MIA. Assistant Mine Manager, Pinyok Tin Mine/Ayer Weng Tin Survey Fields. OC cell Pinyok. Kampong Toh Tin Mine massacre survivor. Death confirmed Ayer Weng (Ayn Weng) Tin Survey Field *c.*1943.
O.2804	ELKAN, Edward Felix	Paul	2/LT (225882) GL	Recruited Malaya	Transferred to Malayan stay-behind-party Operations. Possible courier work. Interned Malaya. Recovered.
O.2000	GENTRY, AA	NA	A/Captain (205742) Nominal roll only	Inactive	Also 2057612. Interned Bangkok. Anglo-Japan prisoner swap. Recovered.
O.2602	GORDON, Roderick	Dombey	Civilian/2/LT or sergeant	Recruited Thailand/ Malaya	Trained Penang. 3IC OC cell Tongkah Dredge/ Nawng Pet Tin (Ronpibon). MIA (Kantang 10/12/41). Death confirmed. Executed Lamsai Beach, Singora, between 13–16 December 1941.

SOE No.	Name	Codename	Rank/ Field Rank	Recruitment Place	Miscellaneous
O.2006	HEMPSON, RD	NA	Nominal roll only	Inactive	Interned Bangkok. Recovered.
O.2751	HOLNESS, HJ	Angus	NFI	NFI	NFI
O.2551	HOWIE, FW	Montgomery	NFI	NFI	Leader Klong Tom Party. NFI
O.2600	KAIN, Maurice C.	Leo		Recruited Malaya	ESOY, OM Penang HQ POC. NFI.
O.2607	KING, Arthur J	Barnaby		Recruited Malaya/ Thailand	Interned Singora Jail, then FIC. Recovered.
O.2704	LAUB, Georg Christian Haae	Scott	Civilian/sergeant	Recruited Malaya	Trained Penang (Tommy Gun specialisation). AKA George Lamb. Commissioned Johore Volunteer Engineers as Major. Cover: Chief Chemist Pinyok Tin Mine. OC cell Pinyok. Kampong Toh Tin Mine massacre survivor. Death confirmed by ambush, Thai–Malay border area, after 13/12/41.
O.2011	MATTHEWS, JV	NA	Nominal roll only	Inactive	MIA. Interned Bangkok. Recovered.
O.2552	MISSELBROOK, Frank A	Cagney	Sergeant (781714)	Possibly unknown Burma operation	STS101, Operation Cleeves (Phuket), Lashio party. Cover: Dredge Engineer, Phuket. OC cell Phuket. NFI
O.2651	MELHUISH, Leslie	McFee	Civilian/2/LT	Unknown SIS operation	Reported MIA Malaya with J. Regan. Death confirmed. Place unknown.
O.2801	NOONE, RO	Owen	Civilian	Recruited Malaya	Transferred to Malayan stay-behind-party operations.
O.2610	OMAY, James	Watson	Civilian/2/LT	Recruited Thailand/ Malaya	Thai Tin Syndicate Mine sites. Also erroneously listed as O.2603. Interned Bangkok. Recovered.
O.2601	ORTON, RL	Rudge	Civilian/2/LT	Recruited Thailand/ Malaya	I/C OC cell Tongkah Dredge/Nawng Pet Tin (Ronpibon). Interned Bangkok. Recovered.

O.2550	PARSONS, WJ	Cable		Recruited Thailand/ Malaya, evacuated.	OC cell Phuket and outstations. Anglo-Japan prisoner swap. Recovered.
O.2606	PATTULLO, AC	Weller	Civilian/sergeant	Recruited Thailand/ Malaya	Trained Penang. Tongkah Dredge/Nawng Pet Tin (Ronpibon). AKA Patillo/AG Patullo. Interned Bangkok. Recovered.
O.2703	PETERS, Edward Valentine	Quentin	Civilian/sergeant	Recruited III Corps Malaya; originally recruited London	Trained STS101. Cover: Shift Engineer, Pinyok Tin Mine. OC cell Pinyok. Kampong Toh Tin Mine massacre survivor. Interned Changi. Death confirmed Changi *c.*1943.
O.2005	PFORTDEN, PB	NA	Nominal roll only	Inactive	AKA Pfoedten/Pfordten. Interned Bangkok. Recovered.
O.2650	POWELL, George	Conrad	Civilian/sergeant	Recruited III Corps Malaya	Trained Penang. Engineer Huey Mot/Yot Bandinlan Tin Mines. MIA (Kantang 10/12/41). Death confirmed. Place unknown.
O.2702	RAVENWOOD, George Albert	Roy	Civilian/sergeant	Recruited Singapore/Thailand	Trained STS101. MIA. Cover: Shift Engineer Pinyok Tin Mine. 8/12/41 part of STS Scapula staff. Involved in military vehicle incident and later interned Singapore. Recovered.
O.2603	REDFORD, AR	Peggotty	Civilian/sergeant	Recruited Thailand/ Malaya	Trained STS101. AKA AR Radford. Ronpibon Tin. OC cell Ronpibon. Interned Bangkok. Recovered.
O.2609	REGAN, Daniel	Chuckster	Civilian/sergeant	Recruited III Corps Malaya	Trained Penang. MIA. Kantang (10/12/41). Executed Lamsai Beach, Singora, between 13 and 16 December 1941.
O.2005	RICHARDSON, NA	NA	Nominal roll only	Inactive	AKA WA Richardson. Interned Bangkok. Recovered.
O.2611	SARRELL, RG	Sherlock	Civilian/sergeant	Recruited Thailand/ Malaya	Huey Mott (Thai Tin Syndicate). Interned Bangkok. Recovered.

SOE No.	Name	Codename	Rank/ Field Rank	Recruitment Place	Miscellaneous
O.2008	SMALL, H	NA	Nominal roll only	Inactive	Reported to have disappeared possibly escaped. NFI.
O.2705	THOMAS, Harding John	Durward	Civilian/sergeant	Recruited Thailand/ Malaya	Pinyok Tin Mine, Mine Superintendent. Death confirmed. Kampong Toh Tin Mine massacre 13/12/41.
O.2604	TURNER, R Keith	Dorritt	Civilian/sergeant	Recruited Thailand/ Malaya	OC cell Ronpibon. Interned Bangkok. Recovered.
O.2500	WEIR, THOMAS R	Tommy	A/Captain GL (211179)	Recruited Malaya	Eastern manager, Thai Tin Syndicate (ESOY), Penang. Confirmed drowned while escaping from Burma 24/6/42.
O.2802	WHITEHEAD, George	George	NFI	NFI	NFI
O.2501	WHITTAKER, AH	Jimmy	NFI	NFI	NFI
O.2605	WRIGHT, ES	Heep	Sergeant (2321201)	Recruited London or Malaya	Royal Signals. Death erroneously reported June 1944. Interned Bangkok as civilian. Tin miner cover intact. Recovered. Operation Scapula, Puma and Cleeves.
O.2620	WRIGHT, Herbert Charles	Brownlow	Civilian/sergeant	Recruited III Corps Malaya	Trained Penang. MIA (Kantang 10/12/41). Executed Lamsai Beach, Singora, between 13 and 16 December 1941.

Other SOE Operatives Southern Thailand

SOE No.	Name	Codename	Rank/ Field Rank	Recruitment Place	Miscellaneous
O.217	COYNE, T	Doyle	A/2LT (237197) GL		See O.2612.
O.216	CUMMINS, Horace Travis	Fergus	LT (205699) GL (ISRB)	Recruited London or Malaya	AKA Cummings. Death erroneously reported. Kampong Toh Massacre (13/12/41) survivor. Cover Plantation Manager Yala Rubber Estates intact. Interned Bangkok, Recovered.
O.214	HATTON, WJ		A/LT	Singapore	Died heart failure/exhaustion while escaping from Burma.
O.8642	HIGGINS, David H				MIA. Interned. Possibly part of unknown Ottoway Mission Thai-Burma border. Recovered.
O.210	KINGDON-WARD, Frank				July 1941 OC scoping/talent scounting mission. Evacuated.
O.212	RICHARDSON, WA			Recruited London	MIA. Interned. Recovered.
O.211	WINDRED, George Loftus		A/Captain (183201)	Recruited London	Interned Bangkok. Cover Journalist intact. Recovered.

Recruited But Not in Thailand

SOE No.	Name	Codename	Rank/ Field Rank	Recruitment Place	Miscellaneous
	BRISTOW, FJ	'V'			MIA Malaya with O.2651 by O.505
	CUMMINS				Operative number not assigned. Brother of Horace T Cummins.
	JOYNSON, AL	'U'			
	MARTIN, J	'T'			
	REGAN, J	'W'	Civilian/2/LT	Unknown SIS operation	Operative number not assigned. Confirmed death Malaya.
	STORKEY, RJ				

Compilation Sources:
NAA: A981 DEF 613 Defence Stranded Australians D Higgins.
TNA FO 369/3697 Siam 1946 File No. 9113
TNA HS1/111 Far East Malaya Casualties – OM Personnel – Tin Miners.
TNA HS1/112 Far East Malayan Casualties – OM Personnel – Tin Miners, OM: Casualties in the Far East 1943-1946 Annex
TNA HS 1/115 SOE Far East: Malaya No. 76, vol. 2 Subject: Far East Malaya General Intelligence; Policy; Progress Reports.

Acknowledgements

There are many who have helped me in this writing journey, but there are some who deserve credit where credit is due. That begins with thanking a group of fishermen on the east Malaysian coast at Terengganu Beach, who first sparked my curiosity about a local myth of hungry wartime European ghosts lingering in the jungles of the Thai-Malaysia border, to an old craftsman in Penang, who shared stories he had heard about wartime massacres in Southern Thailand of tin miners soon after Japan's wartime invasion. Putting pen to paper is one thing, but producing good work is another, and I have to in the first instance thank the wonderful staff at Pen & Sword for that, but more importantly, my many thanks for the professionalism, support and guidance of Tara Moran, Harriet Fielding and numerous others for helping me in this endeavour. I also thank the staff both at The National Archives in Kew and the National Archives of Australia in Canberra, for their respective and attentive aid in putting up with some of my more challenging information requests, and who at all times went out of their way to help me track down obscure and often well hidden archival information crucial to my research. Many thanks also go to Paul McCue, the SOE Historical Association's archivist who patiently offered his salient guidance, support and help along the way. To Patsy and John Kitchen, and HM Bertie, who went out of their way to ensure the mad woman writing fervently in their loft from dusk to dawn was well looked after, I can only offer much well deserved praise, affection and the promised fulfilment of my end of the bargain, by cooking a mouth watering haunch of venison for dinner. None of this would have even been made possible without the absolute support provided by Lieutenant Commander Edward CC Smith, RAN, boat driver, bad golfer and all round good egg.

My deepest and heartfelt thanks however, go to Steve and Ally Wright, Klaas du Randt and Venessa De Boer, for granting me access and allowing me the privilege of glimpsing into what remain private, personal and painful family wartime histories, of fathers and grandfathers and uncles who never came home. I thank you for your faith and trust in me, and I hope that I have been able to lay some of those hidden unknown historical demons to rest.

Kate Reid-Smith

Bibliography

Personal Archives

Courtesy De Boer Family Collection
Courtesy Wright Family Collection

Books, Journals and Other Publications

Beevor, JG, *SOE Recollections and Reflections 1940–45*. London: The Bodley Head, 1981.

Bell, Philip MH, *A Certain Eventuality: Britain and the Fall of France*. Farnborough: Saxon House, 1974.

Blackburn, Kevin, 'The Collective Memory of the Sook Ching Massacre and the Creation of the Civilian War Memorial of Singapore'. *Journal of the Malaysian Branch of the Royal Asiatic Society*. Vol. 73, No. 2 (279) (2000) 71–90, www.jstor.org/stable/41493428 (accessed 3 September 2023).

Carswell, Richard, 'France in 1940 in British Eyes; London-Paris, 1918–2018: Revisiting Franco-British Relations' (Paris-Londres, 1918–2018 : les relations franco-britanniques revisitées) XXVII-1. *Open Edition Journals* (2022). https://doi.org/10.4000/rfcb.8492 (accessed 21 November 2023).

Chang, Iris, *The Rape of Nanking: The Forgotten Holocaust of World War II.* New York: Basic Books, 2011.

Cheng, Goh Eck, (ed), *Thomas Kitching, Life and Death in Changi: the war and internment diary of Thomas Kitching (1942–1944).* Singapore: Landmark Books, 2002.

Cruickshank, Charles, *SOE in the Far East*. Oxford: Oxford University Press, 1983.

Chung, Ong Chit, 'Major General William Dobbie and the Defence of Malaya, 1935–38'. *Journal of Southeast Asian Studies*. Vol. 17, No. 2 (Sep., 1986), 282–306.

'D/S Hafthor'. www.warsailors.com/singleships/hafthor.html (accessed 4 November 2023).

Dreifort, John E, 'Japan's Advance into Indochina, 1940: The French Response'. *Journal of Southeast Asian Studies*. Vol. 13, No. 2 (Sep., 1982) www.jstor.org/stable/20070499 (accessed 21 November 2023).

Ferguson, Niall, *Empire: How Britain Made the Modern World.* London: Penguin Books, 2003.

Flood, E Thadeus, 'The 1940 Franco-Thai Border Dispute and Phibuun Sonkhraam's Commitment to Japan'. *Journal of Southeast Asian History*. Vol. 10, No. 2 (Sep., 1969) www.jstor.org/stable/20067747 (accessed 21 November 2023).

Francis, Ric & Colin Ganley, *Penang Trams, Trolley Buses & Railways, Municipal Transport History 1880s–1963*. Penang: Areca Books, 2006.

Gough, Richard, *SOE Singapore 1941–42*. London: William Kimber & Co. Ltd, 1985.

Gough, Richard, *The Escape from Singapore*. Singapore: SNP Editions Pte Ltd, 2000.

'Hafthor SS (1921–1941) Niyo Maru (+1942)'. https://wrecksite.eu (accessed 2 November 2023).

Hebditch, David, *Covert Radio Agents 1939–1945*. Yorkshire: Pen & Sword, 2023.

Hembry, Boris, *Malayan Spymaster.* Singapore: Monsoon Books, 2017.

Hong, Tan Kim, *The Chinese in Penang: A Pictorial History.* Penang: Areca Books, 2007.

Howarth, Patrick, *Undercover The Men and Women of the SOE*. London: Arrow Books Ltd, 1990.

Kee, Onn Chin, *Malaya Upside Down*. Kuala Lumpur: Federal Publications Sdn. Bhd, 1976.

Krause, Richard Lee, 'The Iron and Steel Industry in Wartime Japan, 1931–1945'. Master of Arts Thesis, Oklahoma State University, 1972.

Magness, Maureen, Evidentiary Document No. 5156, Summary of Examination of Maureen Joy Margaret Magness, Bangkok, 8 January 1945, www.legal-tools.org/doc/6cd2b9 (accessed 11 August 2021).

Malaya Tribune, 10 May 1941. NewspaperSG.

Milton, Giles, *Churchill's Ministry of Ungentlemanly Warfare*. New York: Picador, 2016.

Moynahan, Brian, *Jungle Soldier*. London: Quercus, 2009.

New Straits Times, 10 May 2022, www.nst.com.my/news/nation/2022/05/794880/house-tin-built (accessed 28 September 2023). NewspaperSG.

Nicolson, Nigel. (ed), *Harold Nicolson Diaries and Letters 1930–1939.* London: Collins, 1996.

'Phu Quoc Island', in www.lonelyplanet.com/vietnam/mekong-delta/phu-quoc-island (accessed 9 September 2023).

Piccigallo, Phillip R, *The Japanese on Trial: Allied War Crimes Operations in the East.* Austin: University of Texas Press, 1979.

Pramoj, MR Seni, The Hon, 'Thailand and Japan'. *Far Eastern Survey.* Vol. 12, No. 21 (20 Oct 1943) 204-208 https://doi.org/10.2307/3022873 (accessed 26 October 2024)

Rönnbäck, Klas, Brobert, Oskar and Stefania Galli, 'A colonial cash cow: the return on investments in British Malaya, 1889-1969'. *Cliometrica.* chrome-extension://efaidnbmnnnibpcajpcglclefindmkaj/http://eprints.lse.ac.uk/112145/1/Galli_a_colonial_cash_cow_published.pdf (accessed 26 October 2024) pdf e-prints LSE

Santaputra, Charivat, 'Thai Foreign Policy 1932–1942'. PhD Thesis, Southampton University, 1982.

Simson, Ivan. *Singapore Too Little, Too Late*. London: Leo Cooper, 1970.

Steinberg, David Joel (ed), *In Search of Southeast Asia A Modern History*. Revised Edition, Sydney: Allen & Unwin, 1987.

Swan, William L, 'Japan's Intentions for Its Greater East Asia Co-Prosperity Sphere as Indicated in Its Policy Plans for Thailand.'. *Journal of Southeast Asian Studies*. 27, No. 1 (1996): 139–49. www.jstor.org/stable/20071764 (accessed 7 June 2023).

Swan, William L, 'The Imperial Japanese Consulate in Songkhla, Thailand'. *Journal of Asia-Pacific Studies*. (Waseda University) No. 43 (February 2022). www.jstage.jst.go.jp/article/wiapstokyu/43/0/43_1/pdf (accessed 7 June 2023).

Tantalum Producers International Study Center, *Quarterly Bulletin*. Issue No. 33, March 1983, First Quarter, 2-3,tanb.org/images/Bulletin33.pdf (accessed 28 November 2023).

The Mail (Adelaide SA), 20 December 1941, Trove.

The Singapore Free Press and Mercantile Advertiser, (1884–1942). 4 October 1933. NewspaperSG.

Thomas, RT, *Britain and Vichy: The Dilemma of Anglo-French Relations 1940-42*. New York: St Martin's Press, 1979.

Townsville Daily Bulletin, 29 April 1941. Trove.

Tsuji, Masanobu, *Singapore: The Japanese Version*. New York: St Martin's Press, 1961.

United Nations War Crimes Commission (UNWCC) Military Court for the Trial of War Criminals, 2/LT. Murakami Shuji of the Imperial Japanese Army, [Trial against Murakami Shuji] Trial Report, DJAG SEALF Case No. 65082, UNWCC10.csv; 528, Kuala Lumpur, dated 1-2/7/46 https://www.legal-tools.org/eng/browse/record/f1045 (accessed 23 January 2018)

Ward, Ian, *Snaring the Tiger*. Singapore: Media Masters Pte, Ltd, 1996.

Wilkinson, Peter and Bright Astley, Joan, *Gubbins & SOE*. London: Leo Cooper, 1997.

Wright, Arnold, *Twentieth century impressions of British Malaya: its history, people, commerce, industries, and resources*. London: Lloyds Greater Britain Publishing Company, Limited, 1908.

Yellen, Jeremy A, *The Greater East Asia Co-Prosperity Sphere: When Total Empire Met Total War*. Ithaca: Cornell University Press, 2019.

The National Archives (United Kingdom)

AIR 23/4636 Operation Matador

AIR 81/10852 Flight Lieutenant JAB Dobson, Sergeant GW Smith, Sergeant EFW Fowler; missing believed killed; aircraft shot down and crashed near Singora, Siam, Blenheim V5931, 34 Squadron, 11 December 1941; Sergeant A Mc Johnstone, Flying Officer PN Kingwill, Sergeant GW Gregory: prisoners of war: aircraft shot down and crashed near Singora, Siam, Blenheim V5598, 34 Squadron, 11 December 1941

CAB 101/164 War Cabinet and Cabinet Office: Historical Section, SW Kirby, The War Against Japan, Volume 1

CAB 106/53 Colonel AML Harrison, 11 Ind. Div. Malaya, Chapters I-IV

CAB 106/54 Colonel AML Harrison, 11 Ind. Div. Malaya, Chapters V-X

CAB 121/317 SOE activities in India and the Far East, 1941–1945

FO 369/3697 Siam 1946 File No. 9113

FO 371/154030 General Correspondence from 1906-1966 WESTERN (W): German (WG)

HS 1/69 Siam: Top Level Planning Tin Destruction

HS 1/111 Far East: Malaya, Casualties – OM Personnel – Tin Miners

HS 1/112 Far East Malaya Casualties – OM Personnel – Tin Miners, OM

HS 1/115 SOE Far East: Malaya No. 76, vol. 2 General Intelligence: policy; progress reports

HS 1/169 Special Operations Executive: Far East

HS 1/207 SOE Far East India/General No. 131 vol. 3 Subject: Far East: India/General History of SOE Oriental Mission Killery Mission, 26/2/41-4/10/44

HS 1/212 SOE Far East: India/General No. 134 Vol. 2

HS 1/226 Special Operations Executive. Far East: India/General No. 143 Volume 1

HS 1/348 AD/SI Far East SOE in Thailand

HS 7/51 Training Section 1940–1945 Industrial Sabotage Training 1941–1945

HS 9/839/5 Valentine St John Killery, SOE Record

PREM 3/169/1 1941 Far East (Principle Telegrams)

WO 106/2441 Malaya: Reports and Correspondence

WO 106/2506 Operations 'Matador' and 'Sandwich' 1 August 1941 - 30 November 1941

WO 106/2509 Operation 'Etonian' 1 December 1941–31 December 1941

WO 106/2540 Operations of Malaya Command 8 Dec 41–15 Feb 42

WO 193/602 Denny's Mission (204 Military Mission)

WO 193/606 MO1 Collation File SOE Far Eastern Series, SOE/FE/4 Thailand

WO 193/631 MO1 Collation SOE Series General

WO 208/1905 Thailand CH. II Geography 202 Topographical Description by Provinces (b) South Thailand 26 April 1941

WO 208/2838 Far East Not South East Asian Command, Japan

WO 325/54 Sadao Case

WO 325/75 Singora, Siam Killing of POW's 1 March 1946–31 March 1947

WO 325/93 Execution of Europeans in Singora 1941–1942 Witness Statements

Royal Botanical Gardens Kew Archive

Kingdon-Ward, Frank. RMI, Frank Kingdon-Ward Papers, Registered File 2/IND/60

National Archives of Australia

A981 DEF 613 Defence Stranded Australians, D Higgins

A989 1943/520/2 Malaya – Malayan Research Bureau, 8a Castlereagh Street, Sydney, Revised List 15 February 1943 [37 pages]

A989 1943/80/9/7 Australian Legation to Japan

A1066 IC45/20/1/71/ Protection of Australian Nationals Abroad. Repatriation and Relief Payments. Thailand

A1608 AC47/1/1 Tin ore from Thailand 1940–1941

A3317 442/1946 Yala Incident [re Japanese atrocities against British civilians (mining company personnel) at Yala, South Thailand, in December 1941]

A3978 KUSKIE, B., Officers (RANVR [Royal Australian Naval Volunteer Reserve]) personal record

A6769, KUSKIE B, enlistment details

M 1455, 74 [Personal Papers of Prime Minister Chifley] Correspondence 'H', Part 3 [EV Hill - Horan Bros Garage (Bathurst), includes representations from Hinchinbrook Shire Council, EJ Holloway (Minister for Labour and National Services) and relating to reported death of Norman Holt at Yala (Southern Thailand), Clear Vale field firing range (Bathurst)] [255 pages].

MP729/6 22/401/253 Japan Reports from Australian Legation Tokyo

Notes

Chapter 1

1. Peter Wilkinson and Joan Bright Astley, *Gubbins & SOE* (London: Leo Cooper, 1997) 75.
2. TNA HS7/51 Training Section 1940–1945 Industrial Sabotage Training 1941–1945, Report on the Development of Industrial Sabotage Training at STS17 August 1941–August 1944, Chapter 1, 2. Giles Milton, *Churchill's Ministry of Ungentlemanly Warfare* (New York: Picador, 2016) 87.
3. Milton, *Churchill's Ministry*, 87. HS7/51, Report, II, 6.
4. Wilkinson and Astley, *Gubbins*, 76-8, 85. JG Beevor, *SOE Recollections and Reflections 1940–45* (London: The Bodley Head, 1981) 7.
5. HS7/51, Report STS 17, Chapter II, 2.
6. HS7/51, Report STS 17, 1, 1.
7. HS7/51, Report STS 17, 1, 1. HS7/51, Report STS 17, II, 2.
8. Rönnbäck, Klas, Brobert, Oskar and Stefania Galli, 'A colonial cash cow: the return on investments in British Malaya, 1889-1969'. Cliometrica. chrome-extension://efaidnbmnnnibpcajpcglclefindmkaj/http://eprints.lse.ac.uk/112145/1/Galli_a_colonial_cash_cow_published.pdf accessed 26/10/24 pdf e-prints LSE 150. Arnold Wright, *Twentieth century impressions of British Malaya: its history, people, commerce, industries, and resources* (London: Lloyds Greater Britain Publishing Company, Limited, 1908) 674.
9. Niall Ferguson, *Empire: How Britain Made the Modern World* (London: Penguin Books, 2003) 241.

Chapter 2

1. At the time Britain's focus centred around the potential impact of the emergence of the Vichy Government on French colonies in

Africa, especially as Germany was continuing its sweep into North Africa. French colonies elsewhere hardly rated a mention. Richard Carswell, 'France in 1940 in British Eyes', in London-Paris, 1918–2018: Revisiting Franco-British Relations (Paris-Londres, 1918–2018: les relations franco-britanniques revisitées), XXVII-1, *Open Edition Journals*, 2022, https://doi.org/10.4000/rfcb.8492 (accessed 21 November 2023). Philip MH Bell, *A Certain Eventuality: Britain and the Fall of France* (Farnborough, Saxon House, 1974), 31. RT Thomas, Britain and Vichy: The Dilemma of Anglo-French Relations 1940–42 (New York, St Martin's Press, 1979) 29.

2. King Chulalongkorn did the same in 1909 when he signed the Bangkok Treaty with Britain, essentially relinquishing Thailand's claims to sovereignty and ceding its southernmost frontier provinces of Kedah, Kelantan, Perlis and Terengganu. E Thadeus Flood, 'The 1940 Franco-Thai Border Dispute and Phibun Sonkhraam's Commitment to Japan', in *Journal of Southeast Asian History*, Vol. 10, No. 2 (Sep., 1969) www.jstor.org/stable/20067747 (accessed 21 November 2023) 305.
3. David P Chandler, William R Roff, John RW Smail, David Joel Steinberg, Robert H Taylor, Alexander Woodside, David K Wyatt, David Joel Steinberg (ed.), 'Siam' in *In Search of Southeast Asia, A Modern History*, Revised Edition (Sydney: Allen & Unwin, 1987) 330.
4. Charivat Santaputra, 'Thai Foreign Policy 1932–1942' (PhD Thesis, Southampton University, 1982) 201.
5. Santaputra, Thai Foreign Policy, 1982, 201.
6. Santaputra, Foreign Policy, 201.
7. Santaputra, Foreign Policy, 202.
8. John E Dreifort, 'Japan's Advance into Indochina, 1940: The French Response', in *Journal of Southeast Asian Studies*, Vol. 13, No. 2 (Sep., 1982), www.jstor.org/stable/20070499 (accessed November, 21) 279.
9. Dreifort, 'Japan's Advance into Indochina,' 281.
10. It was essentially Japan's attempt to establish a pan-Asian union under its tutelage, and create a new non-Western world order for the region. Jeremy A Yellen, *The Greater East Asia Co-Prosperity Sphere: When Total Empire Met Total War* (Ithaca: Cornell University Press, 2019) 76.
11. The Hon. MR Seni Pramoj, 'Thailand and Japan', in *Far Eastern Survey*, Vol. 12, No. 21 (Oct 20, 1943) https://doi.org/10.2307/3022983, www.jstor.org/stable/3022873 (accessed 23 November 2023) 204.

12. TNA WO 325/75 Singora, Siam Killing of POW's 1 March 1946 – 31 March 1947, Summary of Examination Dr Sam Thomas, Haadyai, 21 July 1946, 2.
13. WO 325/75 Thomas, Statement, 21/7/42, 1.
14. WO 325/75 Thomas, 21/7/46, 1.

Chapter 3

1. NAA: A981 DEF 613 Defence Stranded Australians, D Higgins, Letter Director Sakioka Yuasa Trading Co., Limited to Messrs. Nawng Pet Tin Limited, Nakorn Srithamaraj, Thailand, Subject: Importation Tin Ore and Tungsten Ore to Japan, dated Kobe, (sic) June 2nd 1941.
2. A981 DEF 613 Letter AHW/CS Nawng Pet Tin. Ltd to Yuasa Trading Co., Ltd, Kobe, Japan, Subject: Importation Tin Ore and Tungsten Ore to Japan dated 19 July 1941.
3. Richard Lee Krause, 'The Iron and Steel Industry in Wartime Japan, 1931–1945' (Master of Arts Thesis, Oklahoma State University, 1972), 20.
4. Harold Nicolson, (Nigel Nicolson, ed.), *Harold Nicolson Diaries and Letters 1930–1939* (London: Collins, 1996) 404.
5. TNA WO 106/2509 Operation 'Etonian' 1 December 1941– 31 December 1941, Memo MO.10 to unknown dated 7/4/41.

Chapter 4

1. WO 106/2509 Cipher No.184 Sir R Craigie (Tokyo) to DDMO dated 4/2/41, 1.
2. WO 106/2509 Cipher No. 248 Foreign Office to Sir J Crosby (Bangkok) dated 17/11/40. WO 106/2509 Cipher No. 93 Foreign Office to Sir J Crosby (Bangkok) dated 23/2/41.
3. WO 106/2509 Craigie, Cipher 184, 4/2/41, 1. TNA HS 1/212 SOE Far East: India General No. 134 Vol. 2 Letter 45/203/41 J Crosby, British Legation Bangkok to Valentine St. J. Killery, etc., etc., etc., c/- Far East Mission, Ministry of Economic Warfare, Singapore dated 31 October 1941. HS 1/212 K/L.6 to CD, AD, ADW O/X, O Subject: Report on Far East Mission dated 16/12/41, 6-8.
4. Originating during the First World War, the 'Maginot Line' euphemism describes a defensive barrier or conceptual defensive strategy inspiring

a false sense of security, often abrogating or downplaying external threat perceptions. WO 106/2509 Craigie, 4/2/41, 2.

5. NAA: MP729/6, 22/401/253 Japan Reports from Australian Legation Tokyo.
6. NAA: A989, 1943/80/9/7 Australian Legation to Japan.
7. WO 106/2509 Cipher No. 50019 War Office to CIC (FE) dated 3/2/41.
8. WO 106/2509 CICFE, Annex B Estimated Requirements in Land Forces When the RAF have Reached Their Full Strength, 1-2.
9. WO 106/2509, Annex B, Estimated Requirements, 3.
10. WO 106/2509 Cipher No. 15568 CIC (FE) to War Office dated 8/2/41, 1.
11. WO 106/2509 Cipher No. 17087 GOC Malaya to War Office dated 24/3/41, 1.
12. WO 106/2509 Memo MO.10 to DMO&P., DF., DDMO (O) dated 7/4/41.
13. WO 106/2509 Cipher No. 60517 War Office to GOC Malaya dated 8/4/41.
14. WO 106/2509 Memo MO.10 to DMO&P, 7/4/41.
15. TNA AIR 23/4636 Operation Matador Cipher 228/4 (WX.2347) CCFE to War Office dated 7/8/41.
16. TNA HS 1/348 AD/SI Far East SOE in Thailand, Cipher 68454 M.O.10 War Office to CICFE dated 27/5/41.
17. TNA WO 193/606 MOI Collation File SOE Far Eastern Series, SOE/FE/4 Thailand, Cipher 68454 War Office MO(10) to CIC FE dated 24/5/41.
18. WO 193/606 Cipher 8591 War Office MO(10) to CIC FE dated 24/5/41.
19. TNA HS 1/207 SOE Far East India/General No 131 vol 3 Subject: Far East: India/General History of SOE Oriental Mission Killery Mission, 26/2/41-4/10/44, Cipher 59 Governor OAG to 235 (Singapore and Straits Settlements) and 161 (Hong Kong) dated 26 Feb 41.

Chapter 5

1. TNA HS 9/839/5 Valentine St John Killery, SOE Record, Memo JDK/OR/657 Major JD Kennedy ISRB to DDSD War Office dated 26/5/41. 'Economic Warfare: Mission for S'pore' in *Malaya Tribune*, 10 May 1941, 2, NewspaperSG. 'Government House', in *The Singapore Free Press and Mercantile Advertiser* (1884-1942), 4 October 1933, 6, NewspaperSG.
2. TNA CAB 121/317 SOE activities in India and the Far East, 1941–1945, Letter War Office to Colonel LC Hollis War Cabinet Offices dated 23/3/41.

3. HS 1/207 Cipher No. 59 sender unidentified London to Governor Straits Settlements and OAG Hong Kong dated 26/2/41. TNA HS 1/115 Special Operations Executive Far East: Malaya General Intelligence; policy; progress reports, O. 105, Report, Subject: Oriental Mission Operations in Malaya April 1942, dated 8 May 1942, 2-3, f.76.
4. HS 1/207 Cipher No. 236 sender unidentified London to Governor Straits Settlements dated 26/2/41.
5. Brian Moynahan, *Jungle Soldier* (London: Quercus, 2009) 119.
6. It was not the first STS to offer unwelcomed training to non-Europeans. The Canadian STS207, for example, had been established to train operatives for various South American and Central American states, and, possibly, USA cohorts as well. The staff were to be a mix of Canadian and British. Listings of British personnel associated with the school are missing from the file. TNA WO 193/631 MO1 Collation SOE Series General, Minute MO1 to MO2 Subject: 207 Military Mission dated 30/10/41. WO 193/631 Minute MO1/BM/1480 MO1 to AG1(d) dated 13/11/41.
7. HS 1/207 Cipher No. 59, London, 26/2/41.
8. HS 1/207 Cipher 59, 26/2/41.
9. HS 1/207 Memo E1/FE/516 E1 to D/Army Subject: Supplies for the East (Puma Mission), 26/3/41. HS 1/207 Cable 56289 WO to CIC FE 14/3/41.
10. HS 1/207 Memo E1/FE/516 E1, Supplies, 26/3/41.
11. Patrick Howarth, *Undercover: the Men and Women of the SOE* (London: Arrow Books Ltd, 1990) 264.
12. When war broke out conscription was introduced immediately, and every male university student was regarded as a potential officer. The OTC's role was to train officers from those university students conscripted into the Army, and to provide basic training for those who remained behind as a Home Guard excepting in this case, Killery's picks. HS 9/839/5 Memo JDK/OR/657 Major JD Kennedy ISRB to DDSD War Office dated 26 May 1941. TNA HS 1/226 Special Operations Executive. Far East: India/General No. 143 Volume 1, Report on S.O.E. activities. Far East Reports (1-5) 1943–1945, Evacuation of Singapore Records – Memorandum, SC Miskin, Detailed Account Singapore Evacuation dated 12 February 1942. Royal Botanical Gardens Kew Archive, FKW, RMI, Frank Kingdon-Ward Papers, Registered File 2/IND/60 'A S Vernay' 1930s correspondence to and from Kingdon-Ward relating to the Burma expedition.
13. HS 1/207 Memo 314 Secretary of State to Governor of Burma dated 28/2/41, 3.

14. TNA HS 1/69 Siam: Top Level Planning Tin Destruction, Note, Mr V. St J Killery dated 28/2/41.
15. HS 1/69 Note, Killery dated 28/2/41.
16. HS 9/839/5 Letter The Borneo Company Ltd to V St. John Killery, Esq., MEW dated 2/4/41.
17. HS 9/839/5 Letter Officer of Commander-in-Chief Western Approaches to V. St. J. Killery MEW dated 7/4/41.
18. HS 1/69 Memo O/FE/592 O. to AD/F Subject: Report on Special Operations dated 27/11/41.
19. HS 1/207 Memo Responsibility For and Liaison With the Killery Mission dated 7/5/41, 1.
20. HS 1/207 Memo, Liaison Killery Mission, 7/5/41, 1. Boris Hembry, *Malayan Spymaster* (Singapore: Monsoon Books, 2017) 130.
21. Richard Gough, *The Escape from Singapore* (Singapore: SNP Editions Pte Ltd, 2000) 22.
22. Wilsons Promontory runs from southernmost Victoria into the Bass Strait. It was an ideal all-terrain fieldcraft teaching environment incorporating dense bushland, eucalypt forests, sand dunes and swamp, grasslands and rock, as well as the 2,500ft Mount Latrobe to hone climbing and ropework skills. In May 1941, the first STS-trained 1st Australian Company finished their training and began training others. HS 1/207 Memo, Liaison, Annex C 'No. 104 Mission to Australia & New Zealand'. Moynahan, *Jungle Soldier*, 115.
23. At the time, a large part of their training also included potentially defending against Communist Fifth Column activities, which in the aftermath of the Second World War would be exploited throughout the Malayan Emergency. HS 1/207 Liaison, Annex C.
24. HS 1/207 Memo, Liaison, Annex C 'No. 104 Mission to Australia & New Zealand'.

Chapter 6

1. Moynahan, *Jungle Soldier*, 114
2. TNA HS 1/169 Special Operations Executive: Far East Memo O/FE/618 from O. to AD/W Subject: SOE Activities dated 9/12/41.
3. HS 1/169 Memo O/FE/618, SOE Activities, 9/12/41.
4. HS 7/51 Report, STS17,14.
5. It seemed Percival and Brooke-Popham's collective requests were finally heard, but only after tensions with Japan in the Far East were escalating.

The War Office was finally despatching reinforcements from India in the hope that increased numbers might act as a deterrence to Japan. But due to the rapid expansion of the British Indian Army throughout 1940 and 1941, many of the Indian divisions lacked adequate training, and there was a massive shortage of experienced troops among them. Despite this, on 8 December 1941, Heath's III Corps consisted of Major-General Arthur Edward Barstow's 9th Infantry Division, and Major-General David Murray-Lyon's 11th Infantry Division. III Corps was also responsible for and the maintenance of northern Malaya's lines of communication area. AIR 23/4636 Cipher 26549 (WX.4989) GOC Malaya to War Office dated 2/12/41. TNA WO 208/2838 Far East Not South East Asian Command, Japan Cipher 17235 CICFE to War Office dated 26/3/41. WO 208/2838 Cipher 17858 CICFE to War Office dated 11/4/41. WO 208/2838 Cipher No. 300 Sir J Crosby to Foreign Office dated 13/5/41.

6. A 'legend' in intelligence terms is usually a claimed background, biography or personal history that is maintained on operations, and is often supported by documentary evidence or memorised details to protect the identity of the operative in question.
7. HS 1/348 Cipher 1138 SOE to Singapore dated 27/11/41.
8. HS 1/69 Captain Nixon OIC Special Operations Southern Thailand, 'Report on Special Operations in Southern Thailand', Singapore, dated 24 December 1941, 5.
9. HS 1/69, Nixon, Report, 24/12/41, 6.

Chapter 7

1. TNA CAB 101/164 War Cabinet and Cabinet Office: Historical Section, SW Kirby, *The War Against Japan*, Volume 1, Interviews with CM Burns; Brigadier EL Marsh-Kellet; Sir Alexander Newbolt; Admiral Sir Percy Noble; Brigadier PW Parker. CAB 101/164 Narratives on operations in Malaya, 1942. CAB 101/164 Report and account of a broadcast by FD Bisseker, Manager Eastern Smelting Company, Penang 1941. CAB 101/164, Major JC Westall RM, Report by SO (I) Singapore, dated 14 May 1942. WO 193/606 Cipher 149/3 CICFE to WO dated 28/5/41.
2. Moynahan, *Jungle Soldier*, 118. TNA WO 106/2506 Cipher 228/4 (WX.2347) CICFE to War Office dated 7/8/41.
3. HS 1/207 Memo, Liaison, Annex B. WO 106/2509 Cipher 50019 WO to CICFE dated 3/2/41. WO 106/2509 Cipher 16476 GOC Malaya to WO dated 4/12/41.

4. HS 1/69, Memo CXG.930 SO2 for OM dated 11/5/41. HS 1/69, Memo CXG.938 SO2 for OM dated 13/5/41.
5. Brooke-Popham had actually been tasked by the War Office and others to undertake preliminary discussions with his regional cohorts, including Crosby and equivalents on circumstances surrounding mounting any infiltration teams into border areas, which he had done, but for some reason had not sent any findings back to London. It seems he may have misunderstood that tasking with tacit approval from London to begin his own infiltration activities. WO 106/2509 Cipher 82341 MO. 10 WO to CIC (FE) dated 5/8/41. WO 106/2509 Cipher 441/4 CICFE to WO dated 28/8/41. WO 193/606 Cipher 149/3 CIC (FE), 28/5/41.
6. WO 193/606 Cipher 149/3 CIC (FE) 28/5/41.
7. TNA WO 208/1905 Thailand CH. II Geography 202 Topographical Description by Provinces (b) South Thailand 26 April 1941, 19.
8. HS 1/348 Cipher 68454 M.O.10 (WO) to CICFE dated 27/5/41.
9. HS 1/348 Cipher 68454 M.O.10 (WO) dated 27/5/41.
10. HS 1/348 Cipher 68454 27/5/41.
11. This was not the first time Brooke-Popham had been trying to become involved with other missions in the region. In March 1941, he had tried and failed to insert himself as an integral player into Brigadier General Lancelot E Denny's British Military Mission 204, also known as 'Tulip Force'. It was essentially a mission to train Chinese guerrillas to fight the Japanese. Brooke-Popham had been sending lengthy proposals out on an assortment of areas, including contracting out for supply and ammunition dumps, and the recruitment of personnel, all of which were promptly shut down by the War Office. CAB 121/317 Cipher unnumbered CICFE to WO 12/3/41. TNA WO 193/602 Denny's Mission (204 Military Mission) Cipher unnumbered MA Chungking to War Office dated 17/3/41. CAB 121/317 Cipher ?587 WO to CICFE dated 21/3/41. WO 193/606 Cipher 70559 MO1 (WO) to CIC FE dated 5/6/41. Richard Gough, *SOE Singapore 1941–42* (London: William Kimber & Co Ltd, 1985), 40.

Chapter 8

1. WO 193/606 Personal Letter FC Scott (WO) to Sterndale Bennet (FO) dated 8/6/41. WO 193/606 Cipher 70559 WO to CIC (FE) dated 5/6/41.
2. Like the scramble for Africa, there had also been the concomitant scramble for the Far East. Although Britain had the edge, having

inherited all of the vast British East India Company assets, expanding into northern Malaya was also inextricably entwined with extending an informal Empire. Pre-First World War commercial negotiations had pushed Thailand into accepting free trade agreements of benefit to Britain's foreign investment earnings, including ceding Thailand's four tin-rich southernmost provinces to Britain. Ferguson, *Empire*, 2003, 241, 245.

3. WO 193/606 Cipher 248/3 CIC (FE) to WO dated 13/6/41.
4. WO 193/606 Personal Letter Wing Commander Sir Frank Nelson (WO) to Lieutenant Colonel C Sugden (MO1) dated 19/6/41.

Chapter 9

1. WO 208/1905 Thailand, II, 1.
2. WO 208/1905 Thailand, II, 19.
3. Masanobu Tsuji, *Singapore: the Japanese Version*, Margaret Lake trans. (Sydney: Ure Smith, 1960) 6.
4. 'Tin Mining in Thailand', in *Townsville Daily Bulletin*, Tuesday, 29 April 1941 (accessed online 11 November 2023) 4. Trove.
5. WO 208/1905 Thailand, II, 19.
6. WO 106/2509 M.O. 10 Note on Operations in the Kra Isthmus Extracts from Telegrams dated 3/12/41.
7. AIR 23/4636 Operation Matador (Malaya) Cipher 26549 GOC Malaya to War Office dated 2/12/41.
8. WO 106/2509 Cipher 26626 GOC Malaya to War Office dated 4/12/42.

Chapter 10

1. Towards the end of 1941, there were now two SOE tin mine denial schemes in play in the Far East. One was the Kailin Mines in China, now known as Operation Conway, and the other in Thailand as Operation Cleeves. Southern Thailand's tin denial schemes were to be a civilian-only affair with ostensibly no military involvement. The destruction of soft coal mines in northern China was supposed to follow suit, but Japan's invasion of Thailand was now raising serious doubts as to whether they should go ahead or not. HS 1/69, Memo O/E/592 O. to AD/F dated 27 November 1941. HS 1/69, Memo D/CE 1 to O. dated 12 December 1941. HS 1/69 Memo O/E/592 from O. to AD/F dated

27 November 1941. HS 1/69 Memo O/FE/619 from O. to D/CE 1 dated 9 December 1941, Subject: Code Names.
2. HS 1/169 Memo O/FE/618 from O. to AD/W Subject: SOE Activities dated 9 December 1941.
3. HS 1/69 Cipher No.SO2/11 O.100 to SO2 dated 28/7/41.
4. HS 1/69 Letter John Keswick (MEW) to NE Young Esq., dated 12 May 1941.

Chapter 11

1. Ivan Simson, *Singapore: Too Little, Too Late* (London: Leo Cooper, 1970) 120.
2. Only a few years earlier Dobbie had tasked his then Chief Staff Officer, Percival, with drawing up a tactical analysis of Malaya's defence should Japan plan to attack Singapore from the north. What emerged a year later in 1937 was a scenario that northern Malaya could become a frontier battlespace, and the east coast the front-line battlefield. Ong Chit Chung, 'Major General William Dobbie and the Defence of Malaya, 1935–38', in *Journal of Southeast Asian Studies*, Vol. 17, No. 2 (Sep., 1986), 282-306. TNA WO 106/2441 Malaya: Reports and Correspondence Letter Major General William Dobbie, GOC Malaya to Brigadier DF Anderson, Directorate of Military Operations and Intelligence WO, dated 17/3/36.
3. CAB 101/164 Report by FD Bisseker, General Manager in the East of Eastern Smelting Co. Ltd, Penang (undated) Covering Period 7 December 1941 to 5 May 1942. CAB 101/164 FD Bisseker, Transcript, Radio Broadcast, Saturday, 20 December 1941.
4. Birch House was named for the former British Resident Perak, Ernest Woodford Birch, who was also the first chairman of the Eastern Smelting Company. In the 1930s it became the company's main administration headquarters in Malaya. In 2023 the former residence was home to an international fast food restaurant chain. 'The house that tin built', in *New Straits Times*, 10 May 2022, www.nst.com.my/news/nation/2022/05/794880/house-tin-built, [accessed 28 September 2023]. Tantalum Producers International Study Center, *Quarterly Bulletin*, Issue No. 33, March 1983, First Quarter, 2-3, tanb.org/images/Bulletin33.pdf [accessed 28 September 2023]. HS 1/69 Nixon, Report, 24/12/41, 6.

5. The site of the smelting factory is now an apartment block. Tan Kim Hong, *The Chinese in Penang: A Pictorial History* (Penang: Areca Books, 2007) 103. Ric Francis & Colin Ganley, *Penang Trams, Trolley Buses & Railways, Municipal Transport History 1880s–1963* (Penang: Areca Books, 2006) 91-95.
6. CAB 101/164 Bisseker, Report, (undated), 2.
7. CAB 101/164 Bisseker, Report, 3.
8. HS 1/169 Cipher 6073 SOE/733 to ACSS Only dated 14/11/41.
9. CAB 101/164 Bisseker, Report, 2-3.
10. HS 1/69 Letter Thomas R Weir to Chas. A Underwood, Esq., Secretary, Thai Tin Syndicate Ltd dated 18/8/41.
11. HS 1/69 Note SO2/186 SO2 to OM dated 9/9/41. HS 1/69 Memo DJSA/FZ/843 Major DJ Stopford Adams to RE Brook, Esq., dated 9/9/41. HS 1/69 Memo SC/2760/69.7 R Brook to O. dated 16/9/41.
12. Charles Cruickshank, *SOE in the Far East* (Oxford: Oxford University Press, 1983) 68.
13. HS 1/69 Cipher SO2/186 SO2 to OM dated 9/9/41.
14. HS 1/348 Cipher 68454 M.O.10 to CICFE 27/5/41.
15. HS 1/69, Weir to Underwood, 18/8/41.

Chapter 12

1. NAA:A1608,AC47/1/1 Tin ore from Thailand 1940-1941, Memorandum 3/250 WE Antrobus UK High Commissioner Canberra to F Strahan, Prime Minister's Department Subject: Tin Denial: Thailand, dated 28 August 1941.
2. Reports vary as to this timing. Anecdotal reports suggest the various operational phases would either begin when the various songs were heard in different places as they began playing on the radio, or it may have been when the song finished.

Chapter 13

1. HS 1/69, Nixon, Report, 24/12/41, 6. TNA HS 1/111 M Kain on list of casualties O.2600, note in red says left SOE Dec 1941 Ref/O/FE/1015 dated 13/6/42.
2. HS 1/69, Nixon, 24/12/41.
3. HS 1/69, Nixon, 24/12/41.

Chapter 14

1. HS 1/69 Nixon, Report, 24/12/41, 1.
2. HS 1/348 Cipher 1138 Cipher SOE London to Singapore dated 27/11/41.
3. HS 1/348 Cipher 6139 SOE FE (Singapore) to ACSS Only SOE dated 26/11/41. HS 1/348 Cipher 6138 O.M. Singapore to ACSS Only SOE dated 26/11/41.
4. HS 1/69 WJ Parsons, Report on Special Operations carried out at Puket (sic) 8.12.41 to 10.12.41, 1.

Chapter 15

1. Tsuji, *Singapore*, 24.
2. Located in the Gulf of Thailand, Phú Quốc is now one of the largest five-star tourist destination islands in Vietnam. 'Phu Quoc Island', in www.lonelyplanet.com/vietnam/mekong-delta/phu-quoc-island (accessed 9 September 2023). Tsuji, *Singapore*, 29.
3. Tsuji, *Singapore*, 61. WO 325/75 Summary of Examination of Colonel Hongo Takeshi, Changi Gaol, dated 19 March 1947.
4. WO 208/1905 Thailand Ch. II Geography South Thailand April 1941, 13.
5. Direction Finding (DF) was a way of using radio waves to determine the direction of a radio wave source, such as might be used on ships using radio transmitters while in transit. It differs from radar in that only the direction of the signal is determined on any given receiver, as opposed to radar, which can also provide distance and range as well. Two or more DF stations would use triangulation to determine the location of a single radio source. During the Second World War, DF was used by both Axis and Allied power to locate and direct aircraft, surface vessels and submarines. David Hebditch, *Covert Radio Agents 1939–1945* (Yorkshire: Pen & Sword, 2023) viii.
6. William L Swan, 'Japan's Intentions for Its Greater East Asia Co-Prosperity Sphere as Indicated in Its Policy Plans for Thailand.' *Journal of Southeast Asian Studies* 27, No. 1 (1996): 139–49. www.jstor.org/stable/20071764 (accessed 4 June 2023) 139.
7. Tsuji, *Singapore*, 61.
8. Tsuji, *Singapore*, 89.
9. Tsuji, *Singapore*, 79.
10. There is some debate as to whether this was Shigeharu Asaeda or Yutaka Asaeda, or indeed if they were the same person. Tsuji identifies him throughout his work as the latter. Tsuji, *Singapore*, 8.

11. Both Tsuji and Tadahiko would later be linked to Japan's Operation Dai Kensho. Known colloquially as the Sook Ching Massacre (Chinese Sùqīng meaning 'to cleanse'), it was a twelve-day ethnic cleansing of Chinese populations in Malaya and Singapore roughly between 21 February and 4 March 1942. The focus was on executing Chinese males between the ages of eighteen and fifty. Many of their names appeared in lists compiled pre-war of potential anti-Japanese suspects that had been maintained by Japanese Intelligence operatives on the Malay Peninsula. Kevin Blackburn, 'The Collective Memory of the Sook Ching Massacre and the Creation of the Civilian War Memorial of Singapore', in *Journal of the Malaysian Branch of the Royal Asiatic Society*, Vol. 73, No. 2 (279) (2000) 71-90, www.jstor.org/stable/41493428 (accessed 3 September 2023), 73. Ian Ward, *Snaring the Tiger* (Singapore: Media Masters Pte, Ltd, 1996) 78.
12. WO 325/75 Hongo, Statement, 19/3/47.
13. WO 325/75 Hongo, 19/3/47.
14. Tsuji, *Singapore*, 84.
15. WO 325/75 Summary of Examination of Katsuno Toshio, Changi Jail, dated 19 March 1947, 1-2, 6. Tsuji, *Singapore*, 83.
16. Tsuji, *Singapore*, 24.
17. Tsuji, *Singapore*, 92.

Chapter 16

1. Tsuji, *Singapore*, 87.
2. Swan, William L, 'The Imperial Japanese Consulate in Songkhla, Thailand'. *Journal of Asia-Pacific Studies*. (Waseda University) No. 43 (February 2022). https://waseda.repo.nii.ac.jp/record/68213/files/AjiaTaiheiyouTokyu_43_2.pdf (accessed 26 October, 2024)
3. WO 325/75 Memo No: 21261/1946 Phra Panoon Nakaranuraksa to The Under Secretary to the Ministry of Interior dated 10 October 1946, 1. TNA WO 325/93 Execution of Europeans in Singora 1941–1942 Witness Statements, 4203/BMWC, LTCOL NDJ Read-Collins, OC British MWCLS, Subject: Singora and Yala (South Siam) Execution 1941–1942 Report On Investigation in Japan dated 18 March 1947. WO 325/93 Nai Taroop, Summary of Examination, Singora, 13 July 1946. WO 325/75 Thai Police Colonel Poon Swat Pisal Statement, Bangkok, 1 October 1946.
4. WO 325/75 Katsuno, Statement, 19/3/47, 4.
5. WO 325/75 Katsuno, 19/3/47, 2.

6. Tsuji, *Singapore*, 89. TNA CAB 106/53 Colonel AML Harrison, 11 Ind. Div. Malaya, Chapters I-IV, III, 38.
7. WO 325/75 Hongo, Statement, 19/3/47, 2. WO 325/75 Summary of Examination of Sub-Lieutenant Swat Kamsuriya dated 15 November 1946.
8. WO 325/75 Swat, Statement, 15/11/46.
9. WO 325/75, Summary of examination, Seto Hisao, civilian, Changi Jail, 2 July 1946, 2.
10. After occupation, Tokyo had awarded the best of Thailand and Malaya's tin mines to Mitsui Kozan Kabushiki Kaisha (MKKK) and the Toyo Kozan Kabushiki Kaisha (TKKK). Lesser tin mines including Chinese tin mines went to associated groups but always under Mitsui patronage. Smelting and other iron works and foundries came under the Nippon Seitetsu Kabushiki Kaisha (NSKK). Conversely, the Mitsubishi Shoji Kabushiki Kaisha (MSKK) held the rice monopoly, while salt and sugar was likewise solely in the hands of Mitsui Bissan Kabushiki Kaisha (MBKK). Dainan Koshi had been established as a rubber shipping agent for sending rubber supplies not only to Japan, but also via Bangkok and Shanghai to Germany. What the Japanese did not have was access to tin. Chin Kee Onn, *Malaya Upside Down* (Kuala Lumpur: Federal Publications Sdn. Bhd, 1976) 83.
11. WO 325/75 Summary of Examination of Mr Heinz F Langfeldt dated 4 September 1946, 1.
12. WO 325/75 Summary of Examination of Antonin Vererka dated 19 June 1946, 1.

Chapter 17

1. WO 325/75 Thomas, Statement, 21/7/46, 3.

Chapter 18

1. Any name plus 'col' is military shorthand for explaining and identifying an infantry column, hence Laycol are Brigadier Lay's troops, and Krohcol are those troops detached and deployed to Kroh and responsible for Kroh force. CAB 106/53 Harrison, II, 29.
2. CAB 106/53 Harrison, II, 29.
3. CAB 106/53 Harrison, II, 19.
4. CAB 106/53 Harrison, II, 19.

5. CAB 106/53 Harrison, III, 29.
6. The railway option from the northernmost Thai–Malay border seemed to have not been eventuated. CAB 106/53 Harrison, III, 29.
7. CAB 106/54 Colonel AML Harrison, 11 Ind. Div. Malaya, Chapters V-X, 37.

Chapter 19

1. CAB 106/54 Harrison, VIII, 8, 26-27.
2. Moorhead had known since at least mid-year 1941 that this area and The Ledge mission were going to be his area of responsibility. Given the paucity of information available about the area, including up-to-date geographical intelligence, Moorhead had taken it upon himself to get to know what might in all probability become his soldiering terrain. CAB 106/53 Harrison, III, 113.
3. CAB 106/54 Harrison,78.
4. According to reports, he later joined the 3/16th in the fighting and was last seen on The Ledge battlefield. The fate of his wife is not mentioned. As far as can be ascertained at the time of writing, Skryne does not appear to be part of Operation Cleeves. CAB 106/54 Harrison, 82.
5. Pathan in this context, may possibly be a British Colonial description for those originating from the Pashtun region of British India, bordering with Afghanistan. It is unclear in the reporting as to what is meant by 'Pathan' style in this instance, but it might possibly allude to traditional fighting styles such as in Islamic martial arts, or a specific Middle Eastern style of sword fighting. CAB 106/54 Harrison, 78.
6. CAB 106/53 Harrison, III, 29.
7. CAB 106/54 Harrison, 79.

Chapter 20

1. HS 1/348 Cipher 6181 O.M. Singapore to ACSS Only dated 8/12/41.
2. HS 1/69 WJ Parsons, 'Report on Special Operations carried out at Puket (sic) 8.12.41 to 10.12.41', undated, 2.
3. As far as Parsons knew, that operation was successfully carried out in the time allotted and well ahead of planning, but there was a problem. The unknown person responsible for that action had not destroyed the parts nor had they been tossed away as directed. For some unknown reason, that person had decided to place them in his evacuation bag, which

within a few days was in the possession of the Japanese, who merely found the offending parts, put them back into the unit and restarted tin mining operations. HS 1/69 Parsons, Report, 1.

4. Cruickshank, *SOE Far East*, 68.
5. This ties in with STS101 signals establishment being transferred to Rangoon in January 1942 as the situation was worsening in Malaya. Cruickshank, *SOE Far East*, 68.
6. TNA WO 325/54 Sworn Statement, TB Snow, unsigned, 19/3/46.
7. HS 1/69 Parsons, Report, 1.
8. WO 325/54 Snow, Statement, 19/3/46.
9. WO 325/54 Snow, 19/3/46.
10. WO 325/54, Lim EE Tian, Plight of 3 Europeans belonging to Takaupa (sic) Valley Tin Dredging NL of Haadyai, South Siam, who were killed at Sadoa (sic) the boundary of Siam, Haadyai, 30/11/45. WO 325/54 Letter (certified true copy), Captain James Rigby, British General List to Mrs Bentley, Southside, Hutton Rugby, Yorks dated 17 April 1945. WO 325/54 Sworn Statement, Tan Ahchu (sic), unsigned, undated.
11. WO 325/54 Tan, Statement, undated.
12. WO 325/54 Tan, Statement.
13. W0 325/75 Summary of Examination of Nai Vichitra Krairiksh dated 20 February 1947, 2.
14. WO 325/54 Letter, Rigby to Mrs Bentley, 17/4/45.

Chapter 21

1. WO 106/2509 Cipher 26626 GOC Malaya to War Office 4/12/42.
2. The reply the next day gave map co-ordinates B 47 L Pattani, map reference Pinyok Y 9869, with Eastings 398000 and Northings 569000. WO 106/2509 Cipher 55631 War Office (MI2) to GOC Malaya 3/12/41 Subject: Immediate Request for Pinyok Co-ordinates. WO 106/2509 Cipher 16476 GOC Malaya to War Office 4/12/41.
3. NAA: A3317 442/1946 Yala Incident [re Japanese atrocities against British civilians (mining company personnel) at Yala, South Thailand, in December 1941], Statement Malcom H Macfarlane, Details of 27 (twenty-seven) people arrested by the Siamese authorities on the 8th December, 1941 at Pinyok, 12/1/46. Maureen Magness, Evidentiary Document No. 5156, Summary of Examination of Maureen Joy Margaret Magness, Bangkok, 8 January 1945, www.legal-tools.org/doc/6cd2b9/ (accessed 11 August 2023) 3.

4. Letter Klaas de Boer, Thailand Tin Mines Ltd, Yala, South Thailand to Hettie, dated 6 November 1941, courtesy de Boer Family Archive. Letter HE Fern, Thailand Tin Mines Ltd. to Principal Witwatersrand University, Johannesburg, South Africa courtesy de Boer Family Archive. NAA: A989, 1943/520/2 Malaya – Malayan Research Bureau, 8a Castlereagh Street, Sydney, Revised List 15 February 1943 [37 pages], 3.
5. A1608, AC47/1/1 Memo Ref: 3/260 WE Antrobus Office of the High Commissioner for the United Kingdom, Canberra, to F. Strahan Esq, Prime Minister's Department, Canberra, Subject: Tin Denial: Thailand dated 19 September 1941.
6. Magness, Evidentiary Statement, 3.
7. Maureen Magness later identified the two Thai police officials as Nai Pring and Nai Pravine Nandwongso. Magness, Evidentiary Statement, 3.
8. Magness, Evidentiary Statement, 3.
9. Magness, Evidentiary Statement, 3.

Chapter 22

1. WO 325/54 Thay Ah Choo (sic), Statement, place unknown, dated 4 May 1946.
2. CAB 106/54 Harrison, 37.
3. WO 325/54 Rigby to Bentley, 17/4/45.

Chapter 23

1. An Assistant Nai Amphur was the British equivalent of an Assistant District Officer. A3317, Macfarlane, Report, 1.
2. Magness, Evidentiary Document, 4.
3. Iris Chang, *The Rape of Nanking: The Forgotten Holocaust of World War II* (New York: Basic Books, 2011) 6.
4. TNA PREM 3/169/1 Far East (Principle Telegrams) Cipher 422/6 CIC (FE) to War Office dated 8/12/41.
5. PREM 3/169/1 Cipher 26903 GOC Malaya to War Office dated 10/12/41. PREM 3/169/1 Cipher 26933 Advanced Headquarters, Malaya Command to War Office dated 11/12/41.

Chapter 24

1. Swan, 'The Imperial', 44. WO 325/75, Katsuno, Statement, 19/3/47, 5-6.
2. WO 325/93 Nai Kalai, Summary of Examination, Singora, 22 July 1946.
3. Swan, 'The Imperial', 45. WO 325/75, Katsuno, 19/3/47, 3.
4. WO 325/75, Katsuno, 19/3/47, 3.
5. Various Thai eyewitness reporting places the first British plane crashing into the sea in this area around this date. Official Air Ministry reporting also indicates one British plane was shot down around this date in the same vicinity, and at least one crew member was reported as bailing out by parachute. TNA AIR 81/10852 Flight Lieutenant JAB Dobson, Sergeant GW Smith, Sergeant EFW Fowler; missing believed killed; aircraft shot down and crashed near Singora, Siam, Blenheim V5931, 34 Squadron, 11 December 1941; Sergeant A Mc Johnstone, Flying Officer PN Kingwill, Sergeant GW Gregory: prisoners of war: aircraft shot down and crashed near Singora, Siam, Blenheim V5598, 34 Squadron, 11 December 1941Partial note AMS.N 357/45 – (enclosure 91B in folder) dated 15 April 1945. AIR 81/10852 Letter P. 364490/41/S.14 Cas. C. BPO/7001/67/Cas. GM Haslem to Base Personnel Office, Air Command, Far East dated 25 July 1947, Subject: Blenheim V5598 missing 9/12/41. WO 325/93 Nai Tobina, Statement, Singora, 12 July 1946. WO 325/93 Nai Taroop, Statement, 13/7/46. WO 325/93 Nai Chalerm Som Chit, Statement, Singora, 14 July 1946. WO 325/75 Summary of Examination of Luang Atakovit, Bangkok, 20 February 1947.
6. King had apparently met RAF Pilot F/LT Andrew M Johnstone in Japan's Cholan prisoner camp in French Indochina sometime in 1942. Johnstone advised he was first downed off Singora, and all three crew were immediately transferred to Vichy Indochina upon capture. That differentiates them from the second downed crew in Ban Pru, who were executed on Singora beach. King informed that he was with British Intelligence in Singapore. AIR 81/10852 Letter F/LT Andrew M Johnstone, Officers' Mess RAF Station Weaton to Under Secretary of State, Air Ministry (Casualty Branch) dated 30 September 1946.
7. Swan, 'The Imperial', 47.
8. WO 325/75 Seto, Statement, 2/7/46.
9. The Japanese renamed the vessel *Niyo Maru* and put it into cargo service until it was sunk in late 1944 off the coast of Burma. 'Hafthor SS (1921–1941) Niyo Maru (+1942) https://wrecksite.eu (accessed

2 November 2023). 'D/S Hafthor', 2. WO 325/75, Thomas, 21/7/46. WO 325/75 Vererka, Statement, 19/6/46.

10. It seems only two boats actually made it back to the shoreline, the first with Andersen and Røstad, and the third possibly with the Second Mate Henry Fredheim. In Vererka's sworn statement he cites the third European survivor was named Henri Frederick. The fate of the second boat carrying Second Engineer Bjarne Jansen and eleven Chinese crew remains unknown. WO 325/75 Vererka, 19/6/46. 'Hafthor SS', 2.
11. Curiously, Parsons later reported that although several of the Takapua Tin Mine personnel including those down in Ban Pru had initially been harassed by Thai officials, he was under the opinion that all had been left alone to continue on with their journey. Where that reporting came from is not known, but on the strength of it he was presuming that all the tin mining communities he was responsible for further south, from Singora to Sadao, had reached safety. Questions still remain if any of them had not been arrested, confined or incarcerated, placed under armed guard, or faced any Japanese threat, why most of the planned small-scale sabotage operations in Parsons' area had seemingly not been undertaken. It seemed all the northern line railways and bridges remained intact, and the communications including between Ronpibon, Phuket, Singora or Haad Yai had not been cut. HS 1/69 Parsons, Report, 2-3.

Chapter 25

1. CAB 106/54 Harrison, 115.
2. The Thai District Officer was never seen again, but it was presumed he was heading north to the Japanese and had either crashed, or perhaps had suffered local justice.
3. HS 1/348 Cipher 6168 O.M. Singapore to ACSS Only dated 8/12/41.
4. HS 1/348 Note SC/3041/69/10 Gladwyn Jebb to A.D. dated 9/12/41.

Chapter 26

1. Swan, 'The Imperial', 46. WO 325/75, Katsuno, 19/3/47, 3.
2. Whether he had any idea about what had happened to his fellow Takuapah Tin Mine employees just a day or so earlier remains unknown. WO 325/75 Summary of Examination of Captain BJ Kemp Malayan

Intelligence Corps 12 WCI(S)227 dated 19 March 1946. WO 325/75, Katsuno, 19/3/47, 1. TNA FO 369/3697 Massacre of Australian tin-miners at Yala, South Siam, in 1941. Code 240, Letter (undated), RL Orton, Rochedale, Sydney to Commonwealth Investigative Branch, Brisbane. FO 369/3697 Letter AG Nicoll, for Deputy Director Commonwealth Investigative Branch, Brisbane, Subject: Massacre of Australian Tin Miners at Yala, South Siam dated 26 March 1946. FO 369/3697 G Sleeth, Report, Subject: Massacre of Australian Tin Miners at Yala, South Siam, undated, 1.

3. CAB 106/54 Harrison, 117.
4. CAB 106/54 Harrison, 119.

Chapter 27

1. A 3317 Macfarlane, 12/1/46, 2.
2. Magness, Evidentiary Document, 4.
3. Tengading village's location is not yet confirmed, although it does suggest it might have been the village that lay adjacent to the road leading into Pinyok Tin Mine.
4. A 3317 Macfarlane, 12/1/46, 3.
5. Maureen Magness recalls the driver as having been a well-known Thai railway official. Macfarlane, on the other hand, describes him as the business manager of a Thai Railways film company. He describes how the Thai driver and his actors had only recently been Pinyok Tin Mine guests for several weeks just prior to Japan's landing. They had stayed in the mine's bungalows, interacted with all the mine's personnel, borrowed the mine's cars to get around and so on, and had used all of them to make a movie about the railways. Whether that movie still exists remains unknown. A3317 Macfarlane, 12/1/46, 3.
6. Magness, Evidentiary Document, 1.
7. Magness, Evidentiary Document, 4.

Chapter 28

1. Magness, Evidentiary Document, 5.
2. Magness, Evidentiary Document, 5.
3. CAB 106/54 Harrison, 82.

Chapter 29

1. WO 325/75 Thomas, 21/7/46. It is unknown whether Settle involved with any tin mine denial operations, or if he was relocated to another civilian internee camp.
2. WO 325/93 Sergeant Major Chamnarn, Statement, Singora, 17 July 1946.
3. Magness, Evidentiary Document, 5. A3317 Macfarlane, 12/1/46, 4.
4. Magness, Evidentiary Document, 2.
5. A 3317 Macfarlane, 12/1/46, 4.
6. Magness, Evidentiary Document, 2.

Chapter 30

1. CAB 106/54 Harrison, 119.
2. CAB 106/54 Harrison, 120.
3. CAB 106/54 Harrison, 121.

Chapter 32

1. Magness, Evidentiary Document, 6.
2. Magness, Evidentiary Document, 6.
3. Magness, Evidentiary Document, 6.
4. Magness, Evidentiary Document, 6.

Chapter 33

1. 'Penang Evacuation Described as Disaster', in *The Mail* (Adelaide, SA), Saturday, 20 December 1941, 2.
2. WO 325/75 Nai Taroop, Statement, 13/7/46.
3. WO 325/93 Nai Chalerm Som Chit, Statement, 14/7/46.
4. WO 325/93 Chamnarn, Statement, 17/7/46. WO 325/93 Teaf, wife of Sergeant Major Chamnarn, Statement, Singora, 23 July 1946. WO 325/93 Sergeant Major Manit Visert Siri, Statement, Bangkok, 22 May 1946. WO 325/75 Nai Beow Suvanratana, Statement, Singora, 3 May 1946.
5. There had been some Roman Catholic priests arrested and incarcerated in Singora Jail in the weeks after Japan's invasion, but Katsuno had

secured release for at least two of them. Dr Sam Thomas recalled one was Dutch and the other was possibly British and both were released along with him on 23 December 1941. They may have possibly then travelled on to Bangkok. It is also possible they may have been black-wearing Chinese guerrilla fighters. WO 325/93 Sergeant Major Nai Kalun, Statement, Singora, 17 July 1946. WO 325/75 Thomas, 21/7/46, 2.

6. WO 325/75 Chamnarn, 17/7/46.
7. WO 325/75 Chamnarn, 17/7/46.
8. The 1941 location of Chinko is unknown. WO 325/93 Ex-Corporal Thai Police Thepa, Statement, place unstated, 14 July 1946.
9. WO 325/93 Chamnarn, 17/7/46. WO 325/93 Teaf, Statement, 23/7/46. WO 325/93 Nai Tobina, Statement, Singora, 12 July 1946. WO 325/93 Nai Chalerm Som Chit, Statement, 14/7/46.
10. Chamnarn had recognised them, especially the airman with the zippered jacket. WO 325/93 Chamnarn, 17/7/46.
11. WO 325/93 Nai Chacom, Statement, Singora, 15 July 1946.
12. WO 325/93 Nai Kalai, Statement, Singora, 22 July 1946.
13. In his 1946 witness statement, Nai Chalerm Som Chit testified to having seen the graves being desecrated and a gold tooth and wristwatch being removed from the grave site. WO 325/93 Nai Chalerm, 14/7/46.

Chapter 34

1. Magness, Evidentiary Document, 6-7.
2. Magness, Evidentiary Document, 7. FO 369/3697 D Bailey, Thailand Tin Mines Ltd, Statement of Claim (Compensation for being disabled), place not stated, dated 30 August 1945.
3. Although the Japanese Army had officially outlawed the rape of enemy women, Japanese military culture usually abrogated those orders, preferring to adhere to superstitions that raping virgins would make them more powerful in battle. Some soldiers were even known to make amulets out of the pubic hair of their victims and wear them when going into combat in the belief it gave them magical invincibility. Chang, *Rape of Nanking*, 49.
4. Magness, Evidentiary Document, 7.
5. Magness, Evidentiary Document, 6.
6. A 3317 Macfarlane, 12/1/46, 5.

Chapter 35

1. Poignantly, in 1946 it would be Macfarlane who would bear witness as authorising authority on all of their death certificates. A 3317 Macfarlane, 12/1/46, 7.
2. Young was the mine manager, Haderup was the mine's accountant, and Beasley an employee. A 3317, Macfarlane, 12/1/46, 9.
3. A3317 Macfarlane, 12/1/46, 9.
4. A3317 Macfarlane, 12/1/46, 2. Goh Eck Cheng (ed), Thomas Kitching, Life and Death in Changi: the war and internment diary of Thomas Kitching (1942-1944) (Singapore: Landmark Books, 2002) 252.
5. Cheng, Thomas Kitching, Life and Death in Changi, 252.
6. It seems after Pudu, and being taken to convalesce at the local convent, on regaining her health Doris had claimed she was Italian. Although the details are obscure, it seems she was in some sort of relationship with a senior Japanese military officer living in Kuala Lumpur, who in mid-1943 had been arrested on bribery charges and sent back to Japan. At the same time Doris had been arrested and taken to one of the Kempetai headquarters, where she was either pushed, or fell, out of a window. Phillip R. Piccigallo, *The Japanese on Trial: Allied War Crimes Operations in the East, 1945–1951* (Austin: University of Texas Press, 1979) 114-115.
7. WO 325/75 Langfeldt, 4/9/46.
8. Curiously, Langfeldt had noticed that on hearing the Allied planes approaching the Japanese soldiers would put on gas masks and all run into the same one building. 325/75 Langfeldt, 4/9/46.

Chapter 36

1. Although the Japanese had made much of playing up to different countries' ideas of neutrality, in Portugal's case it meant nothing in other parts of Portugal's colonies including in East Timor. Japan ignored the fact one half of the island belonged to Portugal, while the other side of West Timor was a Dutch colony. Japan's approach was to converge both European colonies into an island-wide Japanese-occupied Timor Island.
2. HS 1/111 Memo AK2/XX/307, from A.K.2. to AD/8.1 Subject: Anglo-Japanese Exchange: Thailand dated 30/10/42. HS 1/111 Memo author unknown to B/B.100 Subject: Repatriated British Subjects 1943

O.M. Mission dated 22/7/43, 2. HS 1/348 Memo AK2/XX/307 AK2 to AD/S.1 Subject: Anglo-Japanese Exchange: Thailand dated 30/9/42.

3. The other two were possibly George Loftus Windred and Terence Coyne. The Australian Windred had just gone to Bangkok using his cover as a journalist on a MEW and Oriental Mission tasking; Coyne's cover was as a tin miner named Thomas Collins as part of Operation Cleeves. HS 1/111 Memo author unknown to B/B.100 Subject: Repatriated British Subjects 1943 O.M. Mission dated 22/7/43, 2. HS 1/348 Cipher No. 6150 Singapore to ACSS only dated 28/11/41.
4. By the end of the month an ambitious second similar exchange was being negotiated between British and Japanese authorities, but that would not eventuate.
5. Although Gentry had been given a field commission and was ostensibly part of the Oriental Mission's denial schemes, he and the rest of his Bangkok-based cell had organised nor achieved nothing, had not undertaken any training, and seemed to be more under the sway of Crosby's influence, than Killery or anyone else. HS 1/212 Memo V. St. J. Killery to CICFE Subject: Oriental Mission Organisation in the Far East, 1-3. HS 1/212 Note Sir J Crosbie (sic) on the covert activities of the Far Eastern Mission of the Ministry of Economic Warfare ("FEMEW"), 1-3.
6. NAA: A3978, KUSKIE, B., Officers (RANVR[Royal Australian Naval Volunteer Reserve]) personal record – Bernard Kuskie. NAA: A6769, KUSKIE B, enlistment details.
7. MP729/6, 22/401/253 Japan Reports from Australian Legation Tokyo; A989, 1943/80/9/7 Australian Legation to Japan.
8. NAA: M1455, 74 [Personal Papers of Prime Minister Chifley] Correspondence 'H', Part 3 [EV Hill - Horan Bros Garage (Bathurst), includes representations from Hinchinbrook Shire Council, EJ Holloway (Minister for Labour and National Services) and relating to reported death of Norman Holt at Yala (Southern Thailand), Clear Vale field firing range (Bathurst)], Memo 235/2/1/1 Private Secretary Department of External Affairs, Canberra, (name illegible) to The Private Secretary to the Acting Prime Minister, Parliament House, Canberra dated 13 December 1944, page 195 of 255.
9. M1455, 74 [Personal Papers of Prime Minister Chifley], Memo 235/2/1/1/ Department External Affairs to Private Secretary Acting Prime Minister 13/12/44, page 196 of 255.

10. M1455, 74 [Chifley Papers] Memo 235/2/1/1/ Department External Affairs to Private Secretary Acting Prime Minister 13/12/44, page 195 of 255.
11. HS 1/111 Letter Mrs Nancy Fitzgerald, c/o Hongkong & Shanghai Banking Corpn., Gracechurch Street, London, to Mrs Wright dated 21 October 1942.
12. Collins had been working undercover as a tin miner at Huey Muet. HS 1/111 Letter G.L.1996/42, D.C. Orr, Room 055, War Office to Lt Cdr J Senter S.O.E. dated 19 October 1942.

Chapter 37

1. The India Mission was essentially the replacement SOE (Far East) organisation, that had been cobbled together by mid-1942. It's remit was essentially the same as the Oriental Mission's original taskings had been based out of Singapore - behind-enemy-lines, stay-behind-parties and other small-scale sabotage and denial operations in Southeast Asia. HS 1/111 Letter (copy) B. Goodfellow Calcutta to SC Miskin Subject: Casualties dated 31 October 1942. HS 1/111 Memo AK2-CD Subject: Oriental Mission Casualties - Thailand dated 14 October 1942. HS 1/111 Memo BB3/FE/2414 B/B.3 to B/B.100 Subject: Oriental Mission Casualties dated 21 August 1945.
2. Cruickshank, *SOE Far East*,12.
3. HS 1/111 Memo BB3/FE/2414, B/B.3 to B/B.100 Subject: O.M. Casualties dated 21/8/45. HS 1/111 Memo O/FE/948 O. to CD Subject: References AD/OR/172 dated 9 May 1942. HS 1/111 Memo AK2 to D/Mil.3 Subject: Malayan Casualties (Left Behind Parties) dated 19 October 1942. HS 1/111 Oriental Mission Casualty Names List Referred to in Letter No. BB3/FE/2414 to B/B100 dated 21 August 1945 (loose sheet).
4. HS 1/111 Draft Letter Anthony Lincoln Esquire, Colonial Office to unknown dated 5/10/42.
5. HS 1/111 Memo BB3/FE/2456.I, B/B.3 to AG/MR Subject: O.M. Casualties dated 17/9/45.
6. HS 1/111 Note L/10 Subject O.M. Casualties dated 28/11/42.
7. HS 1/111 Memo O.102/PERS/482 O.102 to B/B.100 Subject: O.M. Casualties dated 3/11/42 1.

8. Which two, however, was not recorded, but in all probability may have been Cummins and Butler-Jones, or conversely Windred and/or Coyne/ Collins. HS 1/111 Memo O/FE/948, O. to CD Subject: Reference AD/ OR/1721 dated 9/5/42.
9. Compensation benefits would only be paid to British (white) male personnel, and female personnel benefits would be determined on the merits of each case. HS 1/111 Note, Subject: SOE Disability Benefits, Pensions &c. Arising from Casualties dated 18 December 1942.
10. HS 1/111 Memo L10/PERS/805 L/10 to D/FIN Subject: O.M. Casualties Repatriated 1943 dated 9/7/43, 2.
11. HS 1/111 Memo O.M. Casualties, 9/7/43, 2.
12. Conversely, it was the opposite for those who had been nominally enrolled for Oriental Mission work in Northern Thailand, including in Bangkok. They were not given ranks mainly because it was considered they had not undertaken any of their proposed mission taskings whatsoever. HS 1/111 Memo AD6/XX/58 AD/6. to D/Fin Subject: O.M. Civilian Casualties Tin Miners in Thailand dated 10/12/42.
13. Letter KW 51 Mr Roberts Under-Secretary of State, Foreign Office to Mrs HJ Thomas, c/o JW Lovery, Traffic Headquarters, Khunda Road, Jatni, PO, undated. Courtesy of Wright Family Collection.

Chapter 38

1. HS 1/111 Memo BB.3/FE/2086, B/B.3 to BB Subject: Casualties in Malaya dated 18/4/45.
2. HS 1/111 Memo M/number obscured 3/343, London AG/MR to Kandy AG Subject: Casualties in Malaya dated 20/4/45.
3. NAA: A1066, IC45/20/1/71/ Protection of Australian Nationals Abroad. Repatriation and Relief Payments. Thailand. Letter WP Beahan, Bulls Chambers, 28 Martin Place Sydney NSW to Chas. A Morgan, MHR, Commonwealth Bank Building, Martin Place, Sydney NSW dated 13 November 1944.
4. A1066, IC45/20/1/71/ Letter WP Beahan, Bulls Chambers, 28 Martin Place, Sydney, NSW to CAA Morgan, Esq, MP, Parliament House, Canberra, ACT dated 14 September 1945, page 20 of 25.
5. A1066, IC45/20/1/71/ Letter Prime Minister Australia, Canberra, ACT to Mr CA Morgan, Esq, MP, Federal Member's Rooms, Sydney, NSW,dated 22 October 1945, page 10 of 25.

6. A1066, IC45/20/1/71/ Letter WP Beahan, Bulls' Chambers (sic), 28 Martin Place, Sydney, NSW to Chas. A Morgan, MHR, dated 8 November 1945, page 6 of 25.
7. HS 1/111 Cipher 331, Kandy to Colombo Repeated Calcutta, Chungking, Trincomalee, Kunming, London dated 10/9/45. HS 1/111 Cipher 688 CAW to Kandy dated 15/8/45.
8. That may have included whether or not some operatives may have accrued substantial credit balances, which suggests whatever may have happened to those funds remains a moot point.
9. HS 1/115 Letter HET/FD/6048 Finance Office to War Office, Subject: Officers Missing or Prisoners of War in Malaya, dated 31 October 1943.
10. HS 1/111 Memo BB3/FE/2583, B/B.3. to D/FIN.D dated 5/12/45.
11. HS 1/111 Letter 2041/AG/2Y5, ALFEA/Force 136 Headquarters Kandy to The Under Secretary of State, M.O.1 (SP), War Office dated 19/11/45.

Chapter 39

1. Swan, 'The Imperial', 61.
2. Piccigallo, The Japanese on Trial, 114-115. United Nations War Crimes Commission (UNWCC) Military Court for the Trial of War Criminals, 2/LT. Murakami Shuji of the Imperial Japanese Army, [Trial against Murakami Shuji] Trial Report, DJAG SEALF Case No. 65082, UNWCC10.csv; 528, Kuala Lumpur, dated 1-2/7/46 https://www.legal-tools.org/eng/browse/record/f1045 (accessed 23 January 2018).
3. TNA WO 106/2540 Operations of Malaya Command 8 Dec 41–15 Feb 42, Major General AE Percival, formerly General Officer Commanding Malaya, Despatch on Operation Malaya 8 Dec 41–15 Feb 42, undated. WO 106/2540 Letter Major General Percival to War Office dated 25 April 1946.
4. TNA FO 371/154030 Foreign Office: Political Departments: General Correspondence 1906–1966. Western (W): Germany WG Minute War Office F 292 2 dated 23/7/46. FO 371/154030 Letter 098/4425 (MO1) (R) War Office to Under Secretary of State Foreign Office dated 21/6/46.
5. This was similar to other highly sensitive areas of compartmentalisation where SOE had been operating, including in Germany. FO 371/154030 Memo 216 Registry No. F 9292/594/61 CMA to Under Secretary of State War Office, dated 2/8/46.

6. WO 325/93 Minute 4203/BMWC British Minor War Crimes Liaison Section (Tokyo) to War Crimes Section South East Asia Land Forces Subject: Singora and Yala (South SIAM) Execution 1941–42 Report on Investigation in Japan dated 18/3/47.
7. In Nai Kalai's statement that had been translated from Thai language into English by British investigators, the mine is described as 'Tantoh' tin mine near Betong. This is just one example afflicting several Thai eyewitness statements, when transliteration of places is often problematic, especially when it appeared none of the British seemed to have any idea of Southern Thailand's geography, and even less understanding of Thailand's districts. WO 325/93 Nai Kalai, 27/7/46.

Conclusion

1. E Regan appears to be erroneous. It should possibly read D (Daniel) Regan.